EUROPE'S EXISTENTIAL DILEMMA

EUROPE'S EXISTENTIAL DILEMMA
TO BE OR NOT TO BE AN AMERICAN VASSAL

GUY METTAN

Clarity Press, Inc.

© 2021 Guy Mettan
ISBN: 978-1-949762-40-2
EBOOK ISBN: 978-1-949762-41-9

In-house editor: Diana G. Collier
Cover design: R. Jordan Santos

ALL RIGHTS RESERVED: Except for purposes of review, this book may not be copied, or stored in any information retrieval system, in whole or in part, without permission in writing from the publishers.

Library of Congress Control Number: 2021938213

Clarity Press, Inc.
2625 Piedmont Rd. NE, Suite 56
Atlanta, GA. 30324
http://www.claritypress.com

CONTENTS

FOREWORD
IS THERE LIGHT AT THE END OF THE EUROPEAN TUNNEL? / xi

ACKNOWLEDGMENTS / xv

PART I
A DISAPPOINTING LEARNING PROCESS

CHAPTER 1
EUROPE: FROM ENTHUSIASM TO DISAPPOINTMENT / 3

The End of the European Dream 6
A Disappointing Learning Process 7
The Myth of European Peace Collapses 8
Slipshod Enlargement and Botched Democratic Deepening 11
"Fordization" and Mind Control 13
The Collapse of the German Kultur and Bildung 14
How Can One Be European Today? 16

PART II
THE LESSONS OF HISTORY

CHAPTER 2
FROM CHARLEMAGNE TO STALIN: THE FAILURE OF CONSTRAINT / 21

Europe, a Very Old Idea 23
Charlemagne: The First Attempt to Unite by Force 26
Otto of Saxony and the Successful Second Try 29
The Holy Empire: A Union before the Union 34
Austria and Mitteleuropa 35

  Napoleon: The Second Failed Attempt to Unite Europe
    by Force 37
  Hitler and Stalin: Union through Blood and Tears 38
  Communism: Equality at Any Price 42
  The Failure of Strong-arm Tactics. 45
  No United Europe without Freedom and Equality 48
  Partial Success of the Soft Approach 50

CHAPTER 3

THE GREEK SYNDROME AND EUROPE'S AMERICAN ENCROACHMENT / 54
  Greece: A Miniature Europe? 56
  City-States Vying for Civilization 59
  All Divided but United by Danger and by the Gods 60
  The Peloponnesian War and the Great European
    Civil War. 63
  An Example of a Fatal Spiral of Events 67
  The Broken Springs of Civilization 68
  The Lost Dynamics of Politics and Culture. 71
  A Hidden Fracture. 73
  The Cultural Center of Gravity Shifts Toward the
    United States. 74
  The Nucleus May Be Gone, but the Radiation Continues . . 77
  The Disunited Greeks Call the Romans for Help 79
  The Greek Economy Relocated in the East 83
  Greece Conquered by the "Western Barbarians". 85
  Greece Slain by the Federal Fiasco.... 87

CHAPTER 4

TWO SCENARIOS FOR A DECLINING CONTINENT / 90
  Scenario I: Contraction and Breakup 90
  Scenario II: Europe Absorbed by the United States 92
  Choosing between Insignificance and/or Servitude 94

PART III

A MALFUNCTIONING MACHINE

CHAPTER 5

THE EUROPEAN TECHNOCRATIC DICTATORSHIP / 99

    A Priori, a Logical and Wise Economic Choice 101
    The Dismissal of Democracy or the
        Jean Monnet Method 107
    A Permanent Judiciary Coup d'État 109
    An Obscure Legislative Circuit 111
    Laws Drafted by Non-elected Officials 114
    The Democratic Gap 116
    An Ersatz Constitution 120
    The Betrayal of the Social Model 123
    The Left Betrays the Underprivileged Classes 125
    Third Contradiction: Unbearable Social Inequalities ... 130
    The Spiral of Salary Stagnation and Debt 132

CHAPTER 6

AMERICAN TRUSTEESHIP, RUSSIAN EXCLUSION, GERMAN HEGEMONY / 136

    The Cold War Divides Europe 139
    Military Subjection, Economic Absequience 141
    The Europeans Acquiesce to Vassalization 144
    The Total Flop of Gorbachev's Common
        European Home 146
    Anti-Russian Propaganda Campaigns 149
    The Hypocritical Battle against Nationalism 152
    The Illegal Bombing of Serbia and the Kosovo War 155
    Kosovo Recognized in Defiance of the Law 157
    Hypocrisy Concerning the Right of Peoples to
        Self-determination 159
    Peace Within But Repeated Wars Without 160

A Europe Embarked on Alien Wars 161
Germany's Outsized Influence 163
The Reality of German Oversizing 166
Germany's Demographics Obsession 168

CHAPTER 7
EUROPE'S ABSURD FORM OF GOVERNANCE: BAD PLANNING OR INTENTIONAL? / 174

A Whirlwind of Proposals to Amend European Governance 177
The Democracy Deficit 183
The Countless Layers of Europe's Thousandfold Institutionalization 186
Other Intergovernmental Organizations in Europe .. 187
A Wobbly Institutional Pudding 188
The Europeanists and Populists against Federal Europe 190
Russian Geography and Chinese Demography Require a Strong State 193
The Strengths of the United States: Its Institutions, Its Army and the US Dollar 197
Europe, a "Non-imperial" Empire? 200

PART IV
SCENARIOS FOR THE FUTURE: A DEMOCRATIC INDEPENDENT FEDERATION OR A PROVINCE OF THE EMPIRE?

CHAPTER 8
THE IMPERIAL SCENARIO: THE CHOICE OF INSIGNIFICANCE UNDER AMERICAN ASCENDANCY / 205

A New Era of Post-Truth and Post-Democracy 210
The Impact of the US Imperial Republic on Europe . 213

*The Differences between an Imperial Republic and an
    Empire*..216
A US-Driven Global Corporate Empire 219
Serfdom? A Dubious Fate for Europe................221

CHAPTER 9
THE SCENARIO OF INDEPENDENCE: A DEMOCRATIC RESET AND FULL SOVEREIGNTY / 223

Two Conditions for a European Recovery.............224
*Relative Decline in the United States Opens Up New
    Opportunities* 225
*The Power of the American Narrative is Losing
    Its Impact* 227
*The United States Knows How to Destroy, but Fails
    to Build Peace*................................229
*In Europe, the United States Is Content to Replay
    the Cold War*..................................232
The New Silk Roads Are a Game Changer 234
*China's Rise to Power Opens Up Opportunities
    for Europe*....................................237
How Switzerland Could Inspire Europe 238
*To Trust or Not to Trust the People, This Is the True
    Question* 241
The Security Dimension and The Role of the Army......244
How Switzerland Addressed the Threat of Separatism ...245
A Brief Lesson in Federalism 248
Concordance and Coalitions at Every Level...........251
Innovative Taxation to Finance Federal Europe........253
European Sovereignty 256
Neutrality (or Non-alignment) as a Principle of Action ..257
Europe: The Will Behind the Way 260

EPILOGUE / 262

FOREWORD

IS THERE LIGHT AT THE END OF THE EUROPEAN TUNNEL?

A society begins to decline when the people ask themselves, "What is going to happen?" instead of asking, "What can I do?"
DENIS DE ROUGEMONT

When I wrote the first draft of this book two years ago for my French publisher, the European Union was then in chaos and facing many urgent pressures: the rise of populist parties in Italy, Poland, Hungary, Austria, the Netherlands, and France; the chaotic and endless negotiations with the UK for a post-Brexit agreement; violent mass demonstrations in France; high tensions with the US under the Donald Trump presidency; and the loss of credibility of the European Commission, then chaired by Jose Manuel Barroso and Jean-Claude Juncker.

Today, the sky looks much clearer. Populist movements have failed, especially in Austria and Italy, and are declining in Netherlands and Germany. The Brexit agreement has been achieved, even nobody knows if it is for the better or the worse. The Biden presidency seems to portend a better understanding and cooperation between the US and the European Union. With the new European Union presided by Ursula von der Leyen and Charles Michel, the newly-elected European parliament seems to get better public reception.

And above all, the Covid-19 pandemic has silenced, at least for a while, protest movements like the Yellow Jackets in France. It has also silenced the voice of the austerity countries (Netherlands, Austria, Sweden and Germany) which have been obliged to open their safes! After the looting of Greece in 2015, the Uncle Scrooge countries finally accepted to drop their euros for a common and ambitious recovery plan.

Would this slate of good news be the precursor of a reset of Europe? An evidence that everything is now going ahead for the best?

I don't think so.

For one simple reason. The historical, economic, political and institutional causes which are jeopardizing the future of the European continent have not changed. Even if viewed more favorably by the Europeans, Joe Biden's civility after Donald Trump's rudeness will not suffice to change the basic roots of European politics and deep trends of its relationship with America.

In fact, viewed from a certain perspective, the situation has even worsened. New challenges have appeared: the post-COVID reconstruction of the economy and the society, the giant debt burden, economic relations with a rising China, the loss of international soft power after an erratic management of the pandemic, the growing tensions with Russia, our close neighbor, inflamed by the imprudent epithet of Joe Biden labeling Putin as a killer and increasing sanctions—all these new problems will have to be addressed.

To shed light on our consideration of Europe's future we explore the former attempts made to unify the European continent. Since the collapse of the Roman empire, six attempts have been made—from the Holy Roman Empire to Napoleon, Hitler and Stalin's brutal attempts of dominations. They all failed. It's important to understand why. And notably here, we turn to a historical parallel of the current Europe/US relationship: the trajectory of Ancient Greece which succumbed in gradual stages from fiery independence to utter subservience to the Roman Republic.

Europe today faces the same domestic and global challenges as those of the past. The European project is now confronted by the same flaws and blind alleys as were its previous efforts. The present main dilemma can be summarized as: to be or not to be an American vassal?

Foreword

Given this context, the purpose of this book is threefold.

First, based on the Europe that I know through experience, it provides a study of how the above-mentioned challenges have or have not been taken on in the history of the continent. Faced with similar difficulties, ancient Greece and medieval Europe at times succeeded in coming up with inventive solutions and historical failures. Such lessons learned from the past always prove insightful.

The second part of the book examines in greater depth the problems confronting contemporary Europe—the strengths and weaknesses not only of the European Union but also of Europe's institutional construction; the profound imbalances that keep it from moving forward, namely the democratic "deficit" and the stifling primacy of economics and law over politics; the sprawling expansion of an ever unsatisfactory governance, the military tutelage of the United States and the absence of sovereignty; and the US-exacerbated tensions with Russia and the Mediterranean countries.

The third part addresses the European existential dilemma through examining two possible futures. The first one foresees Europe remaining eaten away with its old evils, unable to reform itself or to make real choices in its own interest. Or to be more precise, Europe chooses to be insignificant, to remain subservient to ever increasing US demands and ascendancy, unable to address its unique concerns in defense or energy policy while being denied potential economic benefits from a rising China and its Belt & Road Initiative, and forced into ever deeper and dangerous confrontation with Russia

The second one is of course my preference, as a European citizen. It postulates that Europeans, fully conscious of what is at stake, will face up to Europe's problems and create an institutional framework that will enable it to emerge from its increasing domination by the United States and stave off its inevitable decline into vassalization—seizing the opportunity of the new space opened by the emerging Chinese power to create a truly democratic and sovereign federal union.

EUROPE'S EXISTENTIAL DILEMMA

This is not impossible. The case of Switzerland after 1815 could be used as a model. At that time, while its institutions were indeed of the federal type, they were muddled, politically unsuitable and hardly democratic. They made Switzerland unfit for resolving the problems posed by a global environment having to deal rapidly with economic changes (industrial revolution) and accelerated political reshuffling, thanks to the emergence of new neighboring powers competing with the traditional French domination. But over time and with struggle, Switzerland evolved a unique and highly democratic Institutional form of governance that successfully set the rules for internal conflict resolution, managed to keep alive the cultural, religious and linguistic diversity of the country and thus preserved a social, economic and political stability without big clashes or adventurous wars over decades. Tiny Switzerland accomplished that in the face of pressures of its larger neighbors. Does Europe have something to learn from Switzerland?

I have therefore not considered Europe solely from the angle of the European Union, but rather from its possibilities, were it to emerge a whole. Indeed, the unwillingness to study Europe's possibility in its geographic totality is also part of the European problem. A strong and efficient Europe cannot be constructed if the other half of the continent is seen as an opponent. The internal construction cannot be dissociated from the external construction and environment, and one cannot succeed without addressing the other.

ACKNOWLEDGMENTS

I would like to thank all those who have helped me in my endeavor with their patient and useful advice, in particular, André Hurst, Honorary Professor at the University of Geneva and great connoisseur of Thucydides and ancient Greece; my colleague, Richard Werly, for whom the complexities of French or Brussels policies have no secrets; my friend and colleague, Arnaud Dotézac, for graciously sharing his long and meticulous investigations of the European Union and NATO; and many others like Slobodan Despot, Richard Labévière, Sergey Pilipenko for their kind support as well as my editors Olimpia Verger and Serge de Pahlen, and my wife and daughter, Myriam and Oxana.

Last but not least, I would also mention my translator Myrna Farage and express my special gratitude to Diana G. Collier for her attentive proofreading and enlightening comments. It brought a wonderful new refreshment to the present edition.

PART I

A DISAPPOINTING LEARNING PROCESS

CHAPTER 1

EUROPE: FROM ENTHUSIASM TO DISAPPOINTMENT

It remains an irrefragable law of history that contemporaries are denied a recognition of the early beginnings of the great movements which determine their times.

STEFAN ZWEIG
THE WORLD OF YESTERDAY: MEMORIES OF A EUROPEAN

I am the same age as Europe. I was born in the fifties and discovered Europe at the age of sixteen in the early seventies. My German teacher had found me a summer job as a Hilfskrankenpleger, or caregiver, at the Sankt-Marienspital in Cologne. For two months, under the orders of the head nurse, a former non-commissioned officer of the Kriegsmarine U-Boote, I came to know Germany and learned German by listening to dying patients tell their life stories. Often I accompanied them to the morgue for their last journey. I even became attached to one of them, the last survivor of the guard of Kaiser William II, a Prussian who died as he had lived, as stiff and straight as a halberd.

The following summer, thanks to the Inter-Rail passport that allowed students to travel around Europe at a reduced rate, I discovered Italy, Pompeii, the Vatican and Castel Gandolfo. A friend who was a Swiss Guard had invited me there, and by an incredible stroke of luck I met Pope Paul VI strolling through the gardens. Then came Greece under the Regime of the Colonels, and the Parthenon, where I spent a night locked in, alone amid the ruins on the hill, admiring the city lights of Athens below. At the time, mass tourism was still limited to the beaches of Rimini, and there was only random surveillance of the UNESCO World Heritage

Sites. A year later I finished high school and passed my baccalaureate in Thonon-les-Bains, France. I went to England, where I spent six weeks working as a gardener's assistant in Hertfordshire, manicuring lawns with tweezers and having tea beneath the lion trophies brought back from what was then Tanganyika by the widows of the colonels who had died in His/Her Majesty's service.

Communism in Europe was to come a bit later over the course of my young loves. In Yugoslavia and Bosnia I discovered Mostar and Sarajevo, sleepy cities that seemed so peaceful before being devastated by nationalism and fundamentalism. They would stir only at dusk, when the crowd of townspeople would emerge to amble in compact clusters along the banks of the Miljacka. Fifteen years later I was to find this same Bosnia ravaged by bombings but also by partisan media in haste to judge who were the good guys and the bad guys. I went on to Prague and Warsaw in October 1980, during the first sizzling weeks of the Solidarity movement when Walesa, Geremek and Michnik, the key personalities of the Polish *Solidarność,* would engage in endless protest meetings.

Between 1984 and 1989 I was diligently visiting Budapest, which was being passed off as the liberal showcase of communism under the regime of János Kádár. As a matter of fact, it was in Hungary on May 2nd, 1989 that I witnessed, dumbfounded and overwhelmed, the first breach in the Iron Curtain, when the Hungarian border guards themselves cut the barbed wires and sawed the posts to let the Trabants, which had come down from East Berlin by way of the steppes around Lake Fertö, cross the Austrian border. In early November 1989, while reporting on the lobbyists of the American Senate, I watched the fall of the Berlin Wall from Washington. An old world was collapsing, a new world was being born, and Europe seemed filled with wonderful promise.

This early European learning experience, much like the initiatory journeys of the *Compagnons* in the Middle Ages, forged me into a staunch European. It had enabled me to taste and feel the tremendous diversity of the continent. I had discovered that the French are linear, straight-line thinkers; that the Germans think in ellipses, with curves; and that the Russians think in spirals, like an endless screw, while the Italians outdo everyone: they don't think, they feel and invent.

Europe was historically dense with an unequalled mix of cultures. Its facilities enabled one to confirm with one's own eyes that the illustrations in Latin grammar, history and language-learning books really existed. This, along with its subtle art of fitting individual trajectories into the evolution of the great history that was in the making and that is specific to old civilizations, gave the continent everything it took to please its youth, at the time so eager to abolish its internal borders.

For all these years, I had seen the European Community as implementing an exhilarating political project and embodying a model of civilization. All the more so because from the mid-1980s, the Commission presided over by Jacques Delors had succeeded, at least at first, in sharing its ambitions with the conquering baby-boomer, post-war generation. At the beginning of the nineties, the end of the Cold War and the reunification of Germany ushered in a wind of hope such as had never been known before.

Thus for fifteen years, I had been a committed pro-European or "euro-turbo," as the partisans of the European Union were called in Switzerland. I was an idealistic pacifist, with ambitions for my country and the continent in full revival. I therefore succeeded in convincing my editors to support the first popular initiative for the accession of Switzerland to the European Community. In the summer of 1990, I strongly militated for the launch of the "Euro-Initiative" by the economic magazine for which I worked. Our battle cry to the Swiss was "Europe needs you!" Eighteen months later, the initiative proved to be a total flop, gleaning only about 50,000 signatures out of the 100,000 required.

Yet nothing seemed able to blunt my enthusiasm. On May 20, 1992, when the Federal Council officially deposited Switzerland's letter of application in Brussels, the front page headline of the newspaper I edited jubilantly read, "Europe Recovers Its Lost Heart!" with a splendid infographic showing Switzerland, flushed with pleasure, beating in the heart of an old but perked-up continent.

The End of the European Dream

The charm very quickly gave way to disillusionment.

In reading Primo Levi's *If This Is a Man*, Vassili Grossman's *Life and Fate* and *The Red Horse* by Eugenio Corti, I had already discovered the other side of the picture. The horrors endured by Soviet prisoners in the Neuengamme camp as related by an old friend of mine, a Bosnian deported from France, had deeply disturbed me. This friend would also help me unravel the hidden threads of the Yugoslavian tragedy and the geography of the hatreds built up during the Nazi and Ottoman occupations and brutally awakened by the outburst of ethnic nationalisms.

The first disappointment came on December 6, 1992, when by 20,000 votes, the Swiss people rejected joining the European Economic Area (EEA), designed as an antechamber to the European Union. Suddenly the dream was shattered by the hard reality of democracy. "Black Sunday," as it was coined by a federal councilor who has remained famous for the term, marked the memories and sounded the death knell of the hopes of all those who, like me, dreamed of being part of Europe in the making.[1]

For my generation, it was a shock. How could we possibly turn down the bet of openness and the promise of a radiant future and let ourselves fall into the trap of the misgivings expressed by "narrow-minded populists"? Should we have gone on dreaming at odds with the people, or on the contrary, admit that the Swiss citizens were right in rejecting the dream? The failure of Communism and the collapse of the Soviet Union, which had just been dismembered before our eyes, showed that opting for the dream was at best a dead end and at worst, a crime. But this took me a while to admit.

---

1 Daniel S. Miéville, *6 décembre 1992. Le non de la Suisse à l'Europe (Switzerland's No to Europe)*. Lausanne, « Savoir Suisse+, PPUR, 2013.

Europe: From Enthusiasm to Disappointment

A Disappointing Learning Process

The Swiss refusal by referendum—an episode the Europeanists would rather forget—nevertheless had great consequences for the destiny of Europe. On the one hand, it ended the inclinations of the Delors Commission to create a second credible body that would accept the host of new states wishing to approach the Union or join it in the long term: Austria, the Scandinavian countries and those of Eastern Europe. The failure of the EEA accelerated a race for expanding the Community that was to upset its internal balances very quickly. Deepening integration, a long and tedious step-by-step process, was hastily put together with a series of very unsatisfying treaties—Maastricht, Amsterdam, Nice, Lisbon—while efforts were focused on enlargement, which was much easier and more gratifying. Having failed to grant itself the means to ensure quality, Europe gave in to the mirages of quantity.

Discredited by the Swiss vote, the EEA became a half-empty shell restricted to Norway, Iceland and Liechtenstein, while the other members of the European Free Trade Association (EFTA), Austria, Sweden and Finland, hastened to join the Union convinced that they had no choice. This snowball effect rapidly affected all the Eastern European countries and the Mediterranean islands—Poland, the Baltic States, Slovenia, Slovakia, the Czech Republic, Hungary, Malta, Cyprus—who jostled to join NATO and, in the process, be admitted to the Union.

But above all, Switzerland's non-acceptance by popular vote gave an unprecedented impetus to all the protest movements and parties opposed to the Union. What was soon to become the "populist surge" had indeed begun on the evening of December 6, 1992 with the victory of the right-wing populist Swiss People's Party (also known as the Democratic Union of the Center, UDC) at the ballot box. This victory of the people was to grant undeniable democratic legitimacy to the diverse movements opposed to the Union and galvanize them in their struggle by showing them that they too could win by the ballot box. Since then, populist parties have continued to grow in the Union's member states, always through elections or referendum votes. The significance of the

Swiss vote on the subsequent development of Europe cannot be stressed strongly enough.

This increasing discrepancy between the exercise of democracy and the pursuit of European integration against all odds, gave rise to a growing wave of doubt and skepticism regarding the merits and legitimacy of the Union and the elite that governed it. How to reconcile democratic rights and the construction of Europe? Was such divergence purely conjectural, due to a temporary inadaptability of the institutions, or was it rather the result of a structural dysfunction of the Union, euphemistically presented as a "democracy deficit"? For Swiss citizens used to exercising their democratic rights practically every month, denying the people's sovereignty and questioning its decisions is inconceivable, however in line with their convictions as they may be. It is no coincidence that in Switzerland, the people are "the sovereign."

The Myth of European Peace Collapses

This first disenchantment was immediately followed by another disillusion; one that was even more serious and shattered my Europeanist ideal for good: the collapse of the myth of European peace. In that same year of 1992, a series of dramatic events had occurred in Russia and Yugoslavia. The former Soviet Union, broken into fifteen pieces since December 1991, had fallen prey to secessions, revolts and massacres. Not having responded favorably to Gorbachev's project for a Common European Home, Europe let Russia sink into chaos and anarchy, pushing it back to its margins. Then, as Russia gradually rebuilt itself, Europe made it an adversary rather than a partner.

In Yugoslavia, the fire smoldering beneath the ashes since 1990 had been stoked by Germany and the Vatican in their haste to recognize the independence of Slovenia and Croatia, proclaimed unilaterally in June 1991. In the summer of 1992, the fire had reached Bosnia, the most fragile of the former republics of the Yugoslav Federation, sparking off a series of wars, sieges, ethnic cleansing and bombings that would end only in the spring of 1999, following the illegal bombardment of Serbia with depleted uranium by

Europe: From Enthusiasm to Disappointment

NATO aviation. This destruction of federal Yugoslavia in the name of nationalism and sovereignty that Europe had moreover claimed to combat, always seemed suspicious to me. As a journalist, I had already been scalded by the way the media manipulated public opinion. For instance, just before the fall of the communist regime in Romania, photos of the corpses of Timişoara wrapped in their white shrouds that had been dug up in the cemetery and presented as the victims of a massacre commissioned by Ceauşescu and his wife created a scandal that rocketed around the world just days before the summary execution of the dictators in December 1989.

Another scandal broke out in October 1990 concerning the false testimonials regarding the supposed atrocities committed by Saddam Hussein's troops just after invading Kuwait. On 14 October, a young Kuwaiti "nurse" testified in tears before the American Congress that Iraqi soldiers had snatched babies from their incubators and let them die on the floor, and that they had destroyed everything in their path and tortured people. This testimonial, which served the United States as a pretext to launch the first Gulf War, turned out to be a set-up organized by a public relations firm financed by Kuwait with the approval of the American services.

There came another round in the summer of 1992, as the crisis in Bosnia festered, when a British television crew filmed Bosnian prisoners in the Tropolnje camp in Bosnia. The group was bare-chested because of the heat. One of the men, Fikret Alić, was gaunt due to a lung disease. The documentary shows the group of men approach the cameras as the journalists call out to them from behind a trellis topped with barbed wire that had been put there to keep the cattle out. The group is filmed and photographed from the waist up with the barbed wire crossing their chests. A photo taken from the film was immediately published on the front page of most western newspapers and magazines with captions and titles such as "Belsen 92," as though referring to a Nazi extermination camp.

The photo was used as an argument before the International Criminal Tribunal for the former Yugoslavia (ICTY) during the trial of Serbian officials and greatly contributed to radicalizing the conflict by unleashing the rage of the Serbian extremists, indignant at having been looked at as Nazis when their country had been devastated by Hitler. A controversy arose some years later around the British magazine *Living Marxism*, which had denounced the abusive use of the photo taken by a team of reporters for the British channel ITN.[2] The courts ruled not on the substance but on the form, thus endorsing a propaganda operation that in any case had not helped to restore peace but rather to demonize a European country...

In 1999, another photo of the same sort, showing the supposed carnage of civilian Kosovars by Serbians in the village of Raçak, served to justify the NATO bombardments of Serbia—itself responsible for dozens of civilian casualties... Yet careful examination of the photo showed that it had been retouched to make it more dramatic and that the bodies were those of soldiers in military fatigues and not of simple peasants.

In 2003 the public opinion hoax campaign took an official turn when American Secretary of State Colin Powell brandished test tubes before the United Nations Security Council to persuade it that Iraq had weapons of mass destruction and to thus justify the second invasion of that country by American troops...

With time, most of such press campaigns turned out to be fake or fallacious. But the damage had been done: the cause for which they had been published had triumphed, in contempt of the truth.

---

2 The author of the article and the magazine *Living Marxism* were both denounced by the entire British mainstream press. The magazine was forced to cease publication due to the exorbitant damages and interests demanded by the courts, which did not rule on the substance but rather on the question of whether or not the journalists had *intentionally* misled public opinion. Only a few independent minds like Noam Chomsky supported the freedom of the press. The behind-the-scenes video of the shooting is unavailable for copyright reasons... For a study of the official version, see David Campbell, "Atrocity, Memory, Photography: Imaging the concentration camps of Bosnia. The Case of ITN versus Living Marxism," in *Journal of Human Rights,* vol. 1, 2002. A critical analysis of the behavior of the media can be found in Peter Brock, *Media Cleansing. Dirty Reporting: Journalism and Tragedy in Yugoslavia*, Los Angeles, GM Books, 2006.

This has always prompted me to question the official truth, whether that of Europe and its worthy sentiments or any other.

Thus in the nineties, Europe, which had always come forward as a project of peace and nationalistic restraint, was revealed in a new, gloomier and more sinister light, by its direct or indirect participation in dismantling—precisely in the name of nationalism—the Federal Republic of Yugoslavia, a federation of peoples recognized by international law. I find that demonizing a specific nationalism—that of Serbia—for the benefit of other, supposedly commendable nationalisms, i.e. those of Slovenia, Croatia, Muslim Bosnia, is in deep contradiction with European values. All the more so as this Balkan fool's game was to continue and culminate with the endorsement of the unilateral independence of Kosovo in 2008.

How to believe in Europe's discourse of peace and its high ideals when they serve to camouflage war and the basest national interests? Behind its rhetoric and its lofty statements on the ending of the Westphalian Order, had Europe not returned to being just like any other power, zealous to promote its interests to the detriment of its asserted values and ready to go to any extremes to succeed in doing so?

A number of incidents only served to confirm this sad reality. There was the bombing of Libya and the support of the Syrian Salafi rebels as from 2011; the economic coercion of Ukraine at the end of 2013, with the financial and technical support given to the champions of regime change in Kyiv; the recognition of the takeover of power by the most radical wing of the Euromaidan on 22 February 2014, despite the agreement signed the day before by the three French, Polish and German representatives with President-elect, Viktor Yanukovych.

Slipshod Enlargement and Botched Democratic Deepening

This contrived democracy and the betrayal of the peace ideal were fissures that perforated the very essence of the European project. In retrospect, it appears that the two options presented in the nineties as complementary and desirable—namely the enlargement (to the East) and democratic deepening (a more transparent and efficient governance)—both led to a situation of extreme tension. Enlargement went only part of the way, for it literally cast aside the Balkans in the southeast, and Ukraine, Belarus and Russia in the northeast, leaving them on their knees. As for the deepening, it never gave rise to a true democratization of the Union.

How can one speak of European Union when some of the essential components of Europe are rejected, ostracized and considered hostile (like Russia)? And how to explain the fact that this European Union so openly welcomes the Muslim migrants while it slams the door in the face of the Slavic Orthodox world that is, culturally speaking, much closer? As for democratic deepening, all the attempts made, however meek, widely fell through for lack of envisaging true solutions and especially for trusting the peoples.

In addition to this geopolitical breakdown, this voluntary subjection to an outside power, and this incapacity to include the politician and the citizens in the construction and the functioning of the European Union, there is yet another great deception, undoubtedly the most significant: the sentiment that the European way of thinking has been vanquished.

Europe failed in instilling in its members—whether States, nations, or individuals—a European ideal. Seven decades after its creation, there is strong evidence that not only the spirit has deserted the Union, but, even worse, the Union has banished the spirit from its antechambers to become a factory of dogmas, norms and procedures.

Yet what is Europe if not a mind and a mindset? The ubiquitous discourse on values—peace, democracy, prosperity, tolerance, openness—not only masks the eviction of the politician, but hides an abysmal void of thinking and vision. Common faith and spiritual impetus have flown, yielding to the myth of technocratic integration.

Contemporary Europe in its momentary embodiment, the Union, has one, huge problem: it was imagined by great romantics but created by shopkeepers and managed by temple merchants including the insignificant Jacques Santer, dismissed from office; Manuel Barroso, the opportunist, who immediately (two months after the 18-month "cooling-off" period for EU officials after they leave their posts) assumed the position of chairman of the international arm of Goldman Sachs after his Brussels mandate; and the intemperate Jean-Claude Juncker, a great promoter of the fiscal paradise of Luxemburg. Spirit of Delors, where are you?

"Fordization" and Mind Control

Thus the decline of the European spirit, linked with the disappearance of the great national intellectuals, was another factor leading to disillusionment, for it seemed to coincide with Brussels' rise in power.

In a few decades the great intellectual tradition of Europe had subsided. As a journalist, I had had the opportunity to meet prominent personalities such as Raymond Aron, whose advice I have never forgotten: "Never stop learning, young man!" France was still gleaming through Sartre, Lévi-Strauss, Dumézil, Lacan, Deleuze, Foucault, Derrida, Yourcenar, Duras, and the great medievalist historians such as Georges Duby and Jacques Le Goff. Italy had its filmmakers and novelists in Dario Fo, Alberto Moravia, Dino Buzzati, Goliarda Sapienza, and Umberto Eco.

After 1945, the intellectual flows began to change directions, speeding up at the end of the seventies. Whereas up until the sixties, it was the Americans—if we remember Ernest Hemingway or Vincente Minnelli and his film *An American in Paris*—who would travel to Europe to draw their inspiration and have their talent recognized, the tendency was later reversed.

As from the eighties, thanks to many very generous scholarships, it was the Europeans who made the pilgrimage to the American universities, returning to Europe (when they did return) to apply the American models. Diversity, creativity, critical thinking seemed to have deserted Europe's university amphitheaters for good, no longer able to attract a public freshly doused with American TV series, slogans and concepts, dished out one after the other.

The Collapse of the German *Kultur* and *Bildung*

The worst catastrophe, however, came from Germany and Austria. At the end of the 19th and the beginning of the 20th centuries, Vienna was the hub of an incomparable intellectual and artistic life that included Kafka, Schiele and Karl Kraus; the Secession style, which was the Austrian version of Art Nouveau; expressionist painting, Robert Musil, Freud and the invention of psychoanalysis. Everything fell to pieces with the two world wars. In Germany, there had been great poets and writers like Goethe, Schiller, Hofmannsthal, Jünger, Thomas Mann and Rilke; prodigious philosophers from Kant to Heidegger and Hegel, Marx and Nietzsche; ingenious musicians as diverse as Bach, Beethoven and Wagner; leading scientists like Humboldt, Einstein, Max Weber and Werner Heisenberg, all of whom had illuminated the world from the end of the 18th century to the 1930s. This Germany that had been the epicenter of European intellectual life for a century and a half, practically disappeared from the scene in less than two generations.

The German intellectual disaster was brought about by the nation's defeat in the two world wars and the rise of Nazism that bled the German and Austrian cultural elite dry, forcing the survivors to emigrate to the Americas. Countless scholars, intellectuals and artists were forced to flee Germany and take refuge in the United States in the interwar period. The reunification of the country and the return of Germany to the summit of the European Union did not succeed in reawakening the great German *Geist*, *Kultur* or *Bildung*. This assertion bears no offense to the great postwar intellectuals, Jürgen Habermas and the Frankfurt School, Hannah Arendt and Martin Heidegger, or to the eminent artists who are no longer with us, Günter Grass, Heinrich Böll, Rainer Werner Fassbinder. Today, the Germanic intellectual life on the European scene boils down to a handful of isolated personalities such as Peter Sloterdijk, Hans Magnus Enzensberger, Axel Honneth and very politically incorrect Peter Handke in Austria.

The dramatic impoverishment of Europe as an intellectual and artistic foyer was quickened by the degradation of the national languages under the influence of English and mass Anglo-Saxon culture. This is something that we prefer to overlook, as it touches the essence of the Atlantic bond and threatens the very being of Europe, namely the cultural and linguistic diversity from which it has drawn its remarkable vitality since the Renaissance.

The deterioration of the national languages, the alteration of their syntax and grammar, the invasion of Anglo-Saxon terms are as impressive as they have been insidious for a generation. The growing usage of poor English is in the process of atrophying the European languages, while the increasing incapacity of the educational systems to teach elementary school children their national languages as they should, will only worsen the situation by constantly lowering the requirements in order to maintain an average.

The generalization of the Bologna Process intended to ensure compatibility in the standards and quality of education, along with the introduction of curricula and academic titles taken from American universities, all with a view to harmonizing higher studies on the continent, also contributed to transforming the universities, hitherto conceived as spaces of critical freedom and settled thinking, into Taylor-system factories of preformatted academic productions. Knowledge, like the armies, had been standardized to be "interoperable." Mind fordization and the systematic formatting thereof were facilitated by the massive recourse to management models and the Anglo-Saxon obsession with ranking. From now on, creativity is measured by the number of articles published in English-speaking journals, all of which are cut out from the same pattern. Thinking out of the box has become a challenge in European universities.

There is not the slightest trace to be found in the corridors of the Berlaymont building in Brussels or the European Parliament in Strasbourg, of Europe's prodigious intellectual life, its passion for debating on ideas, or the thought cult that were its hallmarks. Simply walking down the deserted avenues of the European District of Brussels on a Sunday morning, one can feel the reigning void while the other neighborhoods are rustling with life.

The contrast with the United States, which has always succeeded in galvanizing its creative energies to adapt and enrich its ideal of freedom and personal achievement, is all the more striking. Europe has no equivalent to offer despite its illustrious past. Franchising artworks of the Louvre or the British Museum to the museums of Abu Dhabi may offer some prestige and a few million Euros on the short term but is in no way a great act of European creation. On the contrary, it only serves to divert more visitors from Europe.

How Can One Be European Today?

Twenty years of enchantment, twenty years of disillusion: the European learning process is winding up rather dismally with no happy ending in sight. Being European today amounts basically to posing irritating questions. Can one still believe in Europe in the midst of such mediocrity? Is pessimism leading to fatality? Is the European Union the right tool to prevent the decline? Or has it not become, instead, a terrifying hammer that smashes everything to bits? Should we allow the United States to tell Europeans how they are to progress, with whom they are to collaborate, and against whom they should go to war?

From the turn of the century, we have been faced with ever growing challenges which the "world governance" that has been set up has not been able to curb: unbridled economic growth, insufficient sustainable development, uncontrollable energy and digital transitions, galloping global warming, repeated migratory crises, increasingly unfair redistribution of wealth, misappropriation of fiscal resources for private purposes, the rise of international tensions. If we are to take up these challenges, we have to change methods: improvised tinkering will no longer do.

Weakened by Brexit and flooded by the successive waves of migrants, by the election of Donald Trump and the rise of destabilizing populism, Europe has become a field of tension and contradiction. The European Potemkin village certainly appeals to Erasmus students, globalized CEOs, offline politicians and corrupted media, but it no longer deceives the ordinary citizens of the

Europe: From Enthusiasm to Disappointment

Sicilian countryside, the Hungarian plains or the English suburbs. In contrast to the dreams of Francis Fukuyama,³ the end of the story is not going to happen tomorrow. History will move on with or without Europe. But it would be preferable for Europe to take its place. Being European today means believing in this destiny and making it possible.

---

3 Francis Fukuyama, *La Fin de l'histoire et le dernier homme*, Paris, Flammarion, coll. "Champs," 1992, reed. 2018, pp. 328–542. Peter Sloterdijck, *Colère et Temps. Essai politico-psychologique*, Paris, Libella, 2007 and Slavoj Žižek, "La colère, le ressentiment et l'acte. À propos de Peter Sloterdijck, *Colère et Temps. Essai politico-psychologique*" in *Le Monde. fr*—blogs, 27 February 2008. See also Olivier Renaut, "La fonction du *Thymos* dans *La République* de Platon" in Notomi Noburu and Brisson Luc, *Dialogues on Plato's Politeia (Republic)*, Academia Verlag, pp. 179–188. In *The Republic*, his major political work, Plato distinguishes three major components of human nature according to whether they are dominated by appetite, desire, lust, associated with the body and the flesh; reason, measure, wisdom, associated with the mind; will, anger, courage, associated with the heart. He calls this third force *thumos*, which serves to maintain the balance of the human soul by preventing it from giving in to the tyranny of excessive desires and to the helplessness of disembodied reason. *Thumos* is also what allows one to give a value to oneself and to things and responds to our need to believe that we are "worth" something; that we count in our own eyes and in the eyes of others. It therefore relates to honor, self-esteem and social recognition. *Thumos* can also lose its balance and give rise to resentment and vengeance, as was the case with Nazism (resentment founded on nationalism) or communism (resentment arising from social exclusion), or to an excess of pride in liberalism (the West's desire to humiliate Russia and refuse its admission to NATO and the European Community after 1991). Sloterdijck opposed this need of rivalry, of competition, this desire to be recognized, to the Eros, which responds to the logic of material possession, production and enjoyment. Francis Fukuyama, closer to the Platonic tradition, stresses the need to be recognized, which can either act as a driving force in individuals and society—the desire to be better than others, to be the best in business, sports, art or science drives one on to surpass oneself and to produce excellence—or play a destructive role when left unfettered.

PART II
THE LESSONS OF HISTORY

CHAPTER 2

FROM CHARLEMAGNE TO STALIN: THE FAILURE OF CONSTRAINT

The future belongs to those with the longest memory.
FRIEDRICH NIETZSCHE

*The farther backward you can look,
the farther forward you are likely to see.*
WINSTON CHURCHILL

It was by virtue of this destination of Europe that the Roman Emperors reigned, that Charlemagne, Charles V and Napoleon strived to bring it together, that Hitler determined to impose his crushing domination. How, then, can we fail to see that none of these unifiers succeeded in making the subjected countries give up being themselves? On the contrary, arbitrary centralization will always backlash, triggering the virulence of nationalities. It is my belief that a united Europe could not today, any more than in previous times, be a fusion of its peoples, but that it can and must result from their systematic coming together.
CHARLES DE GAULLE, *MEMOIRS OF HOPE*

For the Europeanists, the past does not exist. History is disturbing. It is banished from texts and official speeches. The reference to Christianity was deleted from the European Constitutional Treaty so as not to offend the atheists, agnostics or non-Christian religious minorities. European history is left to the goodwill of our national textbooks. In the parlors of the elite, the history of the continent has a whiff of evil; it smells of nation, identity, blood, mud, *terroir,* languages and provincial folklore. Anything deep-rooted is highly suspect. Enough of the past, look to the future! *"Tabula rasa!"* That is the official leitmotif.

At best, the history of the continent boils down to a few symbolic terms—Charlemagne, the Renaissance, Erasmus, Hitler, Stalin, Shoah, D-Day, World Wars—that are consensual enough to deserve either being commemorated or used as a collective foil. Indeed, the only history of Europe, the one that counts, dates back to 1951 with the first treaty on coal and steel, and truly begins in 1957 with the Treaty of Rome. Everything before that is bygone protohistory, falling under a dark and obscure, nationalistic *ancien regime*.

Each new generation believes it can outdo the old, and ours is no exception. The "Digital Revolution," the "Fourth Industrial Revolution," the mysticism of Silicon Valley, the mulled promises of artificial intelligence, the gospel of free trade and unlimited growth, the cult of Elon Musk and permanent Innovation, the triumph of liberal democracy and of world governance—all have changed the world, reversed its old paradigms and outdated all the pasts, as the media and other global shapers tell us over and over again. "Don't you understand that nothing will ever be the same again and that our world can no longer be compared to the old one?" This, the apostles of the technological paradise of the future keep preaching, much like the lunatic monks of the Middle Ages who so knowingly painted the hopes of the hereafter in glowing colors to bedazzle the destitute masses.

Indeed this drive to look ahead at any cost with no consideration for the lessons and experiences of the past is obviously deceitful and prone to the worst errors. It inevitably leads to making the same mistakes, like the economists who assure us, after each crisis, that this will be the last one, and that, as opposed to their inept predecessors, they have taken all the precautions necessary to avoid another. When it comes to negating the past, Nietzsche and Churchill are right. Technological prowess has but little influence on the human essence, which has practically not changed since the days of Pericles and Charlemagne, and remains what it is, despite all the technical avatars. And it has even less influence on the planet's ecosystem, other than to destroy it little by little on the pretext of improving it. We know very well that at any rate, the ecosystem will never be able to produce more than what it receives.

But robots, high-frequency financial speculation, Smartphones, hypersonic airplanes and intelligent cars abolish neither history nor humanity; nor has the invention of the steam engine, the telephone and the computer radically changed them. Of course, armies advance at the speed of tanks, planes and cruise missiles instead of at the pace of foot soldiers or horses. But the determination to dominate, the hunger for power, the ambition to rule the world, the pathological and unquenchable thirst for recognition—the "thymotic" passions as Fujuyama and Sloterdijck would call them after Plato—are still at work and keep humanity from throwing off the shackles of history.

If human history is doomed to go on at least until the last man has disappeared—which is what we believe—then Europe as we see it today in no way constitutes a horizon of the Europeans that cannot be overcome. The European Union in particular can succeed or fail, triumph or implode, grow or disappear, gradually reform or undergo a revolution that would change it from top to bottom. These are the prospects that interest us here and that we propose to study in the light of past experience. The Greeks perfectly understood that if we are to know where we are headed, we first have to know where we come from and learn the lessons taught by the failures and achievements of the civilizations before us. To do so, we must try to understand the historic moment of which we are a part.

Europe, a Very Old Idea

So the idea of Europe is not new—far from it. In the fifties, the founders of the European Community were initially concerned with showing that their project fitted into a very old perspective. They sought to justify it by giving it a historical depth and considering it over the long term, as though it were the culmination of a secular dream.

One of the leading initiators, Denis de Rougemont, founder and facilitator of the European Center for Culture,[1] founded in Geneva in 1950 with the support of American capital, dated the European concept back twenty-eight centuries in his census of authors who had contributed to the emergence of a European conscience. His book also contains a list of manifestos in favor of the European Union dating from 1922. Bernard Voyenne, for his part, also cites the poet Hesiod as the first to use the word "Europe"—referring to the nymph, Europa, daughter of Oceanus and Tethys—in a text. There has never been a lack of plans for creating a European federation. From the early Middle Ages to the Age of Enlightenment, many a mind has striven to show the virtues of European unity, at first under the banner of Christianity and later, the universalism of reason. For Innocent III (1198), Europe is embodied in the *Christiana Republica* headed by the Pope: "It is in the supremacy of the apostolic Holy See that the authority of the Empire and of the Ministry are merged."[2]

At the beginning of the 14th century, the lawyer Pierre Dubois aimed to "prevent war through appropriate institutions" and to "organize international arbitration." He advocated creating a secular council or representative assembly to manage the conflicts of what would be the first confederation of kingdoms of Europe. The idea was to be widely taken up later by diverse authors, including William Penn, the Quaker who founded Pennsylvania and who wrote, in 1693, *An Essay towards the present and future Peace of Europe by the establishment of an European Dyet, Parliament or Estates,* with the epitaph, "Blessed are the peacemakers! Let arms yield to the toga."[3]

---

1 Denis de Rougemont, Vingt-huit siècles d'Europe. La conscience européenne à travers les textes, d'Hésiode à nos jours, preface by Jacques Delors, Paris, Christian de Bartillat, 1990 (reprint of the text published in 1961).

2 Bernard Voyenne, Histoire de l'idée européenne, Paris, Payot, 1964, p. 46.

3 Bernard Voyenne, op.cit. p. 84.

From Charlemagne to Stalin: The Failure of Constraint

In the 18th century, the European debate had dealt with perpetual peace projects until the French Revolution popularized the idea of the rights of man and of citizens, and Victor Hugo advanced his formulation in favor of a United States of Europe. More recently, several researchers have corroborated the thinkers who directly contributed to the genesis of the European Community in the 19th and first half of the 20th centuries, including those who were sometimes critical.[4] We should note that the detractors, even when they spoke in the name of the higher interest of European integration, were only marginal and never received the same media audience as the advocates of the official vision. But is this surprising?

The intellectual construction of Europe and the many discourses that forged it are therefore widely known. But strangely enough, none of the historical founders of the European Community took an interest in prior unification ventures, as though nothing had happened for one thousand five hundred years. As if they had never existed or had the slightest heuristic value in the process of engendering modern Europe, the political attempts at integration that had been made over the past fifteen centuries remained in the shadows. Neither the intellectuals nor the politicians of the

---

4 Jean-Luc Chabot, *Aux origines intellectuelles de l'Union européenne. L'idée d'Europe unie de 1919 à 1939,* Grenoble, PUG, coll. "Libre cours," 2013. And, more broadly, Bernard Bruneteau, *Histoire de l'idée européenne au premier XXe siècle à travers les textes,* Paris, Armand Colin, 2008. The author also studied the Nazi period and Hitler's "New Europe" project. We can find a much more critical approach to this propagandist view in *Critique historique de l'idée européenne, vol. 1, Les précurseurs introuvables, Histoire d'une mythologie du Moyen Âge à la fin du XIXe siècle,* François-Xavier de Guibert, 2009, penned by Franciszek Draus, a Polish researcher at the Jacques Delors Institute. The author describes how the tendency to show European integration as the realization of a secular dream is harmful at the intellectual level: it distorts European history by detrimentally depicting certain historical concepts of peace as the foreshadowers of contemporary federalism; and it kills the true European idea by failing to comprehend Europe as an identity and a power. The introductory notice pursues as follows: "The unprecedented crisis that we shall have to face should incite us to reject the ideological constructions of Europe and go back to the historical foundations that alone, might still give some meaning to this civilization that seems to benefit from the lay over brought about by a prolonged decadence!"

European Community's beginnings seemed interested in those efforts. No doubt this was because they had failed and most of them smelled of sulfur, as they had been the fruit of conquering spirits like Charles V or Napoleon, denounced today. Or they stemmed from an abject ideology in the vein of Hitler's "New Europe," or even resulted from a fiercely subversive social eschatology such as Soviet communism.

This refusal to consider past undertakings should nonetheless serve as a warning at a time when the European Union is going through an unprecedented legitimacy crisis, if only to better understand the reasons for their emergence, their short-lived success, and their ultimate failure. We cannot remain indifferent to the roots and legacies inherited from these various endeavors.

The pathetic Nazi experiment has been swept away for seventy years now, and the collapse of Soviet communism has been consummated for a quarter of a century. So we can freely investigate the how and why of the various past attempts to unify Europe, from the earliest to the most recent, with no suspicion of being pro-royalist, pro-Nazi or pro-communist.

Charlemagne: The First Attempt to Unite by Force

Starting from the treaty that established the European Coal and Steel Community (ECSC) in 1951 and the 1957 Treaty of Rome that instituted the common market, the integration of different European States under the same roof is the follow-up of half a dozen extremely varied yet aborted attempts.

Excluding the Roman Empire, which spanned three continents with the Mediterranean serving as its center of gravity, the first initiative to unify Europe dates back to Charlemagne. By forcibly bringing together vast territories that today would encompass northern Spain, France, Belgium, the Netherlands, Switzerland, northern Italy and western Germany, the Carolingian king cut out for himself a state that dominated practically all of Christian Europe of the time. But his empire was extremely heterogeneous. It was a patchwork of very different peoples, languages and traditions lacking a common glue to hold them together.

Charlemagne sought to create this bond and give his domain a new identity by reforming the Christian liturgy and credo—and he was willing to pay the price, namely by instigating the schism with the earliest Orthodox Christianity as defined by the first ecumenical councils.

In supporting Pope Leo III, Charlemagne was able to dictate his terms, namely, that he be crowned emperor and that the liturgy and the formula of the Christian Trinity be renewed. The pope accepted the first condition and crowned him emperor on Christmas night of the year 800 in Rome.

This act, which directly challenged the authority of the Eastern Roman emperor, the one and only legitimate heir to the Roman Empire, laid the foundation of the geopolitical conflict between East and West that exists to this day. It was at that moment that Europe emerged as a conquering and hegemonic power. The contemporary European leaders and extreme right-wing parties have well understood this, and venerate Charlemagne as the tutelary figure of a modern Europe, "sure of itself and domineering," as de Gaulle put it with regard to Israel.

Although an unscrupulous war chief, Charlemagne was also a wise administrator who had perfectly understood the need to give his disparate states a common cohesion and identity. He knew that military force would not suffice to consolidate his conquests and that he would have to mobilize strong intellectual and ideological resources to keep the pieces of his empire together. Consequently, aided by Alcuin, his Minister, he based his propaganda on two cornerstones, opting for a strategy of rupture and continuity at the same time.

The rupture rested on a reviewed and modified version of Christianity that was in direct contradiction with the primeval orthodoxy and tradition of the Eastern Church, and in flagrant violation of the Canon Law established by the Councils. Charlemagne was the first to want to modify the formulation of the Trinity by introducing the *filioque*, (the Son), a term that caused the schism between Catholics and Orthodox two centuries later.

As for the strategy of continuity, he toyed with the idea of restoring the myth of the peace and grandeur of Roman times, for which the enlightened minds of the day were highly nostalgic. For the first time in the history of the continent, the territories of western and central Europe—Latin and Germanic—were brought together in a common structure that was to leave a profound and lasting mark in the European imagination. It is therefore no accident if twelve centuries later in 1957 the Inner Six countries would be mapped out almost exactly as had the Carolingian Empire predecessor (Switzerland alone excluded). Just as that attempt at unification had excluded the eastern Greek and Orthodox Europe, today's attempt excludes Slavic and Russian Europe. At the time, the attempt failed because the Pope had refused to acknowledge Charlemagne's religious claims. But the rot had set in, and the rupture, which was to produce its full impact two hundred years later, as we will see, would create a fracture that has not been mended and divides the continent to this day. Over the centuries, the line has moved eastward, settling today on the border between Roman Catholicism and Orthodoxy and descending from Finland and the Baltic States to Ukraine, Romania and the Balkans.[5]

Charlemagne was thus the first builder of modern Europe, but also its major divider.

What is more, and unfortunately for his successors, Charlemagne's empire suffered from insuperable governmental shortcomings. It was to collapse soon after his death for two reasons. First, in failing to impose his religious reform, Charlemagne was unable to give his states the unitary dynamics that they needed. The ideology of the *filioque*, as appealing as it may have been for his entourage, fell through, rejected by the pope and the Italian bishops. The Catholic schism would have to wait for two more centuries, and the weakening of the Eastern Orthodox Churches by the Arab Muslim conquests, before becoming effective.

A second problem arose from the fact that the Carolingian institutions were not adapted to manage such large and complex

---

5 On this issue, see Guy Mettan, *Creating Russophobia: From the Great Schism to the Anti-Putin Hysteria,* Clarity Press, Inc., 2017.

territories. The procedure for succession to the throne—the weak spot of all monarchies—was full of loopholes. The premature death of his two eldest sons brought about the rise to power of Charlemagne's third son, Louis, called the Pious or the Debonair, who was not at all prepared for the task. Succession to the throne by birthright was not yet firmly established, and no sooner had Louis died than his three sons fell into fratricidal quarrels. At the famous Treaty of Verdun in 843, the empire was divided into three longitudinal bands: West Francia, Lotharingia (the Low Countries, Burgundy and Italy) and East Francia (Germany).

This partition played its part in creating a vertical Europe with communication routes going from north to south across the Alpine passes, but whose longitudinal east-west borders were closed. These internal divisions, specific to what was to become Western Europe, were aggravated by the religious break-up that arose from the 1054 schism, and excluded the entire Orthodox bloc extending from Russia to Greece from the continent. Because of (or thanks to, as some would prefer) Charlemagne, east-west transit has never worked well on the European continent.

Charlemagne's track record is therefore ambivalent. Despite its brilliant conquests and political accomplishments, the Carolingian parenthesis was closed one century after having been opened. Nonetheless, if the first attempt to unify Europe after the fall of Rome had failed, its memory was to live on: it had opened perspectives that would never again be forgotten.

Otto of Saxony and the Successful Second Try

The second try came a century and a half later and turned out to be significantly more promising and enduring. In February 962, King Otto I of Saxony, a distant descendant of Charlemagne's, followed in the footsteps of his ancestor and had himself crowned Emperor in Rome. After a series of victories against the Slavic and Magyar invaders, he was called upon for help by Pope John XII whose states were threatened by the dukes of Lombardy and provided it. Thus, what was later to be known as the Holy Roman Empire of the German Nation was born. It was to last eight hundred and fifty years until Napoleon struck it a fatal blow in 1806.

At its height, the Holy Empire encompassed the territories of East-Central Europe, Germany, the Netherlands, Belgium, Austria, Bohemia, Croatia, Switzerland, Burgundy, the north of Italy and central Italy. Only the western Franks (France), Spanish Aragon and nascent England were not a part of it. In imitation of the Carolingians, the various dynasties that were to rule within It—Ottonian, Salian, Hohenstaufen, and Habsburg—depended on the Roman Church. Thanks to its tight network of parishes, bishoprics and monasteries, the Church had both the administrative infrastructure and the competent subjects to manage so vast and disparate a community. This close interdependence between the Pope and the Emperor, the Church and the Empire, the spiritual and the temporal, was also to have major consequences for the destiny of Europe.

First of all, as mentioned earlier, it was to bring on the definitive rupture with the Orthodox Church and the Byzantine Empire that would be effective in 1054. At the beginning, the Germanic Emperor and the Pope supported each other in an effort to reinforce their power to the detriment of the eastern patriarchs and the emperors of Byzantium. Both figures, the popes and the emperors, were to dominate the historical scene of Western Europe for six centuries up to Charles V, as we can see by rereading Dante's *Divine Comedy* or decoding the first arcane of the Tarot of Marseille...

To a certain extent, the Holy Empire would succeed where Charlemagne had failed, as long as the alliance with Rome proved to be effective and provided, at least in the beginning, a solid political and ideological cohesion.

The situation evolved in two phases. In 962, like Charlemagne, Otto managed to have himself crowned Emperor by the Pope as a reward for the services rendered against the Lombards. The Pope, however, refused the liturgical reform for the same old reason, namely the bishops' resistance. The German Emperors were adamant and fraudulently imposed the *filioque* in the Credo sung during the coronation Mass of Germanic Emperor Henry II on February 14, 1014 in Rome. On the strength of their stature, which gave them prevailing political power in Europe, they had had non-Italian popes who were favorable to their cause elected to the throne of St. Peter. Outraged by such a show of strength, the eastern patriarchs refused to endorse a change that had not been approved by an ecumenical council, as it should have been. It was through the ambition of the sovereign Germans and the popes in their pay, that the schism was consummated.

The cost would prove to be very high in the long term. This time, the church-state complicity would divide Europe forever, cutting it hopelessly in half and allowing the Muslim Arabs and Turkish Ottomans to defeat the Byzantine Empire and the Eastern Christian Churches. The fracture between itself and the Greek-Orthodox and then the Slavic-Orthodox world is so deeply anchored in the European psyche that it continues to wreak havoc even today, as we can see in Russia's continuing ostracism and the Russophobia prevailing in the Western European countries of Catholic or Protestant tradition.

The second outcome, that was much more consequential for the destiny of the young empire, emerged as a bloody conflict between the empire and the papacy. As often occurs in history, the allies would not delay in tearing each other apart after their initial convergence. No sooner had the common Orthodox/Greek/Byzantine adversary been discarded than the two allies of yesteryear found nothing more to say to each other...

In taking a closer look at the scenario, we see that it was the emperor who was in command at first, from 962 to 1075. The imperial administration named the bishops and imposed its will on the popes, controlling their election. The bishoprics and abbeys provided both the framework and the administrative subjects of the empire. For the first time in the history of the continent, a north-south axis was created across the Alps between the Baltic and North Seas and the Mediterranean. The Holy Empire of the German nation thus gradually became the spinal cord of Europe along a vertical axis that would see action during World War II, with the alliance known precisely as the Axis Powers. In 1184, one hundred and thirty years after the official beginning of the schism and thanks to a truce with the Pope, the Empire became hallowed and took the name of Holy Roman Empire (*Sacrum Imperium romanum*), thus consecrating its political and ideological unity against the Greek Orthodox adversary.

This admirable unity would soon break apart once the papacy was no longer bound to share its power with the eastern patriarchs. Just as the German emperors were freed from their commitments towards the Byzantine emperor, the popes also wanted more power and strode towards absolutism to the point of gaining the upper hand over the emperor.

It all began in 1075 with the famous Investiture Controversy where each party claimed the right to choose and install the bishops. Two years later, King and Roman Emperor Henry IV was excommunicated. Disgraced by the scandal and as a sign of penitence, he was forced to go and kneel down before the Pope in Canossa. This symbolic act proved to be disastrous for his authority. The conflict flared up again in the 12th and 13th centuries under Emperors Frederick Barbarossa and Frederick II Hohenstaufen. With them, the Empire had reached its maximal expansion, but neither was able to make the Pope give in: they, too, were convicted and fell from the grace of the sovereign pontiffs. In 1122, the Concordat of Worms put an end to the struggle over investiture. In Italy and Burgundy the Emperor was compelled to accept the free election of bishops by the church but retained the absolute discretion to invest them with their lay attributes. While the emperors certainly lost a lot of prestige in the adventure, they also pulled off the initial separation of church and state regarding their rights and obligations, thus gaining some independence from the religious authority. The Concordat was the first stepping-stone in the budding emancipation of the state from the church. But for the other European monarchies such as France, the benefits reaped were far greater.

In 1231 the emperor's power dwindled even further when the Diet of Worms forced Frederick II to cede certain sovereign rights to the princes, who thereafter recovered the right to mint money, establish customs and even legislate in certain fields.

The conflict with the papacy resumed even more intensely in Italy and Germany after 1240 with the ongoing battle between the Guelphs and the Ghibellines, who supported the Pope and the Emperor respectively. It was to last throughout the Middle Ages, and provided Dante and Machiavelli with the material for their biting chronicles.

In 1356, in order to avoid double elections, the Golden Bull laid down for the first time the principles for the sovereign's election. It also defined the group of prince-electors, declared indivisible so as to prevent an increase in their number. Conversely, the Golden Bull excluded any papal right to the king's election and reduced the right to wage private wars.

The Concordat of 1447 between Pope Nicholas V and Emperor Frederick III once again regulated papal rights and the privileges of the Church and bishops in the Empire, as well as the election of the bishops, abbots and priors. It also provided for the attribution of religious dignities and the financial succession of the abbots and bishops.

The imperial reform concluded by the Diet of Worms on August 7, 1495 was another major advance of the Constitution. It advocated an Eternal Peace forbidding private wars between nobles and attempted to restore the imperial power. Any armed conflict or private justice was henceforth considered to be anti-constitutional. Litigations were to be settled by the territorial jurisdictions or the imperial courts. Any person breaking the Eternal Peace was subject to heavy sentences that could consist of high fines or banishment from the empire.

In 1521, the Imperial Register specified the number of troops that the Imperial Estates had to supply to the Imperial Army and the amounts to be paid for supporting it. In 1555, the Peace of Augsburg (or Augsburg Settlement) extended the perpetual peace to the confessional level and gave up the idea of a religious unit.

In an effort to overrule this weakening process and the *exits* that went with it, the empire constantly reformed its governance, at times quite successfully. Its strategy consisted in gradually withdrawing into the Germanic sector. Thus, in the 15th century, the Holy Roman Empire was to take on the name of "German": the Holy Roman Empire of the German Nation (*Imperium Romanum Sacrum Nationis Germanicae* or *Heiliges Reich der Deutscher Nation*). Under the Habsburg dynasty, particularly under Maximilian I, who ruled from 1508 to 1519 and Charles V, 1519 to 1558, it even enjoyed a certain revival.

Yet in spite of the power boost brought about by the gold from the Americas; despite the sack of Rome and the diverse military interventions in Italy; notwithstanding the immense expanse of its territories, (the first world empire on which the sun never set), Charles V came up against two obstacles: France and the Protestant resistance. His dream of a universal European empire would never dawn. From then on, the Holy Roman Empire of the German Nation would begin a decline that later reforms would be unable to check.

After the Thirty Years' War, the Treaties of Westphalia were declared a perpetual fundamental law in 1654. They confirmed the reorganization and the sovereignty of the internal territories of the Holy Empire, thus further mitigating the central power. They also granted the Calvinists the same recognition as the Catholics and the Lutherans. Dispositions regulating religious peace and denominational parity were set up in the imperial institutions. Peace had returned, but the state power was once again in the hands of the States.

The Holy Empire: A Union before the Union

In its structure, its extent, the way it functioned, as well as in its prodigious capacity to adapt, the Holy Roman Empire of the German Nation is the institution that comes closest to the European Union of today.

It appeared initially as a supra-territorial entity endowed with strong vertical governance embodied by the transcendent figure of the emperor, and governed horizontally through a tight network of ill-defined organs with redundant though closely intertwined competencies.

If we substitute the dukes and lords with the Presidents and Prime Ministers; the Emperor and the Imperial Diet with the Commission, the European Council or the European Parliament; the imperial states by the Member States, we come fairly close to the system of governance of the present-day European Union! Both entities function like one of Tinguely's machine-sculptures, operating mysterious mechanisms as complex as they are improbable. Yet they dialogue and link up with one another through an entanglement of weights and counter-weights according to winding impulse mechanisms with no apparent overall plan.

Like the European Union of today, the Holy Empire was never able to dissolve the local resistances and identities. It wound up integrating them into a confederation that was very formalized in its procedures yet increasingly inconsistent as far as politics were concerned.

Its quirky nature and operation always gave rise to controversy. Jurist Samuel von Pufendorf compared it to a "monster" in his work published under a pseudonym in 1667. One hundred years later, Karl Theodor von Dalberg, Archbishop of Mainz, came to its defense by describing it as "a durable Gothic construction that is not built according to the state of the art, but where one lives securely." Such remarks might well be heard from the lips of Europeanists and anti-Europeanists today!

Austria and Mitteleuropa

As a part of the Holy Empire, and at the same time, a state in its own right, Austria was also an interesting example of European unification. Very quickly it attained a dominant position at the heart of the empire—not unlike Germany and its increasing influence in the European Union today.[6] Austria's course was both parallel and

---

6 The power struggle within the Holy Empire was constantly on the rise, as it is now within the EU and more widely throughout Europe. From a minor little duchy in the 13th century, Austria became a mighty empire that ended up supplanting the original empire of which it was a member. For Bohemia, the opposite occurred. After having played a central role at the height of the Holy

closely bound to the Holy Empire, for from 1438 to 1806 all of its rulers bore the imperial crown. Yet Austria made the wager to move ahead following a different approach that moreover proved to be successful. The Habsburgs had emigrated from Switzerland to Austria in the 12th century, and thanks to an ingenious marriage and dynastic policy, never ceased to expand their domains. After encroaching on their neighbors, they made an alliance with Bohemia before spreading to the south (Italy, Slovenia and Croatia) and to the east (Slovakia, Hungary, Galicia).

In the 18th century, under Marie-Therese and Joseph II, Austria asserted its position as a leading European power. From 1804–1805, its rulers attempted to counter Napoleon, who had just had himself crowned emperor and would accept no contender. The Habsburgs, who were but kings in their states, were compelled to relinquish their imperial title after the forced dissolution of the Holy Empire in 1806. In compensation for the loss, they laid claim to their own imperial crown, that of Austria, which would finally be granted to them with the Treaty of Vienna in 1815.

This unequalled performance was to leave a profound mark in all of central Europe, whose different peoples had never been accustomed to living under the same roof. Although it disappeared after its defeat in 1918, the Austro-Hungarian *Mitteleuropa* had succeeded in creating a very unique climate and culture whose passing many European writers such as Stefan Zweig, Joseph Roth and Claudio Magris would regret despite all of its shortcomings.

From a historical viewpoint, Austria was both ahead of and behind the times. Ahead, because it had successfully created the first multinational modern state; behind, because its governance—its monarchical régime—was unable to carry out simultaneously a containment policy ruling nationalism within and a war-provoking

---

Empire in the 12th and 13th centuries, the Kingdom of Bohemia stepped aside in favor of Austria and became its possession after 1278. Could this be a taste of what might happen to France if Germany should carry on with its hegemony? At this stage, it is impossible to say. One thing is certain: the relationships between the states of a distorted and ill-structured federation are under constant change and contribute to the general imbalance of the entity, as we shall see further on.

policy of expansion without (in the Balkans). Consequently its defeat after World War I struck a fatal blow.

Napoleon: The Second Failed Attempt to Unite Europe by Force

At the end of the 18th century, the French Revolution jostled the old monarchies, leaving them patient and restrained in their ambitions, and opened the way to adventurers. The continental unification project was taken up again by Napoleon. The French emperor aimed to restore the imperial project for his own benefit. And to do so, he used and abused the potent *soft power* of the French Revolution. Drawing on the very promising ideas of the Revolution, he set out to diffuse the principle of citizenship to the detriment of that of individuals as subjects of the prince, and to promulgate the new Civil Code all over Europe.

The Good Word borne by the French—citizenship, equality, fraternity—made its way throughout Europe at the pace of the French victories, somewhat like human rights and democracy following the wheels of American army Humvees today. From this standpoint, Napoleon succeeded, at least at first, in giving Europe a breath of fresh air—to such an extent that Hegel, believing the Absolute was parading beneath his window on the evening of October 13, 1806 at Jena, exclaimed: "I saw the Emperor—this world-soul—riding out of the city on reconnaissance. It is a truly wonderful sensation to see such an individual, who, concentrated here at a single point, astride a horse, reaches out over the world and masters it."[7]

But Hegel was soon disillusioned, and the rest of Europe with him. Napoleon's project was more a tyranny than a liberation of the oppressed. Unable to convince the English and the Russians by persuasion or by force, his short-lived reign abruptly ended in defeat.

As brief as it was, the revolutionary and Napoleonic epic would nevertheless leave Europe a sizable, though very ambivalent,

---

[7] Georg Wilhelm Friedrich Hegel, *Correspondance,* Vol. 1, p. 114, Paris, Gallimard, 1963.

heritage. On the one hand, it sowed the seeds of liberty, equality and citizenship for many European peoples. It brought sovereignty, formerly embodied by the monarchs by divine right, down to the national level. Napoleon had regimented and channeled these principles for his own benefit, but he had also promoted them through his famous codes: the Civil Code, the Commercial Code, the Criminal Code and the Penal Code, thus completely modernizing economic law and the judiciary system. But at the same time, the Revolution and the Empire infected Europe with the virus of nationalism.

The revolutionary and Napoleonic turmoil was followed by the Holy Alliance. This was not a unifying project insofar as it did not aim to establish a single vertical power but rather to share the management of the continent in such a way that each member would be its own master without having to fear a popular uprising. This attempt at governance through consultation proved to be quite effective, for it ensured almost a century of relative peace on the continent. Thanks to this mechanism and to the "concert of nations" that came after 1848, the European states avoided destroying each other and resolved their conflicts through summit conferences or, when that was not possible, by limited wars (the Crimean War of 1853, the Italian wars for independence, the Austro-Prussian War of 1866, the Franco-Prussian War of 1870).

It should also be pointed out that this was the first attempt at European governance established on a conservative, if not reactionary basis, thereby showing that conservative forces, too, could develop a vision of Europe. European construction is not the prerogative of the so-called progressive forces...

Hitler and Stalin: Union through Blood and Tears

As was the case with Napoleon, the last two attempts preceding the project of a European Union also arose in very particular circumstances. Both were carried out by force of arms and the mediation of dictatorships embodied by the great charismatic figures of Hitler and Stalin. It is striking to note that both regimes, with their horrific excesses, were modern hybrids of the ancient

Greek tyrannies: like them, Nazism and Communism were based on mobilizing the popular masses.

In our liberal democratic regimes, it is distasteful to evoke the two above-mentioned figures, as repulsive as they are outrageous, especially with regard to Europe. And yet, from a historiographical perspective, we have to admit that they both set up coherent and ambitious European projects.

Hitler mentioned the New European Order project, *Neuordnung Europas*, as early as 1938, when he met with Mussolini, and then in 1940, when he met with Petain. It was officially launched in 1941 during his speech at the Sports Palace in Berlin: "The year 1941 will be, I am sure, the historic year of a great new European order."[8] According to the Nazi propaganda, it was all about creating a new, economically integrated Europe—like the Greater East Asia Co-Prosperity Sphere of the Imperial Japanese Government—that included the whole of the continent with the exception of the Jews and the Soviet "Judeo-Bolsheviks." The objective was in fact to constitute a Europe under German hegemony. This very restrictive project nevertheless succeeded in appealing to many French intellectuals and pacifists, such as Drieu la Rochelle, who supported the United States of Europe in the interwar period, and who would collaborate with Nazi Germany after France was occupied in June 1940.

Thus, until the turning point of the war in 1943, the reflections on and proposals for a unified Europe bloomed one after the other with highly suggestive titles that could be read under the pen of the contemporary Europeanists: "The Time Has Come for a Unified Europe" (Maurice Lambillotte, 1940); "The Rationalization of the Continental Economy" (Georges Lafond, 1941); "The Economic Order of the New Europe" (Walther Funk, 1941); "The End of the Obstacles to European Union" (Louis Le Fur, 1941); "A Discourse on the Europeist Method" (Henri de Man, 1942); "Integrating Eastern Europe" (Anton Zischka, 1942); "The Great Space, A New

---

8 Yves Durand, *Le Nouvel Ordre européen nazi*, Brussels, Éditions Complexe, 1999. And also Mark A. Mazower, "Hitler's New Order 1939–1945," in Diplomacy and Statecraft, Vol. 7, no 1, 1996.

Order in Global Economy" (Ferdinand Fried, 1942); "Tomorrow, the European Constitution" (*Frankfurter Zeitung*, 1942). These publications demonstrated the importance the Nazis gave their project for a new European order, which they promoted through intensive poster campaigns and numerous public and radio broadcast debates.

As Bernard Bruneteau pointed out, Hitler's project, in spite of the violence, the forced requisitions and the *Service du travail obligatoire (STO*—English: Compulsory Work Service), was

> far from boiling down to a mere issue of opportunism or a purely Fascist engagement. This attitude involved genuine militants for a united Europe who believed they were carrying on with a political struggle that had often begun in the 1920s.
>
> They were pacifists who dreamed of putting an end to state sovereignty; technicians who had confidence in the virtues of an economic government; socialists in the quest for a last, mobilizing Utopia. All were victims of an illusion that made them believe in Hitler's commitment to Europe, blinding them to the monstrous realities of his new order. [...] Vichy's Europeist intellectuals continued the reflections begun in the days of Briand on the conditions of a political and economic federation. At times their terminology was disconcerting: "community of communities," "supra-continental management organ," or "single federal currency." And what if the plans for Europe imagined under the Occupation were the unsettling prehistory of our democratic European construction? [asks the author].[9]

The intellectuals and corporatism enthusiasts who were close to Vichy and who would become references after the war,

---

[9] Bernard Bruneteau, *Les "Collabos" de l'Europe nouvelle,* Paris, CNRS Éditions/Biblis, 2016. By the same author: *L'Europe nouvelle d'Hitler. Une illusion des intellectuels de la France de Vichy,* Paris, Éditions du Rocher, 2003.

like André Siegfried ("The Profound Unity of the 'Western Civilization'")[10] and especially the economist François Perroux ("Federal Authority and Single Currency"[11]), many of whom had attended the Vichy School for Executives in Uriage, would also become close to Jean Monnet and inspire not only post-war thinking but the very conception of the European Project.[12]

Care must be taken not to confuse the Vichy regime with the Nazi regime and Uriage with Vichy, insofar as the school was closed on Laval's orders on 1st January 1943, and several of its students later made the right choice in joining the Resistance. All the same, during at least the first years of the Occupation, many of the founders of the European Community were sympathetic to the National Revolution of which Petain was an emblem, and to corporatism conceived as not only an economic but also a political and antiparliamentarian doctrine. Did Robert Schuman, the "Founding Father of Europe" along with Jean Monnet, not vote for Marshal Petain's full powers on July 10, 1940 and accept the post of Under-Secretary of State in his first government? They

---

10 André Siegfried, "La civilisation occidentale," in Revue des Deux Mondes, September 1941.

11 François Perroux, "La monnaie dans une économie internationale organisée," in Revue de l'économie contemporaine, December 1943.

12 Bernard Bruneteau, *Histoire de l'idée européenne au premier XXe siècle*, op. cit., and especially Antonin Cohen, *De Vichy à la communauté européenne*, Paris, PUF, 2012. The latter shows how communitary Europe's emergence from the Resistance was a far cry from the official historical version. On the contrary, it owed much to the corporatist thinkers who admired the pre-1940 Italian and German corporatisms and thus influenced the genesis of the European construction. He shows in particular what the project of a supranational authority in charge of managing the market economy without parliamentary control, as proposed by Jean Monnet and Robert Schuman on May 9, 1950, inherits from the conception of the economy and of politics arising from the third option: neither capitalism nor socialism. The founding act of the European construction thus appears in a different light, not so much as a beginning but as an end. Incidentally, we should point out that two of François Perroux's major works, removed from his official bibliography, were published in 1938 under the title Capitalisme et communauté de travail) and in 1942 under the title Communauté. The term flourished and was to become the official name of united Europe up until the Treaty of Maastricht (cf. Antonin Cohen, "Du corporatisme au keynésianisme," in Revue française de science politique, Vol. 56, 2006/4, pp. 555–592.

were wary of socialism and communism, and this led them to conceive a strong state that was responsible for regenerating society and arbitrating the opposing interests of the social classes, which is the primary feature of democratic regimes.

Their Christian convictions, influenced by Emmanuel Mounier's personalism, also explain why, after the war, they would belong to the large family of Christian-Democrats, the very one who paved the way for a European Economic Community inspired by the liberalism of the fifties and excluding any other formula. From Konrad Adenauer and Walter Hallstein, diplomat and first president of the European Commission from 1958 to 1967, to Jacques Delors, without forgetting Italy's De Gasperi, Belgium's Paul-Henri Spaak or France's Robert Schuman and Jean Monnet, most of the signatories of the first European treaties had supported, at some time in their lives, this third corporatist option between capitalism and socialism, between fascism and parliamentarianism, before finding themselves under the Christian-Democratic banner.

Communism: Equality at Any Price

As for communism, it operated from the bottom, starting from the lower classes. It sought to conquer the world by constructing a "New Man," rather than a new European order imposed from higher up by a racial and cultural elite convinced that it was superior. From the start its inspirers, Marx and Engels, had placed their ambitions on a global, planetary level. As the most advanced capitalist society, Europe was to serve as a spearhead for the proletarian revolution. Contrary to Marx's theories, however, the revolution did not occur in Germany, Great Britain or even France, which were the most stable countries economically although they harbored the strongest social contradictions, but in the periphery, in backward Russia.

Against all odds, whether Marxist or capitalist, communism took root in that country. In spite of a ruthless civil war widely supported by the outside powers from France to Great Britain and the United States who sent contingents to combat the Bolshevik regime, the country was still semi-feudal. After the victory in 1921 and the need to reconstruct the economy devastated by eight years of war, debates soon raged between the tenants of world revolution led by Trotsky, and Stalin's supporters, who were convinced that the revolution had to be consolidated from within and the country modernized before they could consider exporting it *urbi et orbi*. Moreover, it was of no use counting on a hypothetical collapse of capitalism in Europe or the United States.

With the failure of the Spartacist uprising in Berlin and that of Bela Kun in Hungary, Stalin had understood that the world revolution was not going to happen soon, and that it was safer for the young Bolshevik power to rely on its own forces and construct socialism "in one single country." The Bolsheviks, however, never completely gave up on proletarian internationalism; the Cominform and the Comintern remained essential constituents of their foreign policy.

We know the rest of the story of European communism with its alliances and counter-alliances, its *Internationales* and its fratricidal struggles. Whatever one may think of communism, the fact remains that it was durably established for nearly seventy years in Russia and fifty years in the eastern half of Europe, while holding firm in China, the future leading world power. In this respect, Stalin's Europe—or at least the eastern part of it –lasted as long as the Europe of Charlemagne, Napoleon and Hitler put together. And this, we should not ignore, even if it goes against the conventional wisdom prevailing in today's Europe shaped by capitalism and liberal democracy, and seeking at all costs to close the communist parenthesis. We should note in passing that Stalin never "conquered" Eastern Europe or even the Baltic countries through military aggression. He occupied the three Baltic republics, former tsarist possessions, following the German-Soviet Nonaggression Pact of 1939. We should also point out that the Munich Agreement of 1938, as well as France and Great Britain's refusal to make an alliance with him, put Stalin in a dilemma. It was in this state of mind that he attacked Finland, an ally of Nazi Germany whose cannons were a threat to Leningrad.

The Munich signatories barely masked what European historiography disregards today: the Munich Agreement consisted in far more than simply handing the Sudetenland over to Hitler. It also aimed at leading Hitler to attack Soviet Russia first and turn his attention away from France and Great Britain—exactly what Hitler intended to do immediately after Munich. The 1939 Molotov-Ribbentrop Pact succeeded in making him change his mind at the last minute and postpone his plans to attack the Soviet Union. It was as vital for the East as it was for the West to avoid taking the first German blow. The course of the war showed that they were right.

As for the Soviet stranglehold on Eastern Europe, it was the direct consequence of the German defeat following the invasion of June 1941 and the various Conferences—Tehran, Yalta and Potsdam—held by the victors. The Soviet league scrupulously respected the treaties even after the western camp launched the Cold War. The best proof of this was Stalin's failure to react to the Greek civil war. It had been sparked by the British and the Americans which refused to accept that liberated Greece be governed by the communist resistance members who, like the Yugoslav Partisans, had defeated the Nazi oppression by themselves and were therefore fully legitimate. Defeated in 1949, the communist resistance fighters were deported to camps that rivaled in cruelty with Nazi camps and the Soviet Gulags. For almost five decades, the eastern half of Europe and Russia therefore shared a common market as well as an ideology and military alliance that was perfectly symmetrical to their equivalents in Western Europe: NATO vs. the Warsaw Pact, EEC vs. COMECON, capitalism vs. communism, private property vs. collective property. It is of less importance that this eastern bloc later collapsed in favor of the western model, just as Charlemagne, Frederick Barbarossa, Charles V, Napoleon and Hitler had failed: a historical experiment that lasts seven decades in spite of all its deviances cannot be ignored.

The hatred that the effort for a united, communist Europe generated in the national-conservative elites of Eastern Europe in power today and in the liberal democracies of the West is no reason to elude the fundamental question: why did this system manage to establish itself and remain for so long in Europe, and why did it appeal to such huge masses of peoples in the East as well as in the West before dissolving under Mikhail Gorbachev? Whether rejected or missed, the experiment left its marks, its habits, its nostalgia, and they will all come back one day. Just like the Austro-Hungarian Empire, albeit on another register, the disappearance of communism in Eastern Europe was, at the time, a relief for the newly independent nations and the liberal elite of Western Europe. Yet a quarter of a century later, there also lingers a feeling of loss, of regret, a void.

Politics and quantum mechanics obey the same laws: matter is stronger than antimatter. But the universe remains orphaned by what it has lost, by what has become invisible to the human eye. Without that lost part, it would not have existed. The universe has preserved its trace deep within its fibers and in the laws that govern it. This "dark" matter continues to influence the universe.

The Failure of Strong-arm Tactics

What lessons can we derive from these consecutive non-converted trials, these failures and partial successes? Historians explain that the Carolingian Empire disappeared following dynastic quarrels. Likewise, Charles V, who was always short of money in spite of the gold from the Americas, lost his European battle because he lacked the funds to pay his troops at the fateful moment. It is also said that if Grouchy had arrived in time, Napoleon could have won the Battle of Waterloo. All of these arguments hold some truth. But they have to be taken for what they are: limited explanations that do not paint the whole picture. The immediate causes are like the eyes of an insect: they give partial, multiple and useful visions but inhibit the general view. So things have to be considered at a higher level.

Lesson number one: the worst way to unify Europe is by force. The brutal conquerors like Napoleon or Hitler did not hold out for more than fifteen years in spite of being supported by powerful armies and ideologies. They ended up antagonizing the European nations as a whole: Napoleon, for propagating the ideals of the Age of Enlightenment at bayonet point; Hitler, for his use of gas chambers to promote his theories on the superiority of the Aryan race over "degenerate" peoples. This reasoning clearly shows that the implacable yet shrewd conquerors like Charlemagne and Stalin were more effective and enduring. From Pepin the Short to the Treaty of Verdun in 843, the Carolingian Empire dominated Europe for almost a century thanks to a clever policy of acquisitions, consolidations and alliances, particularly with the pope. The Soviet massacres and military (or police) brutality caused countless—though selective—casualties among carefully defined peoples or "class elements." In parallel, both the Carolingians and the Communists established a new and efficient administration: the former, by resting on the Church and its clergy, monks and abbots; the latter, on the contrary, by fighting the Church and naming a new generation of civil, atheist executives.

Both gave great importance to education, literacy, culture and propaganda. The Carolingians spread the written word by developing the Caroline script, creating schools, and supporting the Catholic theology and liturgy that countered the dominant Orthodox culture of the time. They made their arts and culture shine through illuminated manuscripts, mosaics and goldsmithing. They standardized bookkeeping and currency.

At its beginnings, the Soviet regime did likewise. It brought literacy to the uneducated masses and encouraged the film industry, music and painting. It disseminated a new theology of history and of human development—historical materialism—that appealed to millions of exploited proletarians and peasants deprived of their land.

Lastly, both introduced economic and social reforms that greatly increased the prosperity of many sectors of the population. The Carolingian Empire restored trade between northern and southern Europe across the alpine passes, forming a common market with peoples with whom they had never before had economic relations. For their part, the Bolsheviks hoisted Russia from the Middle Ages to the industrial era and provided electricity in less

From Charlemagne to Stalin: The Failure of Constraint

than two generations. They even succeeded in getting ahead of their American opponents in their space program.

These achievements explain why the systems lasted for a relatively long time, for they were not considered as totally negative. They collapsed as a result of internal but symmetrically opposed factors. In the case of the Carolingian Empire, the outside threats only played a marginal role and were more a consequence than a cause of its fragmentation. Pressure from the "barbarians" had always existed but it had never been able to fell the empire, which was exceedingly stable and unified: in other words, well governed. The Arab invaders in Andalusia were incapable of vanquishing Charles Martel in 732, and their successors lay low.

The major cause was therefore internal and can be resumed in modern terms as follows: the Carolingian Empire suffered from a serious and crippling governance failure. Its institutional architecture did not measure up to the challenges it faced. The succession to the throne has always been the weak point of monarchical systems, which flounder when it comes to setting up clear and widely accepted rules. The legitimacy crisis is a permanent threat.

Division and fratricidal wars due to institutional deficiencies are what weakened the empire and got the better of it, much more than the Norman or Saracen attacks. Strong institutions, however, whether monarchical or democratic, usually survive a mediocre ruler (as long, of course, as the state of mediocrity does not last too long…).

As for the Soviet implosion, it was not caused by an institutional problem—on the contrary, the Soviet Union had a sort of hypergovernance, or "hypertrophied" governance—but by the inability of the regime to ensure the material prosperity and well being of its citizens even though these conditions were stipulated in the official Marxist doctrine. The growing divergence between state ideology and reality from the early 1960s discredited the regime in the eyes of the people far more than Stalin's purges and deportations, the deprivation and famine engendered by forced industrialization, the war against Nazi Germany with its 26 million dead, or the samizdats of the dissidents of the seventies.

No United Europe without Freedom and Equality

But it is also true that one of the reasons for the Nazi and Soviet failures stemmed from their head-on opposition to one or the other tendencies that Europe had displayed over the centuries of its evolution: the desire for both freedom and equality. Hitler's regime in particular flouted the two major values cultivated since the Renaissance that had structured the intellectual and political life of Europe for five centuries and that now fashion its imagination and political practices.

Over the years, the quest for freedom has taken on different forms. In the Middle Ages, it was a struggle for the primacy of the temporal over the spiritual; in modern times, it has become a claim for independence and national sovereignty. At the individual level, the quest first took the form of a fight for freedom of religion and worship with the 1517 Reformation and the emergence of Calvinism in 1536. It later became a struggle for freedom of conscience and human rights with the censure of absolutism, the English Revolution of the 17th century, human rights and the philosophy of the Enlightenment in the 18th century, right up to its triumph with the French proclamation of the Declaration of the Rights of Man and of the Citizen in 1789.

These centuries of fighting for freedom prevailed over every form of religious and political resistance and culminated in the establishment of liberal democracies on practically the entire European continent.

The history of equality, the second of the great principles specified by the French Revolution, is a bit more complex. It goes back to Christianity, which is clearly opposed to the slavery and inequality of the ancient world that created distinct differences between the citizens, who had all the rights; the foreigners, who were deprived of the right to vote and access to land property; and the slaves or helots who were destined to toil and feed everyone else. The Christian Gospel innovated by advocating the principle of the universal equality of all humankind regardless of race, sex, status or social condition. This revolutionary principle—which would be much later considered by Nietzsche as laying the foundations for a religion of slaves—endured all sorts of trials and tribulations and encountered much resistance. Over the centuries, nevertheless, it eventually impregnated the European conscience and was applied—at least partially—at the political level with the dawn of democracy. And the very principle of democracy was based on the formal, if not perfectly effective, equality of all citizens.

Nazism aimed at reversing this secular movement that upheld freedom and equality. Deploying extreme brutality, it did away with freedom and equality for one and all, reserving it exclusively for a small minority (albeit the majority in Germany): the race of the Aryan lords.

Hitler was able to lean on a strong social foundation by joining forces with the most anti-egalitarian members of the bourgeoisie stemming from Calvinism, who believed that eternal salvation is reserved for a predestined minority of chosen ones, and those of the nationalist and colonialist right wing, who considered that the race of white Europeans was superior to the others. At the same time, he disgusted both the most fervent partisans of equality, the Soviet Communists, and the most committed defenders of freedoms: the Anglo-Saxon liberal right wing, the true Christians, and the social democrats, who were the defenders of any and all minorities.

From this standpoint, we can acknowledge that communism embraced, often exaggeratedly, one of the two cardinal values of Europe: equality. This explains its success, at least in its early stages, and the apprehension that it inspired in the right-wing elites as a whole, always very skeptical of equality. However, because of the Russian civil war, the foreign invasions despatched to overthrow it, and the violent elimination of the radical socialist movements embodied by Rosa Luxemburg and Karl Liebknecht in Berlin, and also because of the power struggles that eroded it from the inside, Soviet communism was to sacrifice freedom very quickly on the altar of equality and turn into a vicious dictatorship. In wanting to ensure that equality triumphed by abolishing freedom, communism also ended up going astray. The absence of freedom coupled with economic incompetence brought about its collapse.

Partial conclusion: the failed experiments of Nazism and Communism have taught us that if it is to last, every European construction must meet all the requirements of freedom and equality over the long term. Yet with respect to this freedom and equality, i.e., at the level of democracy, the functioning of the current European Union leaves much to be desired...

Partial Success of the Soft Approach

To understand today's Europe, let us go back to the enlightening examples of the Holy Roman Empire of the German Nation and the Austro-Hungarian Empire. Of all the historic attempts made, they were the most successful, for they spanned the centuries despite all their contradictions. Their longevity owes much to the slow and gradual method of growth that they adopted, although it was not always peaceful and gentle at first. We saw that early on, the Holy Empire, for example, provoked the religious schism with Byzantium in order to justify its secession from the Eastern Roman Empire. But once the great conquests were over, their territorial integration took place over the long term by means of marriages of consent and intelligent matrimonial strategies rather than by the sword. It was not long before ideology was relegated to second place and even gave way to a serious conflict with the Church.

Out of the 844 years, six months and four days that the Holy Roman Empire of the German Nation lasted, it enjoyed territorial expansion for two centuries before eroding almost continuously for the following 650 years. It lost Italy, Burgundy, the Netherlands, Belgium and Switzerland, leaving the Empire with only the territory comprising Austria and West Germany.

Its political evolution followed the same ascending curve only to regularly descend afterwards: centralized and absolute in its early times, the imperial power then began its constant decline. This, however, did not prevent it from preserving its prestige and showing remarkable resilience. In spite of its countless faults, the improbable structure proved to have its use.

Although they were not in a position to engage in offensive wars and thus to expand, the two empires succeeded in ensuring political stability in central Europe and the peaceful resolution of conflicts between its members (with the exception of religious wars). They knew how to curb the power claims of their most ambitious princes, protect their subjects from the despotism of the nobles, and defend everyone from the temptation of foreign conquests (for instance, Louis XIV's France), thus serving to mitigate any centrifugal tendencies. In short, the two empires performed an essential governmental function: security. The empire is indeed, above all, a security architecture. Let us not forget that twice, in the 16th century and again in 1683, the Holy Empire and Austria succeeded in vanquishing the Ottomans who had besieged Vienna and were threatening all of Christian Europe. Later, these empires largely focused on economic integration by developing a single market between northern and southern Europe and in central Europe for Austria. This "common market" made it possible to drain the increasing surplus of agricultural produce as well as the commodities of the fledgling urban industry towards the towns and the ports. Thanks to the monopoly on coin minting, a unique currency, the denier or imperial thaler, was imposed and was highly appreciated by the international merchants of the time. This monopoly, along with the exploitation of silver mines, also allowed the empires to control the "tonlieu," the revenue levied from tolls and local markets. In other words, the empires had complete control over all imports, exports and the circulation of goods.

Finally, there was the incessant creation of legal standards and courts to interpret them, in order to maintain the central power. From the reforms of 1495, the administration of justice, as well as the monopoly on law and the creation of legal framework, were moreover to become the main pillars of imperial power in the Holy Empire. It is worth noting that the courts were also enabled to serve as financial resources by recuperating the revenue from fines or by pronouncing judgments that enriched the imperial treasure.

This normative power is also the underlying force of the European Union today, as we shall see. Piling up laws and regulations anchors the machine and reinforces the power of the judges and the lawyers to the detriment of the executive. However, it also gives rise to a corpus of procedures, practices, customs and traditions that keep the pieces of the system together and justify the bureaucracy that directs it.

Like all supranational ensembles, empires are constantly torn between the centrifugal forces that aim to break them apart, and the centripetal forces—the centralization or the absolutization of power—that strive to keep them together. Their survival therefore depends on a skillful, internal power game of checks and balances. It is obvious that both the Holy Empire and Austria played with these constraints for a long time: they were centralizing and authoritarian when the trend tended towards absolutism; they were decentralizing and more liberal when the aspirations of the day so required.

It should also be noted that the emperors of the Holy Empire were elected, which was not an easy task, for it required the consent of the prince-electors and that of the pope for the coronation. While these multiple allegiances weakened the sovereign, at the same time they reinforced his legitimacy and prevented him from monopolizing public violence for his sole profit. In the case of Austria, the subtle balances between Catholics and Protestants, between Austria and Bohemia, and later between Austria and Hungary, forcing them to respect the other minorities which had their own languages and traditions, also contributed to balancing the omnipotence of the sovereigns and making them arbitrators rather than all-powerful despots.

In conclusion, these two empires managed to last as long as they were capable of ensuring the security of their members, providing a degree of economic prosperity, establishing socially useful standards, and maintaining, through the adequate institutions, a balance of power between the various political forces and the nations that made them up. They disappeared when they were no longer in a position to fulfill one or all of these functions.

With regard to Europe, we can legitimately ask the following questions: Is Europe capable of ensuring security and prosperity? Do its institutions respect the internal political and social balances? Are its standards set to meet the needs of one and all or of only a few? Is it in a position to respond to external pressure? Is it on the side of the very resilient Germanic Roman Empire and the greatly multinational Austrian Empire? Or is it following the fragile wake of Charlemagne and Mikhail Gorbachev?

CHAPTER 3

THE GREEK SYNDROME AND EUROPE'S AMERICAN ENCROACHMENT

> *Preconceived ideas, the gentle, natural, unconscious slopes of the mind will no doubt become insufficient and little used to resolve the new problems. Nationalism, internationalism, individualism run up against stalemates today, whirling through impossibilities, caught up in contradictions that will demand vigorous decision-making and clear-minded soul-searching.*
> ALBERT THIBAUDET, *ON THUCYDIDES*

> *History teaches but it has no pupils!*
> ANTONIO GRAMSCI, *ON ITALY AND SPAIN, ORDINE NUOVO*

> *Do not pay attention or give credit to what others may tell you, nor to the simplified and deceitful chronicles that will be written on this period to serve the logic of a linear and perishable history; true history is circular and goes on forever.*
> CARLOS FUENTES, *TERRA NOSTRA*

On November 2018, Europe celebrated the one hundredth anniversary of the end of World War I. French President Emmanuel Macron invited seventy heads of state to commemorate the end of the greatest massacre in the military history of Europe. A Peace Forum followed that was snubbed by the American President, Donald Trump. Everywhere, there were festivities in honor of the restored peace between France and Germany, ceremonies in honor of those who were killed in action, solemn speeches, exhibitions, and television broadcasts.

But have we really learned the lessons of this terrible war and those that followed it—World War II and the Cold War—and truly grasped what they meant for Europe?

In the preceding chapter, we listed the attempts to unify Europe that preceded the EU and studied the reasons for their success or failure. We are now going to change angles and go even further back in history to ancient Greece, whose great yet tragic destiny shows striking similarities with that of Europe.

After centuries of conquests and unequalled influence, the prestigious Greek civilization shamefully let itself be absorbed by the Romans in 146 BC. Why was Greece incapable of resisting the Roman expansion that displaced its standing in history? Why did the glorious victors of Marathon and Salamis against powerful Persia; the inventors of democracy, philosophy and rationalism; the builders of the temples of Delphi and Epidaurus, the architects of the Olympic stadium and of the Parthenon; Alexander's valiant infantrymen who had made the Hellenic civilization triumph as far as Pamir—why did these highly eminent Greeks come to such a pathetic end? These are questions that have been haunting Europe since World War I.

In his essay, *La Campagne avec Thucydide (On Thucydides)*, written just after the end of the war, the Franco-Swiss Hellenist, Albert Thibaudet, was one of the first to point out how remarkably alike World War I and the Peloponnesian War were, in spite of "the profound difference between a modern state and a Greek city-state."[1] In what way can a 2,400 year-old civil war between two city-states shed light on a war that took place between major European powers at the beginning of the 20th century? In every way—or almost.

Both conflicts—each in its own right—sealed the destiny of the part of the world in which they took place, with similarities

---

1 Albert Thibaudet, "La Campagne avec Thucydide," (On Thucydides) in *Thucydides, Histoire de la guerre du Péloponnèse,* Paris, Robert Laffont, coll. "Bouquins," 1990.

and parallelisms that fire the keen observer's imagination. In several respects, today's Europe and the main confederation of states that make it up, i.e. the European Union, call to mind the situation of Greece after the Peloponnesian War, when, according to Alexander, Greece was struggling to recover its old luster and forming coalitions to reconstruct its unity and preserve its independence in the face of the expansionist threats of its eastern and western neighbors.

Greece: A Miniature Europe?

To begin with, this common destiny of classical Greece and modern Europe is a geographical consequence. On different scales, both entities are peninsulas with their face to the sea, and their backs to a vast hinterland. The bays and mountainous promontories of Greece plunge into the heart of the Mediterranean Sea just as Europe projects itself into the Atlantic Ocean with the British Isles and into the Mediterranean with the Iberian Peninsula and the Italian mainland.

Both combine the solidity and gravity of land with the spirit of adventure and enterprise at sea. Both present "a continental mass with interior plains that feed the farming populations, and an agricultural evolution that puts it in contact with the routes of human circulation," says Thibaudet. He goes on: "We have often shown how Greece is a miniature of Europe, and how within Greece itself, Attica is a reduction of all of Greece."[2]

These similar geographies produced a history and a civilization that manifestly share common characteristics. The Greek peninsula and the extensive European peninsula alike, have nooks and crannies providing ideal conditions for human expansion to develop strong and diversified local cultures. These lands are neither rich nor uniform nor easily accessible enough to favor the emergence of hegemonic powers that would dominate enormous human populations. Above all, they are open to vast sea horizons that facilitate contact, unlock perspectives, break the chains of tradition, in short, that beckon to exploration and adventure.

---

2 Ibid., p. 123.

The Greek Syndrome and Europe's American Encroachment

This topography engendered very distinct local peculiarities that were embodied in city-states and states endowed with strong roots and well-established identities, while cultivating the feeling of sharing a common universe thanks to one language, one religion and their own institutions. The Greeks shared the alphabet, their gods, the Olympic games, and amphictyonies or religious councils to manage the greater temples. The Europeans had the Latin language, the Christian faith, the Church, and Roman law in common—at least up until the Renaissance.

Even the practice of date determination was similar. It was indexed on religion rather than on the reign of kings. In Greece, it was determined by the first Olympic games, which had a religious origin and were supposedly inaugurated in 776 BC on the initiative of the king of Elis. The first Olympiad served as the basis for dating the Greek calendar, just as the presumed birth date of Christ served to designate the year 1 in the European calendar.

If the characteristic geography of Greece impeded the emergence of huge empires ruled by absolute monarchies dominating masses of illiterate peasants and slaves, it was, however, propitious for the rise of very diverse political regimes, whether simple or double monarchies, aristocracies, oligarchies, tyrannies or democracies. The constant emulation/rivalry between them stimulated innovation, creativity, and inventiveness.

At the intellectual level, literature progressed rapidly with Homer and Hesiod thanks to the adoption of the Phoenician alphabet. The arts flourished, painting and sculpture thrived, uninhibited, and dozens of gods and goddesses enriched the divine pantheon. With the mastery of geometry and the invention of the Doric and Ionic columns in architecture, imposing temples and elegant public monuments sprang up, just like the Romanesque and Gothic cathedrals which would typify Europe in the Middles Ages.

Writing and arithmetic also boosted agriculture and industry: farmlands were manured, vases and amphorae were manufactured to transport wine and olive oil. New techniques such as the mill, the rudder and the anchor improved trade. There was a demographic explosion, and the population multiplied tenfold in four centuries between 800 and 350 BC. Vying in boldness, the cities stretched far out and founded colonies, one after the other, on the coasts of Asia Minor (Ionia), Africa (Cyrenaica), the Adriatic coast and Sicily, southern Italy (Magna Graecia), Provence, Spain, and even around the Black Sea in Crimea (Chersonese).

In 500 BC, Greece fanned out and established settlements everywhere in the eastern Mediterranean and on the shores of the Black Sea. At first, these colonies had close ties with their founding metropolises and engaged in economic, human and political trade on a regular basis. The division of labor between farmers on the one hand and the manufacturers of handicrafts and weapons on the other was intensified. Barter was no longer sufficient, and a monetary economy was set up thanks to Croesus, a sovereign of Asia Minor who was close to the Greeks, and his invention of state currency and the public monopoly of coin minting.

Maritime trade grew nonstop. Two monetary systems made their appearance based on the Aeginetan mina and the Euboean mina. The ports became major economic and political centers. With the opening of Piraeus, Athens soon became the leading maritime power thanks to its location at the heart of Attica and at the crossroads of the trade routes between the continent, Ionia, Crete, and the Bosporus.

It was also at this time that the institutions and laws that would make ancient Greece famous were established. Sparta, under the impulse of Lycurgus, invented a particular regime that was aristocratic, military and strictly egalitarian at the same time, while headed by a double monarchy. The semi-legendary Spartan lawgiver created the Gerousia, a sort of council of elders made up of men over sixty that functioned somewhat like a Supreme Court or final appeals court focused on balancing the power between the two kings and the assembly of citizens. It divided the Spartan territory into inalienable lots that each family was responsible for farming. The Spartan ruling class was formed by a few thousand citizens, who were forbidden to work and obliged to eat together, were compelled to dedicate themselves exclusively to the art of war.

In Athens in 621, Draco innovated by laying down the law in writing, thus making it available to the literate. He established a clear distinction between murder and involuntary homicide that eased the tension between the city-states and enabled them to free themselves from the infernal cycle of private vengeance. Two generations later, Solon abolished slavery due to debt, instituted a lay jury in the courts, and defined the poll-based tax according to each social class. As the popular assembly was open to everyone, the poll tax gave access to the magistracies. Thus Athens laid the foundations for a true democracy by entrusting the sovereign power to the citizens' assembly (excluding, however, slaves, women and foreigners).

A bit later in Locres, a colony of Magna Graecia in Calabria, Zaleucus also reformed the penal laws and enacted the sumptuary laws. In an effort to stave off the accumulation of wealth by the rich and to preserve the city from political disturbances, he forbade the citizens, in particular, from selling their patrimony, thus achieving a period of stability that was acknowledged and praised throughout Antiquity. Locres is also known for having invented a tradition of political economy that modern legislators, with their long-winded, questionable legislative innovation, would do well to draw on. Whoever wished to change a law or propose a new one, had to come before the assembly with a rope around his neck. If he failed to convince the majority of the citizens to accept his reform, he faced being hanged...

City-States Vying for Civilization

The European continent was to experience a similar evolution. After the fall of the Roman Empire in 476, Europe was faced with having to digest and assimilate the barbaric peoples. With Roman unity out of the picture, Europe had to reconstruct locally and deal with princes jealous of each other's authority. Christianity was established as the common religion, and Latin, in spite of having to compete with the vernacular languages, gained ground in culture, diplomacy, administration, philosophy and religious practice.

We shall not go over the entire intellectual and political history of Europe at this point. From Saint Augustine's *The City of God,* to Thomas More's *Utopia*; from Machiavelli and Baltasar Gracian to Montesquieu and Rousseau; from Hobbes, from Bodin and Kant to Hegel and Marx, the thinkers and philosophers who were at the origin of the state and of the modern political institutions of Europe are innumerable.

It can be acknowledged, all the same, that Europe's progression was analogous to that of Greece, for it went from a religiously inspired (St. Augustine, Abelard, St. Thomas Aquinas) political vision to a secular, lay and rational conception of politics. This gradual passage from religion to reason, from myth to critical thinking, from pope to emperor, from church to state, and from priest to officials elected by popular vote, follows the same process with Europe as with Greece.

Likewise, at the economic level, the European economy, which was purely agricultural and continental from the 5th century AD, slowly developed around the ports and through trade. In the South, there was Italy with Sicily, Genoa, Venice, Amalfi or Ragusa; in the North, the Hanseatic League took its first steps, followed by Spain, Portugal and France, before England became the new Atlantic Athens and superseded them all.

All Divided but United by Danger and by the Gods

Like the Europe states 2000 years later, the Greek city-states were constantly at war, though curbed by peace negotiations, Olympic truces, religious feasts and prohibitions, agricultural obligations, and codes of conduct that thwarted systemic massacres. Whenever a serious threat arose, ambassadors or delegates from the amphictyonies—like that of the temple of Delphi—would meet to find common solutions.

At the turn of the 500s, the external threat for Greece became more evident. Its expansion collided with that of the Persian Empire in Asia Minor (Turkey) that placed the Greek colonies and large cities of the Ionian coast under its guardianship. Spurred on by Athens, the Greeks led a first expedition to support the

Milesians, who had rebelled against Persia. Darius responded by crossing the Aegean Sea to Attica, but he was pushed back at Marathon and failed to take Athens (490). Ten years later Xerxes, determined to expunge the affront, landed a huge amount of troops in Thrace (Heredotus mentioned one million). They succeeded in taking Athens and Attica in spite of Leonidas' sacrifice at the Thermopylae pass. In the end, the Medes were totally defeated. At sea, the Greek admiral Themistocles succeeded in luring the Persian fleet into the trap laid in the strait of Salamis; on land, the Spartans beat the Persian army in the Battle of Plataea. The Median Wars ended with a resounding victory for the Greeks.

There is no need for lengthy explanations to draw a parallel with the history of Europe. After the turmoil that followed the fall of Rome, Europe progressively resurfaced with the Carolingian victory over the Arab invaders, Charlemagne's attempt to restore an empire, the conversion of the "Barbarians" to Christianity, the expansion of Roman Catholicism, and with renewed demographic growth. Then came the first Crusades in the Middle East. With the construction of cathedrals, Romanesque and Gothic art burgeoned, preceding the artistic and intellectual audacity of the Renaissance. Finally, the oceans were crossed, and powerful imperial colonies were created following the great discoveries made possible by the progress in navigation. In seven centuries, like Greece between 1,000 and 500 BC, obscure and marginal Europe moved into the limelight on the world scene.

This slow progression of events produced similar effects in both cases. The conquest of new territories and the sudden influx of wealth incurred the same benefits, but also the same ills. In Greece, the victory over the Medians opened the markets of the East and confirmed Athens as the dominant power over the freed cities of Ionia. As could be expected, Athens would not take long to use and abuse its position.

The people of Athens, who had supplied most of the sailors of the fleet, demanded their share, both economically and politically, of the new wealth. The advent of democracy loosened tongues and boosted ambitions. Contesting the power of the much more conservative rich landowners, the people soon asserted themselves as the most loyal supporters of Athenian imperialism—for better or for worse.

At the time of Pericles (450-430 BC), Athens became the center of literature, philosophy and the arts in Greece. Through Aeschylus, Euripides, Sophocles, Herodotus, Socrates, Plato, Thucydides, Xenophon, Phidias and the great architects, the name of the city was to radiate across the centuries. But there was a somber side to the coin. In 454 BC, Athens decided to bring the treasure of the Delian League (the heritage from the Median Wars that belonged to the victorious cities as a whole) back to the Acropolis. Twenty years later, in 336 BC, Pericles embezzled the public treasure for the sole benefit of the Athenians by dipping into it to finance the building of the Parthenon. The Athenian republic had turned into an authoritarian empire that both irritated and daunted the other Greek cities, especially Sparta and Corinth. One disastrous decision after another led to a civil war that would prove suicidal. Through its causes, its unfolding and its consequences, it calls to mind the two world wars that ravaged Europe in the 20th century. To quote Thibaudet: "When one of these peninsulas will be engaged in a general war, in a war of life and death, it will have been for a question of hegemony, arisen from an even more general issue: the dominion of the seas." This fatal sequence occurred in 432 BC, when Sparta and Corinth, exasperated by its hegemonic behavior, declared war on Athens. The same logic would go into action in 1914.

Thucydides is very explicit: "I believe that the true motive, and also the least admitted, was the Athenians' increase in power and the fear they inspired in the Lacedemonians, thus forcing them to engage in war." As for Thibaudet, "War is inevitable because the continual growth of the greatest maritime power is inevitable, because the distrust of this growth and the barrier set up by the greatest military state at a time it considered the most propitious, are inevitable. We touch upon Euclid's Elements of history."[3]

---

3 Ibid., p. 38.

The events in 432 BC and 1914 AD shared the same profound and circumstantial causes. In both cases the continental powers were the first to attack: Sparta against Athens in the first case, Russia against Austria-Hungary, and Germany against France and Great Britain in the second. Russia refused to accept the Austrian progression in the Balkans (annexation of Bosnia) and the ultimatum given to Serbia. Germany was exasperated by England's dominion of the seas and its unlimited colonial pretentions, while Great Britain was extremely alarmed by the development of the German navy that posed a direct threat to its maritime hegemony. Like in ancient Greece, the play of alliances did the rest.

The Peloponnesian War and the Great European Civil War

The two civil wars broke out for minor, peripheral reasons: the shift of alliance of Corinth's far-off colony, Corfu, as regards the Peloponnesian War, and the assassination of an Austrian crown prince in the obscure province of Bosnia as regards World War I. In both cases the question of who was responsible for triggering the hostilities is misleading, for either side could have made the first move. Corinth could not accept losing Corfu to Athens any more than France could accept giving up Alsace-Lorraine to Germany; or than Russia could let its Serbian ally be swallowed up by Austria-Hungary; or than England could allow William II to build a fleet greater than its own.

The wars shared the same causes, the same devastating game of alliances, the same disastrous effects for the belligerents and the destiny of their respective peninsulas.

In both cases the conflict would last some thirty years, from 432 to 404 BC for the Peloponnesian War, and from 1914 to 1945 AD for the two world wars, with lulls imposed by truces. The inadequate Peace of Nicias lasted only eight years, and the calamitous Treaty of Versailles, twenty years.

Thucydides, like the observers of the First World War, immediately understood that the treaties that had ended the first phase of the conflict were too precarious to restore peace. Although the pact of 421 had provided for fifty years of pacification and the return to the *status quo ante* for all the Greek belligerents, it had left too many grudges and unsolved problems—just like the Treaty of Versailles in 1919.

With a bit of hindsight, the two world wars should indeed be considered as one, single war. By splitting it into two distinct events, contemporary historians masked its profound continuity. The two phases of the conflict that cleaved the 20th century naturally form a single entity. The first phase led directly to the second one with its ruinous consequences for Europe: the Cold War and the division of the continent between two opposing hegemonies, the United States and the Soviet Union.

Morally speaking, both the Great Greek War and the Great European War instigated mass murders and let to the committing of monstrosities that provoked general disbelief and shock. In both conflicts the belligerents were led to betray the values of civilization.

> A people governed for so long more by haughtiness than by wisdom and who thereby finds every excuse to take its revenge, commits all the excesses that can be expected; all the abuses stirred by the desire to abruptly escape long years of hardship by seizing the property of others; and all the brutalities, all the barbarisms inborn to people who ruthlessly hound their rivals, not to satisfy their ambitions but rather because they are driven by a blind feeling of equality.[4]

Does this excerpt from Thucydides on the massacres of Corfu not perfectly apply to the abominations of trench warfare, the cruelties of the Bolshevik Revolution and even more so to the appalling atrocities committed by the Nazis against the Jews, the Slavs and the Gypsies?

The unfolding of the two wars, moreover, followed similar logics. In both cases, they were total wars that mobilized all the

---

4 Thucydides, *La Guerre du Péloponnèse* (*The Peloponnesian War*), III, pp. 73. 76.

The Greek Syndrome and Europe's American Encroachment

combatants' human, economic and technical resources and took place on a global battlefield (on the scale of the antique world), largely overrunning the initial boundaries of the warring states: the colonies (Sicily, Italy, Dalmatia, Ionia and the Bosporus in the 5th century BC; and in the 20th century, Africa, the Middle East, India and Australia), as well as the great neighboring powers (the kingdoms of Asia and of Thrace, the Persian Empire, Egypt, Carthage and the Etruscans; the United States, Japan, China, Latin America). All were made to contribute, either by furnishing resources or as allies and partners.

As far as the military operations are concerned, the two wars spread out over unprecedented territories and lasted for exceptional time spans, on land as on sea. Both camps mobilized ground and naval forces: continental Sparta was allied to Corinth, Greece's second maritime power, while Athens leaned on Argos, a land power in the Peloponnese, and other Greek provinces inland.

During the Great World War, continental Russia was the ally of semi-continental France and the American and English maritime empires, against the coalition of the very continental Germany, Austria-Hungary and Turkey that extended to the Japanese naval empire from 1939 to 1945. Both conflicts exhausted every possible means of combat, whether on the side of the victors or of the vanquished: all-out war, total war, unexpected defeats and victories, spectacular turnarounds, attrition warfare and interminable sieges, maneuver and trench warfare, and the unprecedented massacre of innocent civilians (Hiroshima, Nagasaki and the bombing of Dresden by the Allies). And in both cases, it was chiefly the third parties who had initially kept out of the picture but had subsequently emerged, that were to reap the profits: Thebes and Macedonia in the first case, and the United States and the Soviet Union in the second.

Twenty years after its victory over Athens, in fact, triumphant Sparta was conquered by the Theban general, Epaminondas. Not much later, it would be the whole of Greece's turn to be conquered and subjected by the rough-hewn (though educated by Aristotle) Greeks, Philip of Macedon and Alexander the Great. Following the Macedonian example, the United States, which had taken advantage of the first phase of both episodes of the Great World War to make profits at the expense of Europe, was very quick to impose its supremacy upon all the warring nations, whether friends or foes. The Soviet Union, as the second victor, did likewise in the part of the world attributed to it at Yalta, at least until its collapse in 1991. The states responsible for the hostilities were exhausted, and this favored the surfacing and the subsequent domination of the peripheral powers of the conflict: Macedon in one instance, the United States and Soviet Russia in the other.

The only difference between the two conflicts is how they ended. The Peloponnesian War saw the victory of Sparta, a land power, while the Great World War terminated with the triumph of the Anglo-Saxon sea power. But here again, appearances are deceiving. We should remember that Sparta was able to impose itself only from the time when it decided to enter maritime warfare. As long as it was limited to the spears and shields of its hoplites, Sparta remained powerless before Athens. It was only after dispatching its most brilliant generals—Brasidas, on the one hand, on a mad expedition to the ends of Thrace, and Gylippos and his triremes, on the other, to help the besieged Syracusans resist Athens—in other words, only after taking up maneuver warfare both on land and at sea, was Sparta able to defeat the Athenian army and fleet.

In Europe, it was also maintained that the war had ended with the victory of the sea powers both in 1918 and in 1945. But this is the Western victors' partial version of the story that does not correspond to the military reality. In the summer of 1914, without the Russian war effort and its hundreds of thousands dead on the East European continental front, France would have been vanquished from the moment it joined the war in August-September 1914.

As for the 1939–1945 phase, we saw that Nazi Germany was part of allied maritime powers that included Italy and Japan, while the Allies' final victory was achieved only because the Soviets sacrificed 26 million soldiers (the Americans lost half a million men on the European and Asian fronts combined).

Europe's Great World War was won in Stalingrad and Kursk in 1943 much more than thanks to the Anglo-Saxon landings in Sicily and Normandy. We can see then, that also in Europe, the land and sea powers played equal roles and that neither force was solely responsible for any victory.

An Example of a Fatal Spiral of Events

Thucydides' carefully detailed account of one of the best-known episodes of the Peloponnesian War, the dialogue between Athens and Melos, illustrates how this fatal spiral of events leads to the moral suicide of a civilization. At some point during the war in 416, a squadron of 3,000 Athenians landed on the small island of Melos, a former Spartan colony that had remained neutral during the conflict. Negotiations took place between the aggressors and the besieged. The former explained to the latter that in order to preserve their goods and their lives, they had better surrender, and that in return for the payment of a tribute, they would be left alone.

The Melians put forward their neutrality and the fact that they were in no way a threat for Athens. They also stressed how dishonorable it would be for them to give up their independence and their freedom. They persisted in placing their values above their interests and even their lives. Convinced that they were doing the right thing, the Athenians specified that personally, they had nothing against the Melians, but that their imperial hegemony was at stake. They were in no position to accept Melian amity: "Your hostility is less harmful to us than your friendship, for in the eyes of the world, the latter makes us appear weak, while your hatred is proof of our power." For Athens, it was

> absolutely impossible to let a small, independent island that appears to taunt us in front of all of our subjects and gives an unfitting example, subsist. […] If you remain independent, it will appear that we are afraid to attack you because of your power. So it would be doubly beneficial for us to dominate you: our power would be even greater, and so would the respect of our subjects—for we should

have proved our strength—and thereby we would increase our security. This conquest is all the more necessary because you are islanders, and we are the masters of the sea. And you are weaker than others. Your independence is therefore inadmissible.

This was, in essence, the discourse of the Athenians, who proceeded to attack, shattering the resistance of the Melians, slaughtering the population and razing the city to the ground. Indeed, they won a resounding victory, but one that scandalized the Greeks of the time and contributed to making Athens lose the moral battle.

This episode is typical of the moral trap into which the imperialistic powers lock themselves, especially when they claim to fight for freedom and human rights. It can be related to many recent invasions that have taken place in the modern history of imperialism: the Franco-British expedition against China in 1905; the French massacres in Setif and Madagascar in 1945 and 1947; the American invasion of Grenada in 1983 and the European bombing of Libya in 2011, after the blockade on Cuba and the overthrow of Saddam Hussein in 2003.

The Broken Springs of Civilization

With the war over and peace restored, Greece and Europe continued their paths in analogous directions. The Greek trajectory after the Peloponnesian War and that of Europe after the Great War ran parallel to each other.

Because of the human and moral damage caused, the Peloponnesian War and the Great World War crushed the deep-rooted springs of the civilizations that had started them. In both cases, human losses were gigantic as much for the victors as for the vanquished. Sparta, whose very institutions tended to curb its demographic growth, never really recovered from the bleeding of its military aristocracy, which was the cornerstone of its entire social organization. Athens, deprived of its colonies and its Long

The Greek Syndrome and Europe's American Encroachment

Walls that protected Piraeus from military invasions, was never able to reconstitute its former maritime power.

The actors of the intellectual and political life did not delay in withdrawing into themselves and rigidifying, leaving way for the oligarchic or authoritarian structures—the tyrannies—to get the upper hand over the democratic experiments and the audacity of thinking. The Greek momentum had passed. From the creation of the portico and Zeno's movement of Stoicism in 301, Greek philosophy focused on utilitarianism, the techniques of personal development and the search for individual happiness. As commendable as they may have been, Epicureanism and Hedonism, the dialectician heirs of the Sophists and Cynics and later the Stoics who followed Epictetus and Seneca, fall under the category of the wise art of life rather than of philosophy. The tree still offered enticing fruit, but its roots no longer plunged deeply enough into the earth of Attica to make it grow.

As far as politics were concerned, the relative weakening of Athens and the limitations of Sparta, whose institutions were unsuitable for managing an empire, were propitious for the emergence of new contenders. The Boeotian League around Thebes was the first to try to take advantage of the situation. Thanks to Epaminondas, who was an unequalled strategist, the Thebans took Sparta in 371. Sparta would never completely recover and withered away.

Athens, for its part, had tried to seize the opportunity afforded by the war with Sparta to reestablish its imperial supremacy. But that attempt would also be short lived. From 360 BC on, Athens' reputation of invincibility was definitely ruined. The revolt of its allies supported by the king of Persia put an end to its imperialist dreams: the Athenians had lost on every front, for they had been incapable of proposing a durable alliance. From that moment on, "the history of Greece becomes unintelligible," as Xenophon, who died in 354 BC, had to admit. Of course, the history of Greece continued, but the independence of its cities was over. Athens, Sparta, Corinth, Thebes and the others found themselves a new master in the king of Macedon, who had gained growing influence through the 4th century. Greece was no longer quite within Greece. Its cultural influence remained enormous and even continued to expand, but its destiny was being determined elsewhere, in Macedon, before being passed on to Rome. A new era of decline/expansion that historians would qualify as Hellenistic was beginning, and it would end two centuries later with the annexation to Rome.

Phillip II of Macedon had been educated in Thebes and was therefore able to become involved in Greek matters thanks to his command of the Greek culture and language. He won over supporters through skillfully arranged subsidies and gained a foothold first in Thessaly and Thrace, then beat the Thebans and the Athenians at Chersonese in 338. He was assassinated before he could carry out his project to conquer Persia.

His son Alexander took up the torch with the success that we all know. He began his career by putting down a Theban revolt and razing the city, with the exception of the poet Pindar's house. The warning was clear: either Greece submitted, thus preserving its culture and having it recognized, or it would be wiped out. The message came across. Greece submitted. In a dozen years, thanks to the rallying of the cavalry and the Greek navy, the formidable Macedonian Phalanx would conquer Central Asia all the way to the Indus.

After his sudden death in 323, Alexander's successors, the Diadochi, agreed to divide the empire that was now too big for them. But they didn't take long to quarrel. After a long civil war, they managed to found three dynasties after all—the Lagid in Egypt, the Seleucid in Babylonia and the Antigonid in Macedon—that lasted for a relatively long time (they would disappear only with the Roman conquests of the 2nd and 1st centuries BC).

Alexander's dream was to fuse the Greek and Persian empires into one. He had taken the first steps in this direction by marrying Persian princesses and encouraging his generals and soldiers to marry women of the conquered aristocracy. He died too soon to fulfill his dream. But his heirs were quite successful in carrying out his wishes, and on these foundations the Hellenistic Civilization, a mix of Greek and Oriental cultures, was born. It would diffuse the values, philosophy, arts, architecture, urban planning, sciences, religion and language of the Greek civilization as far as its borders with China and India. The *koinè* language derived from the Ionian-Attic tongue would replace the ancient local dialects, and along with Aramaic, become the main vehicular language of the eastern Mediterranean Basin from Egypt and Syria to India. It would serve to underpin the influence of the Greek civilization in this immense expanse for a very long time, remaining in use until the end of the Byzantine Empire in 1453.

The Lost Dynamics of Politics and Culture

But before studying what is called the Hellenic period of Greek history in greater detail, let us come back to the consequences the Peloponnesian War had on Greece proper.

Initially, the damage went unnoticed. In Greece and in Europe, the return to peace had enabled the economy to recover and the commercial channels to be reactivated. This was thanks to the capital repatriated from the colonies and the neighboring powers that had been spared by the war in Greece and to the Marshall Plan in post-1945 Europe (the plan was financed by the capital flight from Europe to purchase American products and armaments during the war). The Soviet Union, for its part, which had been the main liberator of Europe, reconstructed with practically no outside aid thanks to the technical and industrial capital accumulated in the 1930s by the forced labor of the peasants and the deportees of the gulags.

At the moral and intellectual level, the war did not seem at first to have affected the vital forces of the belligerents. There appeared to be only material damages for Greece: the Walls and the Athenian fleet were destroyed; the overseas territories were lost, heavy war compensations were paid, and the military potential of the vanquished cities was severely limited. At the outset, Greece seemed to recover its economic and artistic vitality.

In the immediate post-war period and the relief brought about by restored peace, economic and intellectual activity seemed to resume. There were raging debates between Socrates and the

Sophists. Philosophy became a political issue to such an extent that in 399 the people of Athens condemned Socrates to death for corrupting their youth. With Plato, who was born during the war and died in 348, metaphysics and the great Greek thinking reached their climax. But one generation later, while maintaining its importance, reflection began to take a more practical turn with Aristotle. His death in 322 was to consecrate the last of the Greek geniuses. Athens and Greece would remain a hotbed of culture for centuries to come, with their schools of philosophy and rhetoricians attracting numerous pupils, especially among the aristocracy and the Roman ruling classes. But the flame of creative genius had been lost.

In Greece, during and following the Peloponnesian War, tragedy with Aeschylus, Sophocles and Euripides, comedy with Aristophanes and Menander, philosophy with Socrates, Plato and later Aristotle and Diogenes; rhetoric with Demosthenes; medicine with Hippocrates; history with Herodotus, Thucydides, Xenophon and later Polybius, thrived. Likewise in Europe, the truce in the interwar period was the occasion for a new blossoming in the arts, science, philosophy and the humanities. Art Deco with the Paris Exhibition in 1925, cubism with Picasso, surrealism with André Breton, psychoanalysis with Freud, abstract art, Russian avant-garde with Kandinski and Malevitch, quantum mechanics with Planck, Bohr, Einstein and Heisenberg, and architecture with Le Corbusier and the Bauhaus, flourished during the whole time, as well as the more classical arts like cinema, music and literature.

Europe also seemed to flourish in the immediate post-war period from 1945 to 1960: existentialism, phenomenology, the New Wave and the New Novel, the Frankfurt School and the great Russian writers from Pasternak to Solzhenitsyn emerged. Science sent the first men in space and on the moon, and the May 68 "revolution" led many to believe that times were changing and that the future of Europe would be forever young and radiant.

Up until the 1970s, Europe was able to belie the impression that these intuitions were not quite right. Europe remained at the forefront of thinking with its great intellectuals, historians, painters, filmmakers, and fashion designers.

A Hidden Fracture

In the history of civilizations, this post-war boom is indeed only temporary. It often masks a fracture, a deep and irreversible rupture with the prior world. Everything seems to go on like before but nothing is the same any longer. The more perceptive minds cannot be fooled. From 1918, philosophers and writers felt that an irreparable wound had been inflicted. In France, Paul Valéry realized that "civilizations are mortal." In Germany, it was Oswald Spengler who sketched "the decline of the West" in a masterpiece that would be strongly contested but that, over time, would prove to be right.

In his quest to formulate the laws of history, Spengler sought to draft a "morphology of universal history" according to which the great historical cultures, like biological organisms, are born, grow, decline and die, and maintained that Western civilization is no exception. According to Spengler, the latter is in the process of reaching its final stage since entering its Faustian phase and is open to any and all compromises to satisfy its Promethean desires of grandeur and domination, harbingers of its final fall.[5]

Stefan Zweig, a staunch nationalist in 1914, also gradually realized the inanity of war and the drift of European civilization following the advent of National Socialism, and wound up

---

5 Later, the appeals of the Club of Rome, concerned about the ravages of industrial capitalism on resource depletion and the degradation of the natural environment, would take over a plan that had been more global though still tied to the West. The theory of catastrophism that appeared in the 1970s, and more recently the discipline of collapsology, are symptoms of this feeling of inevitable decline reflected in the bestselling novels of authors like Michel Houllebecq. In the Anglo-Saxon world, after British historian Arnold Toynbee, American scholar Jared Diamond and his thesis of "collapse"—the eloquent title of one his works—popularized the idea that no matter how advanced societies may be, they can collapse because they are incapable of responding to the disintegration factors undermining them: environmental degradation, climate change, growing rivalries and hostilities with their neighbors, loss of traditional trade partners, and inappropriate solutions to these threats.

committing suicide in Brazil in 1942. Meanwhile, the Russians converted to Bolshevism, and strove to cut all ties with the old world in their own way, resorting to violence to reconstruct a "new man" who would definitively mark his distance with the corrupted society of capitalism and of profit for profit. And again, it was a great philosopher, Edmund Husserl, who in *The Crisis of European Sciences and Transcendental Phenomenology*[6] was alarmed about the radical crisis of life and the "skeptical shipwreck" of European reason.

The Cultural Center of Gravity Shifts towards the United States

This apparent vitality actually camouflaged deeper ills. First of all, since the end of the Great World War, the economic, moral and intellectual center of gravity of the world was changing axes and tilting towards the United States of America. A 1950 film entitled *An American in Rome* by Italian filmmaker Steno well illustrates this change of perception. Released in 1954, the movie tells the emblematic story of an Italian seized with an irrepressible penchant for everything coming from the United States, from John Wayne to popcorn. He threatens to throw himself from the top of the Coliseum if he is not granted an American visa. Indeed, between 1914 and 1945, the foremost victor of the Great European War had not only become prodigiously rich thanks to the purchase of weapons by the Allies and to the French and British capital that had found refuge on its soil, but it had multiplied its human and cultural capital as well, following the massive emigration of the European—and especially German and Jewish—intellectuals, thinkers, artists and writers who had fled the war and Nazi persecution. In the fifties, the majority of the great directors and actors in Hollywood, from Capra and Lubitsch to Marlene Dietrich and Greta Garbo, as well as the great American scientists, from Albert Einstein and Enrico Fermi, John von Neumann and Oskar Morgenstern (the fathers of game theory) to the father of the space

---

6 Published in French: Paris, Gallimard, 1989.

discovery, Werner von Braun, or the well-known psychoanalyst, Bruno Bettelheim, were European emigrants.

Within a generation, the United States had literally vampirized German science and the pick of the European intelligentsia. Europe would not recover. The movement had been irrevocably reversed, now seeing Europeans flocking to American universities and art galleries in order to be recognized, published and knighted. Today, Europe no longer sets the pace, and from henceforward, the Americans can't care less what the European intellectuals and artists think and do. They may be briefly infatuated with *French Theory* and invite a few stars to their universities, and their movie studios might adapt a few good novels to the screen, but this is only to better affirm their universality and their cultural hegemony. Going forward, the clocks of the intellectual life of Europe, from France and Great Britain to Italy and Germany, have been set to the American time, as shown by the minimal space that the movie theaters of Europe allot for European creations.

Let us quote the great German playwright, Botho Strauss, with these heart-wrenching lines:

> I sometimes have the feeling, when I am with Germans, of being only with ancestors. I am like the secluded monk of Heisterbach or a sixty-year-old deserter who, after the end of the war, leaves his hiding place and goes back to a country that, to his bitter disbelief, is still called Germany. I think I am the last German. A vagabond, a ghost rummaging in the sacred ruins of cities, of land and of the spirit. A homeless soul.[7]

We can date the end of the great European intellectual epic with the death of Italian philologist and author Umberto Eco, who was probably the last figure of the *honnête homme*, or the complete European intellectual. The intellectual influence of Europe

---

7 Botho Strauss, "La disparition de la civilisation allemande" (English: "The Passing of the German Civilization"), translated by Antonin Moeri for Antipresse, excerpt from "Der letzte Deutsche," in *Der Spiegel*, 2 October 2015.

today is limited to exclusively national personalities, prisoners of their mother tongue, who every now and again sign an article in English in the *New York Times* in the hope of proving to their readers that they still hold a place in the world.

In the East, the other victor, the Soviet Union, held its own. Thanks to the German technicians brought willingly or forcibly to Russia, it launched the first satellite into space followed by the first man, Yuri Gagarin. For a while it was the rival of the United States. But, as is well known, the Khrushchev Thaw did not last, and the Soviet Union went into a phase of intellectual decline even more rapidly than that of Western Europe.

It was therefore at the moral and political level that, in European terms, was actually a great civil war, proved the most disastrous for Europe. In organizing systematic massacres and the genocide of millions of men, women and children because of their faith, skin color, sexual orientation or political convictions, Hitler's Germany and its accomplices had gone too far beyond civilization and the values that had founded the moral and spiritual magisterium of Europe. The Shoah against the Jews, the genocide of the Slavs, Gypsies, homosexuals and communists defied all logic and the *Lumières, Aufklärung* and *Enlightenment* that Europe had adhered to since the 18th century. The same held true for the atrocities and ravages of the Peloponnesian War that had undermined the pillars of reason and the ideal of beauty of Classical Greece.

The effect of this rupture was not brought to light immediately, not until two or three decades after the war, when the first testimonials by Raul Hillberg and Primo Levi in particular, and the first studies by Hannah Arendt, began to be heard. But the rupture itself had been weakening Europe since 1945. One consequence of the loss of moral magisterium, among others, was an accelerated decolonization. How to justify the dominion over the other peoples of the world in the name of civilization when such crimes had been committed?

The Greek Syndrome and Europe's American Encroachment

The Nucleus May Be Gone, but the Radiation Continues

Like in Greece after the year 400, the impact of the European Great Civil War was not only to reinforce the victorious powers from the periphery of the continent (i.e. USA and USSR) to the detriment of the core (UK, France, Italy and Germany), but also to weaken the center by stimulating the colonies' legitimate desire for emancipation. Again like in ancient Greece, the cycle of colonial emancipation from Europe had already begun much earlier. The declaration of independence of the United States in 1776, that of Haiti in 1804, and the liberation wars led by Simon Bolivar in the Spanish colonies of Latin America had already given a signal. Although colonization had vigorously resumed in the 19th century with the Industrial Revolution and the resurgence of economic and military power in Europe, the Great Civil War would strike a fatal blow to Europe's dominion over the world. Having been obliged to mobilize the soldiers of its colonies, Europe thereby aroused their military spirit. At the same time, it shattered both its reputation of being invincible and the legitimacy of its domination, already jostled in the Americas and the Far East with the Japanese victories over Russia. The situation was all the more uncomfortable in that the two former allies, the United States and the Soviet Union, supported the struggles of the colonies against their metropoles.

This is how the British lost India in 1947 and the rest of their colonies in the sixties. The Dutch, the Belgians and the French, at the price of two calamitous colonial wars in Indochina and Algeria, followed suit. The Portuguese in turn had to give up their colonies in 1974. The last European empire forced to decolonize was Soviet Russia at the beginning of the 1990s, when the countries of Eastern Europe and Central Asia won their independence, after communism, though the 1945 victory had frozen the process of decolonization for a time.[8] It should be noted that Greece had

---

8 In this respect, we can quote Soviet dissident Andrei Amalrik's intuitive statement: "Just as the adoption of Christianity postponed the fall of the Roman Empire without saving it from an inevitable end, likewise the Marxist doctrine delayed the dismemberment of the Russian Empire—this third Rome—but it did not have the power to prevent it." In André Amalrik, *L'URSS survivra-t-elle en*

also gone through an analogous evolution by gradually losing its colonies in Greater Greece, Sicily, southern Italy, Spain and Provence (Marseille).

This slow and painful process, however, did not imply the end of all European influence in the former colonies—far from it. Similar to ancient Greece, the languages of the invaders continued to be spoken, and trade, security alliances, and the free—or forced—movement of people remained intense. The ancient Greek city-states as well as the European metropoles had retained their power of attraction. But they were no longer the hubs around which subjected, peripheral nations gravitated.

It is precisely at the political level that the consequences of the Great European Civil War were the most dramatic, for "the Macedonian syndrome" was beginning to be felt more and more. We saw how the void left by the Peloponnesian War, the weakening of Athens, and the suppression of the Spartan power by Thebes in 380 had served to trigger the rise to power of Macedon and its complete domination over Greece 75 years after the end of the war. In Europe, the Europeans lost control of their destiny in less than ten years, between 1945 and the early fifties.

Not only had Europe lost its colonies, but it had also given up its independence by accepting that its western sector be placed under the trusteeship of the United States through the Marshall Plan, by the breakout of the Cold War at the end of 1945, and later, by the creation of the North Atlantic Treaty Organization (NATO) in 1949. The United States imposed the *de facto* economic and military vassalization of Western Europe in the name of preserving Europe's interests and security in the face of the supposed threat posed by the Soviet Union.

Symmetrically, the latter retaliated by doing the same with the territories it had liberated in 1944 and 1945, imposing its economic and military hegemony in various countries of Eastern Europe: the Baltic States as from 1944, Albania and Yugoslavia in 1945 followed by Bulgaria and Poland in 1946, Romania in 1947,

---

1984? (Will the USSR survive in 1984?), Paris, Fayard, 1970.

Czechoslovakia in 1948, and East Germany (via the creation of the Warsaw Pact and COMECON) in 1949.

This subordination of the former holder of world power by two states which had remained on the fringes until then is the mirror image of Macedon's gradual control over Greece. It is striking to note that in both cases, trusteeship led to internal divisions, prompting one of the camps to ally with outside powers that ended up completely dominating both camps. In Greece, the Romans intervened twice in response to an appeal from one part of Greece and never left again after their third intervention. In Europe, the Americans intervened twice at the request of France and Great Britain, and they're still around. The only difference is that in Europe, matters went ahead a great deal faster than in Greece.

The Disunited Greeks Call the Romans for Help

Let us study in detail how what happened during the last days of Greece resonates with the evolution of Europe today.

The Hellenic period is characterized by the domination of Macedon and an unprecedented expansion of the Greek civilization in the East. Let us not forget that the Macedonians, in spite of their rough manners, were also Greeks. As violent and brutal as their domination may have been, it never represented a bloodthirsty, homogenous, centralized and monolithic dictatorship. In many respects, it allowed inconsistent treatments, various forms of liberties and autonomy, and at times even substantial privileges to subsist. Some cities remained very independent, others were granted the statute of allies, still others, that of subjects. This did not keep them, throughout the entire period, from engaging in rebellion, making rear alliances with Ptolemaic Egypt or Seleucid Syria, and playing complicated games of influence among the various Greek leagues. Despite that, they never really interrupted their economic and cultural exchanges. Beyond the superficial political issues, the Hellenic era was also marked by intense, long-term tendencies that are equally present in contemporary European society. In the first place, the cultural exchanges were double-edged: the Hellenization of the East found its very symmetrical counterpart in the Orientalization of Greece. The influence of eastern customs modified Greek society in at least two important ways: it weakened democracy and contributed to transforming the city-states into authoritarian, oligarchic regimes.

As opposed to the so-called enlightened despotism, a frequent model where a single person monopolized the power but was clever enough to be supported by the people, the oriental type of monarchy did not acknowledge the people's delegation. It wasn't even a corrupted form of democracy. "Oriental despotism," as it would later be called, does not stem from the bottom, but from the top, proceeding from the gods and the fortune that allowed its rivals to be vanquished. It rests on an oligarchic social basis of rich landowners, high officials, major merchants, and top financiers.

The second profound transformation was economic. The globalization of trade and the sudden access to the Asian markets that followed the conquests of Alexander had the same effects as the great discoveries or the fall of the Berlin Wall in 1989 in Europe. They provoked a strong indraft. First of all, the economic center of gravity was moved eastward, from Greece to Alexandria and Antioch, while Rhodes tended to replace the port of Piraeus as the hub of international maritime transportation.

This same process has been observed for thirty years now with the progressive balance of the world economic center of gravity tilting towards Asia: Japan and the Asian Tigers at first, then China and Vietnam from the year 2000. From the 4th century BC, Alexandria, Rhodes and Antioch were to the Hellenic world what Shanghai, Singapore and Yokohama are to world trade today. This new order naturally engendered deep socio-economic changes. It led in particular to the massive relocation of production centers to the East. The local production of Greek vases moved east of the Mediterranean while the Greek agricultural economy collapsed due to the competition from Egyptian wheat and Palestinian and Syrian wines.

There ensued a general impoverishment of the countryside and the appearance of urban proletariats as well as growing economic and political instability, with the unemployed local

The Greek Syndrome and Europe's American Encroachment

labor force seeking to expatriate to the East as settlers, sailors or artisans. The bravest among them signed up as mercenaries, which gave them the right to cultivate land in their new country of residence after fulfilling their regulatory years of military service. This "globalization" of the Greek economy generated depopulation and an impressive increase in inequalities within the Greek city-states, where the masses of poor citizens had to face rich, arrogant, cosmopolitan elites who were less and less "patriotic" and increasingly indifferent to what lay in store for the cities. The cities also experienced the typical evolution of "liberal" societies, that consists in going from the common good to the private good, from the manufacture of goods to finance, from agriculture to trade, from the public sector to the private sector, from the state to the multinational corporation, from mercantilism to free exchange, from Colbertism to neoliberalism and from there, to an acceleration in the privatization of the public services and the economy as a whole, theorized by the corporation of economists who had, from then on, taken precedence over the philosophers.

This transition from public authority to private power, that affected even the army with the suspension of the draft and recourse to private mercenaries, is typical of today's Western world. But it could also be observed when Classical Greece was on the decline and the Hellenic kingdoms were burgeoning. At the political level, the Greeks obviously sought to react to these tectonic changes and the feeling of fleeting leadership, but without being able to sever their local roots or achieve the unification that would have allowed them to restore their influence of yesteryear. After Alexander's death, the Hellenic world was divided into three more or less equivalent powers: Ptolemaic Egypt, Seleucid Syria/Mesopotamia, and Greece under Macedonian influence. The three were constantly at war. After 280 BC, the major rivals were the Ptolemies and the Seleucids, with each side trying to attract or bribe the Greeks against the other. Greece, for its part, was also divided into three opposing, regional powers with the Macedonian kings trying to maintain their authority over the reluctant Greeks, organized into two rival leagues, the Achaean, centered on the

Peloponnese and Corinth, and the Aetolian, that grouped together the cities and peoples of central Greece. The formation of these leagues, or confederations, dated far back in Greek history, as we have seen, with the creation of the Athenian and Spartan Leagues during the Peloponnesian War. But the latter were to play a leading role in the post-war period which, in the decline followed the spurt of Alexander's campaigns, was to end with the Roman conquest and the clinical death of Ancient Greece in 146 BC.

These federalist attempts at unification clearly recall the 1957 Treaty of Rome and the creation of the European Community. They had an economic and political function at the same time, the idea being to resist foreign invasion attempts and preserve the Greek identity and independence. The Greco-Roman historian Polybius, a fierce Achaean patriot who was taken hostage in Rome, clearly describes how the Achaean confederation functioned. It was not unlike that of the European Union:

> Already, in the course of the preceding period [before 250], several efforts had been made to bring the Peloponnesian cities to come together, but nobody had succeeded in convincing them, for instead of endeavoring to achieve freedom for all, each city strove only to increase its own power."[9]

Denis Roussel, who translated Polybius, stated, for his part, that the antique Achaean League, dissolved in 324 by Alexander and reconstituted in 280 to drive off the tyrants and the Macedonian garrisons, had later grown considerably with the adhesion of Arcadia, Argos and Sicyon. The member cities "were grouped on strictly equal footing within a *sympoliteia* (sympolity); in other words, they remained citizens of their home city, but were at the same time citizens of Achaea" (as is the case in the European Union today). It does not seem that an absolutely uniform type of constitution was imposed on all of them, although a tyrannical or overly oligarchic regime would not have been compatible with

---

9 Polybius, *Histoire* (*History*), Paris, Gallimard, "Quarto" coll., p. 206.94.

membership in the Confederation. They maintained their laws and their own courts, but they were also subjected to the confederate justice and laws.

The Greek Economy Relocated in the East

They continued to coin money, but this money was the same everywhere, apart from certain symbols and letters on the pieces that indicated the city where the coins had been minted (in this respect, the Euro is nothing new!). At the head of the federal government was a *strategos*, elected by the Achaean Assembly for one year. He was re-eligible for office after a one-year interval. His acolytes were a secretary, a financial administrator, and a *hipparchos* (cavalry commander), who were also elected. With the ten magistrates (*demiourgos*) that were permanent representatives of the city, these magistrates constituted the Executive Council of the Confederation.[10] We can note in passing that the integration of the Greek confederations was more advanced than in modern Europe, for it was extended to the army whereas today, defense is entrusted to a separate organization, NATO, headed by a foreign power.

As we saw above, once the effects of the economic boom prompted by Alexander's conquests had abated, the socio-economic situation of the metropole continued to decline, slowly but surely. Emigration and depopulation could be felt in the countryside, where "the large properties that the democratic institutions had succeeded in dismantling were reconstituted. This regime brought with it the ills that accompanied it at all times throughout Antiquity."[11] In other words, there was stagnation, or even a decrease in production, promoted by the lack of the incentive to innovate and increase productivity due to the massive recourse to bonded labor in the major sectors.

The backlash of these new political and social conditions was also felt in industry and the arts and crafts, while a financial and

---

10 Ibid., pp. 206–207.

11 Jean Hatzfeld, *Histoire de la Grèce ancienne* (*The History of Ancient Greece*), Paris, Payot, 1931, pp. 370–371.

commercial "capitalism" as well as a very wealthy elite likely to establish a devoted clientele (the HNWI or High Net Wealth Individuals, as modern bankers call them) emerged. Only navigation flourished, as illustrated by the greatest "supertanker" of its day, the *Syracuse,* a 5,000-ton ship built by the tyrant Hiero to ensure the transit of merchandise from Sicily to Alexandria in every season.

We know less about how the Aetolian League was organized and functioned, but there is no doubt that it was inspired by the same principles. Only its foreign policy, determined by its geographical location closer to Italy and the Romans, was different: the Aetolians almost always preferred a strategic alliance with the Romans against the other ethnic Greeks, Achaeans or Macedonians. Other leagues appeared (the Boeotian and the Arcadian), but they were short-lived.

The economic and political decline and the incessant play of one league against the other that alternated alliances with Egypt, the Seleucids or the Macedonians and soon with the Romans, proved fatal for the Greece of Europe. At first, from 280 to the end of the second Punic War in 212, these rivalries were limited to the Hellenic area. They were intra-Greek, with the Greeks of Europe allying with the eastern Greeks. But with the rise of the Romans, who annihilated the Etruscan kingdom at the beginning of the 3rd century and soon directed their ambitions towards southern Italy and Sicily which were under Greek and Carthaginian influence, the Greek Leagues did not take long to turn to Rome. By 266, Rome had already subjected the Greek cities and provinces of southern Italy as a whole. In 264, it went to war with Carthage, sparking the first Punic War that ended in 241 with a treaty that disadvantaged Carthage and made of Rome a maritime power. After several misadventures, the Romans, whose strength rested first and foremost on their army, acquired a navy that very quickly rivaled that of Carthage and Greece.

Heeding the call of the merchant cities of southern Italy subjected to Illyrian piracy, Rome intervened in the Adriatic and in Illyria, obtaining a foothold in the Balkan Peninsula and posing as the protector of the Greek cities of Epirus. In 218 the Punic War resumed. During the war, the Macedonians allied with the Carthaginians in the hope of evincing the influence of nearby Roman Illyria. Rome reacted by contracting an alliance with the Aetolians and devastating several Greek islands and cities in Aegina and the Peloponnese, thus opening the door to Roman interference in Greek affairs.

Greece Conquered by the "Western Barbarians"

This first Greco-Roman conflict, however, ended in peace with Macedon. Rome maintained its advantages in Illyria, and Illyria opened its ports to the Macedonian traders. This incursion of the "Western Barbarians" had nevertheless made a bad impression on the Greeks due to the ravages caused by the Roman army. It had aroused their national feeling and opened the debate on the necessity to preserve the Greek "identity," civilization and freedom in the face of the invader. But the Greeks were incapable of constituting a single, vast confederation, and this, along with their natural propensity to divide, was to the benefit of Roman interests.

The Second Punic War ended in 201 with a resounding defeat for the Carthaginians, conferring immense prestige on Rome, which had become a hegemonic power in the western Mediterranean. In 200, the Romans, allied to Attalus, king of Pergamum and an opponent of Macedon, seized the first opportunity to attack the latter.[12] In the great Battle of Cynoscephalae in 197, the famous,

---

12 The ambivalence (duplicity?) of the Romans towards the Greeks is obvious, just like that of the Americans towards Europe later on. Their reticence to intervene is due more to their situation than to any anti-imperialistic scruple. In Rome, like in Washington or Brussels today, they knew how to force a people to accept unwanted laws or wars of conquest. "The proposition of the law relative to the Macedonian War (the second, that of 199, A.N.) was rejected by practically all the centuriates of the first assemblies to which it was presented. No doubt exhausted by the length and the weight of the previous war, the people spontaneously voted the way they did, weary of the dangers and fatigue (...). The resentful senators personally exhorted the consul to convoke the assemblies once again, to admonish the people's complacency and make them understand how prejudicial and dishonorable it would be to adjourn the war. The consul made a grand speech invoking the gods and the omens and, after this speech, the people were made to vote, and they approved the draft law." This is substantially what

invincible Macedonian Phalanx gave way for the first time before the Roman legions. Macedonia had to resign itself to signing an unfavorable peace that excluded it from Greek affairs. Flaminius, the Roman consul, shrewdly proclaimed the unrestricted freedom of the Greek cities and states under Macedonian domination, with Rome retreating from Greece...at least in words! For Rome had thus favored the Achaean League to the detriment of their Aetolian allies. All the Greek cities began their pilgrimage to Rome in an effort to acquire advantages and privileges from the Senate at the expense of the other Greek cities. Polybius relates very well how these embassies from European Greece and the Hellenic monarchies tried to nail profitable concessions from the Romans, who had only to act as referees and make their choice. The same course of events can be seen today as European presidents and prime ministers rush to Washington to obtain a military alliance, a fighter aircraft or a trade agreement in their favor.

In 191 BC the conflict resumed, this time on Macedon's initiative. The effort entailed combatting the troops of Antiochus, the Seleucid king, who had designs on Greece. It ended in 188 with the defeat of Antiochus and the Greek liberties restored, but also with a durable alliance between Rome and the kingdom of Pergamum. In less than forty years, the Romans had not only settled in Illyria, they had also just taken a firm foothold in Asia Minor.

In principle, Rome was to retreat from the Greek territories, but in actuality, Rome had every intention of directing the foreign policy of the Greek states, which obviously violated their sovereignty. The freedom restored was therefore conditional and constituted a *de facto* domination that greatly displeased many Greeks. The Rhodians, who were allies of Rome, were angry over the support that the Romans gave their Lycian opponents while Perseus, a new Macedonian king, took up the torch in the struggle for Greek independence against the Roman invader, and by the same token, alarmed his traditional Greek rivals. The parade of

---

Livy relates, cited by David Engels in *Le Déclin. La crise de l'Union européenne et la chute de la République romaine, analogies historiques,* Paris, L'Artilleur, 2003, p.168.

ambassadors resumed, and Rome lost no time in taking advantage of the occasion to engage in a new war against Macedon, defeating it in 168.

This time Rome imposed draconian conditions: Macedon and Epirus were completely dismantled, the major cities were destroyed, it was forbidden to exploit gold and silver mines, and tens of thousands of Achaean patriots, allies of Macedon, including the historian Polybius, were deported to Rome. Rhodes paid a heavy toll for its insubordination: in 167, the Romans created the free port of Delos, thus depriving Rhodes of its customs revenue, making it a second-rate market and naval power.

The Greeks realized too late the disastrous consequences that this new defeat would entail for them. They reacted by a final burst of patriotism, in solidarity with the deported and with king Perseus, who had died in a Roman prison. As the third and last Punic War between Rome and the Carthaginians had resumed and given new hope to the Greek patriots, they rose up again against the Romans. But in 146 Carthage was definitively vanquished and razed. It would not be long before Greece suffered the same fate: Macedon became a Roman province under the authority of a praetor, who governed *de facto* European Greece as a whole.

Greece had ceased to exist as an independent political entity.

Only Hellenism survived the Roman guardianship. If it was emptied of its creative force, if poetry, eloquence, and philosophy were extinguished for good, it subsisted thanks to the rhetoricians, the professors of philosophy and those who popularized the great thinking of Antiquity. The victors appropriated the knowledge and the values of the vanquished. Nonetheless, we must grant the Roman occupants the merit of having ensured the transmission of Greek culture to posterity.

Greece Slain by the Federal Fiasco

This brief overview of the history of ancient Greece evokes, without replicating it, the trajectory of modern Europe. Both experienced:

- the prosperity and the expansion of a brilliant civilization founded on the individual and the principle of the autonomous city (nation);
- a disastrous Great Civil War with a spiritual crisis and loss of centrality for both the victors and the vanquished;
- the rise to power of outside peripheral states that led to a "globalization" of trade and a concentration of wealth that in turn led to new conflicts; and
- domination followed by the definitive conquest of the central hearth of civilization by outside forces that wound up fighting each other to the benefit of the hegemony of a monopolistic hyperpower.

It was Rome versus Macedon in the case of Greece, the United States of America versus Soviet Russia in the case of Europe.

To conclude this chapter and resume with our topic—the capacity of modern Europe to continue to make history and of the European Union to fulfill this mission—the last words of Hellenist Jean Hatzfeld, written in 1931, are probably the most pertinent:

> One might ask whether it is worth the trouble today, for a man of culture, to investigate the political history of a small people whose economic development was different from ours, who never achieved a stable form of politics, and whose existence was nothing more than a long conflict between jealous cities and fleeting States. And there is certainly something disappointing in seeing the Greeks come so close, so often, to an organization that would have enabled them to constitute a vast and solid state, without ever being able to see it through durably. But first, it is perhaps worthwhile to acknowledge these endeavors, to seek the cause of these failures, to tell oneself that all that Athens lacked in the 5th century was a greater concern for public education and a sincere application of the principle of representation of the allied cities. As for the Achaean League, a better military legislation and a bit more civic

The Greek Syndrome and Europe's American Encroachment

spirit would have sufficed to change the destinies of the Greek world.

But what is even more striking in the history of Greece is to discover political forms and tendencies that we are familiar with. Within the States, there was royalty, aristocracy through birth or through wealth, and diversely nuanced democracies. In the relations between the States, we saw impassioned nationalism; vigorous and awkward imperialism; the dream, fulfilled for a few years, of conquering and organizing the world; federalism that might have ensured the welfare of Greece if it had been properly developed; and finally, a spirit of cosmopolitanism and human brotherhood (*even though limited to the upper class of citizens*).

It is telling to see these tendencies and forms confront each other in a people who were very close to us intellectually, coming forward with remarkable clarity and in an astounding shortcut; for we find them in our contemporary Europe, and the future of our civilization no doubt depends on the outcome of their conflict.

We will agree that ninety years after having been written, this text on the end of Ancient Greece is extremely pertinent to the Europe of today…

CHAPTER 4

TWO SCENARIOS FOR A DECLINING CONTINENT

Courage means looking for the truth and speaking it out.

JEAN JAURES[1]

Since a man without memory is a man without a life, a people without memory is a people without a future.

FERDINAND FOCH

At this stage of our historical observations, we can see that there are two possible scenarios forecasting what the Europe of tomorrow might be like: Roman Germanic or Greek.

Scenario I: Contraction and Breakup

The first draws on the evolution of the Holy Roman German Empire. Its foundation was followed by a phase of economic and territorial expansion, then stagnation that led to a long period of political weakening, territorial shrinkage and institutional waning, studded by reforms aimed at prolonging the survival of the whole.

This scenario conforms quite well to the developments of the European Union from the end of the 1940s, subsequent to the first economic treaties and the creation of NATO. Once the EU was established, there was continuous economic and territorial expansion: the European Coal and Steel Community (ECSC) of the six founding states in 1951; the creation of the European Economic

---

1 Jean Garrigues, *Les Grands discours de la Troisième République de Victor Hugo à Clémenceau,* Paris, Armand Colin, 2004.

Two Scenarios for a Declining Continent

Community and the Atomic Energy Community in 1957; the lifting of customs duties in 1968; the enlargement to include nine member states (the United Kingdom, Ireland and Denmark) in 1963, Greece in 1981, the countries of southern Europe (Spain and Portugal) in 1986, Austria, Finland and Sweden in 1995. This territorial expansion accelerated with the introduction of the euro in 2002 and the sudden extension to ten new states in 2004, followed by the accession of Bulgaria and Romania (2007), and finally Croatia in 2013. Other countries submitted their candidacy, particularly in the Balkans, while negotiations even commenced with Turkey.

But in 2010–2016, this expansion came to an abrupt economic halt. The financial crisis generated by the global crisis of 2008 put the euro and deeply-indebted Greece under pressure, as did Great Britain's decision to leave the Union after the 2016 referendum. It is worth noting that NATO, whose mandate since its creation In 1949 was supposedly limited to defending the North Atlantic, extended its military intervention even more rapidly thereafter, before slackening the pace and getting bogged down in an endless war in Afghanistan.

At the same time, the European institutions, as we shall see later on, also went through a series of intense, complex and remote crafting that needn't envy the complicated institutions of the Holy Roman German Empire. Indeed, in three decades, united Europe was transformed into a bureaucratic monster that was even more complex than the Holy Empire after the 16th century. If its achievements are commendable, its efficiency and especially its sustainability are seriously questionable. In any case, the cracking observed since 2010 poses serious doubts. Brexit, effective since 2021, as well as the increasing acts of rebellion in certain countries of Eastern Europe—Hungary, Poland or Italy until to 2019— lead one to believe that Europe has already entered its phase of contraction and begun to retreat towards its Franco-German hard core. This withdrawal greatly resembles that of the Holy Empire when it refocused on the Germanic space.

It is also interesting to note that this feeling of recurrence is amplified by the economic "satellization" of France and Germany's constant rise to power. The only question, if this scenario really materializes, will be to know how long this phase will last before the European Union falls completely under German influence, to the point of splitting up with those who would refuse such an option.

Scenario II: Europe Absorbed by the United States

The second scenario is just as pessimistic as far as its consequences are concerned, viz., complete and utter absorption by a larger, stronger power, with the American Republic absorbing modern Europe, paralleling the Roman Republic absorbing Greece. History may not repeat itself, but it has a fierce tendency to serve a similar dish...

Greek history and European history are duplicates of each other: after an anonymous gestation period, there is a phase of economic innovation and intellectual creativity entailing a territorial expansion that runs into the neighboring empires. Thanks to its victory, an influx of wealth streams into the metropole that is at its peak. Its social and political structures are modified, creating internal rivalries that eventually lead to civil war.

After a brief phase of recovery, the decline begins, with alternating periods of prosperity and regression. The core gradually loses its creative forces, democracy withers and wanes, the inequality gap widens, the oligarchy takes over, while the former peripheries sparkle and shine. Increasing external interferences end up annihilating the old metropole, which loses its political independence, its productive vitality and its creative energy.

Ancient Greece first lost its liberty and its independence to Macedon, a half-Greek neighboring power, before being conquered and dominated by the Romans. This subjugation occurred in four successive stages, concentrated between 215 and 146 BC and according to a uniform plan: Macedon and its Greek allies were at war with another Greek coalition that called the Romans to the rescue. Whether by calculation or by skill, the Romans

Two Scenarios for a Declining Continent

intervened, albeit giving the impression that this was done almost grudgingly. They took advantage of the situation to meddle in Greek affairs but pulled out at the end of the war, as though they were not really interested and their only ambition had been to ensure their own security which had been threatened by the then empires of evil, i.e. the Carthaginians and Seleucids that would later correspond to the Serbs, the Taliban and Iraqi and Syrian Ba'athists for the Americans.

During the first Macedonian war, however, the Romans had set foot in Illyria, supposedly to fight the pirates. During the second war, they downright settled in Pergamum, Asia Minor on the pretext of protecting their allies. As from the third war, recklessly launched by Perseus, king of Macedon, they didn't even bother to make excuses: Perseus was conquered, and Macedon divided into four republics governed by puppets working for Rome. The fourth and last war (148-146) ended with the collapse of Macedon and the transformation of Greece into a Roman province controlled by the legions stationed there.

Is this scenario not substantially like that of the two phases of the Great War of Europe? At the request of some of the Europeans, the United States intervened in the conflict for the first time in 1917, claiming to be reluctant and acting in self-defense, as though they in no way wished to interfere in European quarrels (though they made a huge profit by exporting arms and goods to warring Europe).

In a surge of generosity in 1918–1919, they proposed a peace program (Wilson's Fourteen Points and the creation of the League of Nations) from which they would soon distance themselves in the name of isolationism and non-intervention—though they kept a close eye on Europe, if only to make sure they were reimbursed the huge sums they had loaned their Allies...

When World War II broke out, history seemed to repeat itself. At first the United States did not appear to be interested in the conflict (although their industries were operating full speed) that had, moreover, been started through the Europeans' own fault and by one of their most demented tyrants, Adolf Hitler. The United

States would intervene in Europe as cautiously as the Romans had, centuries earlier, not before July 1943, long after the attack on Pearl Harbor by the Japanese navy. And still they waited patiently until June 6, 1944, when the war against Nazi Germany was already in the process of being won by the Soviets, to land in Normandy and strike a fatal blow to an already greatly weakened enemy.

Once the war was won, this time the Americans, like the Romans in Greece, would not leave Europe. They stationed their troops and established military bases there by the dozens on the pretext of protecting the Europeans from a new enemy, even more frightening than the previous one: their former ally, the Soviet Union.

Again, one might object that there is no comparison, for nothing is the same as it was in ancient times, and that the digital revolution and global mobility make any comparison with the past obsolete. The Atlanticists maintain (while ignoring Russia's crucial contribution!) that the United States saved the Europeans twice from self-inflicted disasters.

The above statements may be true, but they in no way alter the general picture. The weft of the fabric of European 20th century history is no different from that of Ancient Greece, spotted with civil war, appeals for outside help, interventions, and "benevolent" occupations for the good of the subdued peoples…

Choosing between Insignificance and/or Servitude

Two equally disturbing perspectives confront us. On the one hand, there is a withdrawal towards an increasingly fragmented Europe that is slowly defederalizing, like the Holy Empire that was gradually emptied of its substance through a number of reforms and treaties. From this standpoint, Europe's future would consist simply in administrating its decline and managing its crises in such a way as to make the system and those who benefit from it last as long as possible. In a nutshell, a constrained destiny with no vision, no project; a limited, truncated Europe, doomed to be steadily put aside by the vigorous upswing of ever more powerful peripheral states (the United States, China and Russia).

In a world caught up in imperial and Neo-Westphalian reconstruction, with the United States wanting to keep all the power levers (the dollar, arms, economic sanctions and customs taxes) at their disposal, a scheme well defined by Donald Trump's slogan, "Make America Great Again," and with China showing its ambition to become the first economic world power, Europe has little influence with its management oversight of now 27 states bent on their own, short-term interests.

The second scenario isn't any more comforting. It boils down to endorsing the progressive but inexorable vassalization of Europe by the new tutelary power of the day, the United States of America, which is so close and so friendly that America gladly sucks in Europe's culture and creative energy and clutches it with all the might of its benevolent tentacles...

Ancient Greece was drained of its blood, of its economic and political vitality, even as it Hellenized its neighbors. By transmitting its values, its ideas, its talent for trade and navigation, and its mercenaries to make war, Greece had conquered the spirit and sometimes the heart of the other nations, but it had lost itself in the process.

Modern Europe, which invented so much of what has constituted the modern world, is following suit: it gave the world its principles of democratic governance, its political and economic doctrines, its intellectual genius and artistic creativity, but all the while sapping its own vital energies. The rest of the world is Europeanizing, just like Asia and Rome Hellenized yesterday, even as Europe is exemplifying the Theorem of Cylon:[2] it is being

---

2 The Theorem of Cylon goes as follows: "North and South are coming closer together, but not the way we think." Actually, it's the North that is coming closer to the South, and not the contrary. In other words, it is the North that is "de-civilizing" while the South is civilizing, with the colonialist becoming colonized in turn. It can also be interpreted as follows: "Every advanced civilization ends up being overtaken by those whom it considers to be barbarians." The Theorem comes from a Greek first name and originated in a remark between Brazilian sociologists struck by how the behavior of civilians and public infrastructures

Americanized, Sinicized and, by opening its ports, schools and theaters without restriction to the ubiquity of products Made in USA or Made in China, and in becoming the great melting-pot of globalization, it is slowly on the way to Third-Worldization, applauded by its governors and its media...

Good souls may bellow at this observation, but can one really contest this inverted colonization? Are there no other more efficient, more humane and more sustainable ways to safeguard brotherhood and compassion?

At this point in our synthesis, the issues are as follows: is Europe, and more specifically the political entity that represents it, i.e., the EU, irretrievably doomed to political insignificance and servitude? Or is it capable of reawakening with a start and bouncing back to recover its independence and its sovereignty and win back its status as a great democratic power? Could we see a Europe that would no longer be imperial but rather act to balance and stabilize a world increasingly weakened by the United States/China faceoff? The answer lies in the following chapters.

---

in many Northern countries has degraded, while some formerly underdeveloped countries have brand new infrastructures and encourage hyper-policed behavior, such as China, Singapore, the Gulf States and certain "third-world" cities.

PART III

A MALFUNCTIONING MACHINE

CHAPTER 5

THE EUROPEAN TECHNOCRATIC DICTATORSHIP

Populism has something to do with the memory of peoples: it's a way of calling out to their unconscious, laden with memories left by history.
JEAN-CHRISTOPHE RUFIN[1]

There are two ways for a democracy to abdicate: handing power over to a man or to a commission who will exercise it in the name of technology.
PIERRE MENDÈS FRANCE

There can be no choice against the European treaties.
JEAN-CLAUDE JUNCKER[2]

It is for us, the living (to resolve)… that government of the people, by the people, for the people, shall not perish from the earth.
ABRAHAM LINCOLN[3]

Is Europe prepared to ward off the slow decline that past experiences seem to predict for it? Is the European Union the proper tool to do that?

---

1 "Voyage dans l'Europe qui a peur" (A Journey in Fearful Europe), *Paris-Match,* 22–28 November 2018.
2 *Le Figaro,* 28 January 2015.
3 The Gettysburg Address, 1863.

EUROPE'S EXISTENTIAL DILEMMA

A priori, Europe has what it takes. At the economic level, it succeeded in getting back on its feet after its disastrous civil war and in reconstructing an economy (*"Les Trente Glorieuses"*—"The Glorious Thirty"!) that has become the world's leading economy in terms of consolidated national product and average per capita income. At the political level, it managed to reunite by expanding eastwards and southwards after the fall of the Iron Curtain. And at the cultural, technological, normative and scientific level, it hoisted itself to second place on the world scene, after the United States but before China, at least for a while. Such significant performances are truly commendable.

Yet upon closer study, the continent shows very alarming flaws in its conception and construction, which can only worsen with time.

The first of these deficiencies, and the most annoying, is the conscious and willing rejection of the political aspect. In granting the economy and the judicial absolute precedence, the founding fathers of Europe, from Jean Monnet to Jacques Delors and Walter Hallstein, may have given the impression that they had done the right thing. But in disregarding the peoples, the citizens or the nations—whichever—they led Europe to a dead end. On the long term, this calculation is proving to be more and more dangerous.

The second major problem comes from the profound geopolitical imbalance that has marked European construction from its beginnings and that now threatens to make it collapse. Like the Tower of Pisa, built on unduly soft ground, the European house very soon leaned westwards, towards the United States. Instead of being corrected, this inclination increased after the fall of the Soviet Union and now threatens the stability of the edifice, given the reluctance to secure its Eastern Russian, Turkish, and now Indian and Chinese flank. This structural imbalance is exacerbated by a faulty distribution of internal spaces: the lower floors of the European tower are being increasingly monopolized by Germany, with its tendency to relegate its co-tenants to the basement, like Greece, or to the top floors with no elevator leading there, while the British have just terminated their lease…

The third major flaw is the great institutional hodgepodge characteristic of European (mal)governance. With its "drawer" constitution that has become impossible to amend, Europe has set up dysfunctional institutions that overlap, duplicate, compete with each other, and interpenetrate without respecting the separation of powers that democracy has required since Montesquieu.

Let us see in more detail how and why this excessively economic and legal approach is in the process of slowly killing Europe by depriving it of its major resource that is both inexhaustible and free: the energy of its citizens and its peoples.

A Priori, a Logical and Wise Economic Choice

At the end of the 1940s, the choice made by Europe's founding fathers may have seemed logical and wise. After all, wasn't the economy in an emergency? And after years of war, wasn't it time to rebuild? It wouldn't be fair to hold their decision against them years later. We can blame them, however, for making their choice an exclusive one and for transforming their orientation into an ideology—a new, secular religion—when there were other options, as we saw with the many thinkers that militated for a regional Europe or for a federal Europe based on the Swiss model. The economy could have been a temporary priority instead of being established as a dogma.

In his 2013 book, the economist Robert Salais clearly shows how Europe, from the time of the Bretton Woods Agreement imposed by the United States in 1944, had at every crucial moment chosen the economy over the political options, as though the conditions prevailing at the time of its birth had imposed that one and only choice forever.[4]

Instead of accepting John Keynes' proposal advocating an international system of trade that would have provided a balance between importers and exporters, Washington defended a system

---

4 Robert Salais, *Le Viol d'Europe. Enquête sur la disparition d'une idée* (*The Rape of Europe. An Investigation into the Disappearance of an Idea*), Paris, PUF, 2013.

regulated by the International Monetary Fund (IMF).[5] The latter announced the liberalization of capital movements, the generalization of conditional loans for indebted countries and the neo-liberal opening of international trade by the General Agreement on Tariffs and Trade (GATT). The Marshall Plan, proposed at a time when the Americans sought to supervise European post-war economic reconstruction and counter Soviet influence, speeded up Europe's conversion to the American model of liberal Fordism.

The second mistake was made during the Cold War, when the United States decided to create and arm the new Federal Republic of Germany (FRG), to the horror of the other Europeans. The "German problem" immediately arose because the American aims were contrary to the objectives of some European countries like France. The Schuman Plan for the European Coal and Steel Community (ECSC) was conceived as a response meant to resolve issues such as the French occupation of Saarland and the Ruhr. It was also supposed to be complemented by a Defense Community less dependent on the United States. If the European response provisionally resolved some problems, it created others for the long term. The ECSC institutions included a High Authority—a forerunner of the European Community—that could apolitically regulate the coal and steel industries of the Member States. These institutions, designed by Jean Monnet, deliberately excluded citizens' participation and engendered the generalized depoliticization of the European institutions that we are enduring today.

It was the Treaty of Rome (1957) with its creation of a common market between the six Member States of the ECSC that marked the great shift of emphasis towards the economy. The interests of Benelux and the FRG converged in favor of opening up the markets. Rather reluctant to accept the project, France signed the Treaty of Rome after having made sure that a common

---

5 George Ross, book review of Robert Salais' *Le Viol d'Europe. Enquête sur la disparition d'une idée* (*The Rape of Europe. An Investigation into the Disappearance of an Idea*), Paris, PUF, 2013, in *Sociologie du travail,* vol. 56, N° 2, April–June 2014.

agricultural policy (CAP) would be established and that its future ex-colonies would be integrated into the new market.

These three agreements that reinforced GATT's program to liberalize commerce placed Europe on the rails toward economic liberalism and technocracy. Soon it would no longer be possible to change tracks. As former French Minister of National Education and Defense Jean-Pierre Chevènement stated:

> Conciliating the national economic prerogatives with the intelligent opening up of trade could have allowed room for democratic participation, but because of the international crises of the 1970s, it did not. The United States set up a messianic neoliberal program that was followed by several members of the EEC and restructured the conditions that all of Europe would have to meet. But it was the French left wing and François Mitterrand who made the decisive political choices of the 1980s.
>
> After 1983, when the radical program of the left was thwarted by the European Monetary System (EMS) and the German monetary power, France adopted a competitive deflation policy in the hopes of reducing the German monetary benefit. The French strategy aimed, moreover, at renewing European integration whereby France would regain its initiative if all went well. From 1985 the single market was finalized. It was the only political process possible to reengage the Member States in renewed Europeanization. Thus began the construction of what is today the most open market in the world, at the cost of a maze of abstract regulations written by a European Commission whose stated purpose was to help the EEC face the challenges of globalization. The next great step was the Economic and Monetary Union (EMU) that France hoped would curb Germany's monetary power.[6] The creation of the Euro, once again, would disregard a more political orientation and chain Europe to the

---

6 Ibid.

economy. In hindsight, we can see that these choices were hardly haphazard and were somehow engraved in the DNA of Europe as its genitors had conceived it. From the outset, Jean Monnet had deliberately put politics aside to favor the economy and technology. At the CECA Conference of 20 June 1950 he stated: "The members of the High Authority will not represent the governments, for the principle of national representation appears, in this case, as a source of division. They will act in virtue of a collective mandate and ensure common responsibility. (…)"[7]

The British prime minister of the time, Labour Party leader Clement Attlee, had sensed the danger:

Democracy cannot abdicate entirely into the hands of a few supposedly competent people. Even if we substitute a unique European framework for several national frameworks, there is no reason to substitute a dogma of infallibility for the principle of responsibility that is the law of the democracies. Everyone can make mistakes, even the *most prominent leading international* experts.[8]

To understand the reason why politics and democracy were put in parentheses, one has to go back to the ideology behind the European project. In a study published in 2014, journalist Arnaud Dotézac brilliantly summarized the how and the why of the antinational and antidemocratic orientation of the European construction. The following pages are the gist of his analysis.[9]

---

[7] Jean-Pierre Chevènement, *La Faute de M. Monnet* (*Mr. Monnet's Fault*), Paris, Fayard, 2006. And also Eric Roussel, Jean Monnet, Paris, Fayard, 1996, p. 555.

[8] Ibid., p. 29.

[9] Arnaud Dotézac, "Le déficit démocratique de l'Europe" (Europe's Democratic Deficit) in *Market Magazine*, N° 117, 2014.

Among Jean Monnet's close co-workers were Pierre Uri and Paul Reuter. They had all attended the Uriage Staff College in Isere in the early 1940s, the former as a student and the latter as a teacher. The college was a training center founded by the Vichy regime to train the Militia and the future executives of the National Revolution. In a way, it was an ancestor of today's ENA (École nationale d'administration—National School of Administration). The doctrine of the "Third Way," a vast political project under Vichy aimed at freeing or liberating the nation from of capitalist individualism and communist collectivism, was actively professed. It also contemplated the making of a "new man," possessing both the qualities of an elite senior official and a businessman.

One of the major themes of the Uriage study cycle in 1942 was the various aspects of the community: there was the blood community, the labor community, the social peace community, the community of France (the "Communauté nationale") and of the Empire, but also the community of Europe. It is in fact in Uriage that the concept of the "European Community," a term that was adopted exactly as it was and in full knowledge of the facts by Jean Monnet via his friend Paul Reuter, was invented. As early as 1943, Pétain was promoting it, primarily in his speech at Mont-Dore:

> Europe is a group of nations that could create a community that today is only virtual. We want to give it its institutions and its means of existence. (…) Moreover, the institutions we are dealing with are viable only if the States making up the community voluntarily assign part of their sovereignty (…) to the benefit of a communitarian system (…). The very idea of a community between nations excludes any inside or outside imperialism. It is therefore in itself a prime factor for peace.

The communitarian institutions described by Pétain were intended to be composed of teams of independent men who would voluntarily detach their competency from political options. These are the institutions that Reuter directly integrated into the founding treaties when Monnet called upon him when setting up the European Coal and Steel Community (ECSC). Having been one of the co-authors, with Jean Monnet, of the Schuman Plan in 1950, Paul Reuter was to be the sole designer of the High Authority that would become the supranational executive, legislative and jurisdictional organ of the CECA.

The High Authority became the Commission of Communities, which in turn became the European Commission that we know today. Its genetic code, dating back to Uriage, has remained intact.

Considering the ideology that motivated Paul Reuter and his many colleagues, it is not surprising that democracy was the Commission's great absentee. As he saw it, the European supranational organization had to be the chosen domain of the technicians, a field reserved for the specialists, conceived to enable them to surface from their subordinate role and assume the responsibilities of power. Reuter and Monnet were therefore perfectly aware of their model's democratic deficit from the start.

What is more, they made no effort to hide this in their comments: "The independent, and if we dare say apolitical, nature of the High Authority was greatly remarked. Some saw a direct threat to the democratic spirit; others came out with the terrible accusation of technocracy." (*Revue française de science politique—French Political Science Revue,* 1951). And "But the action of the Community brings up too many technical considerations to serve as an occasion for continuous political discussion." (*Le Monde,* 1955). It is interesting to note that on the German side, Walter Hallstein, the first president of the European Commission (1958–1967), also came from the same circles and was in fact not far from the ideas of Uriage, having actively contributed to a "third way" policy for Europe. From 21-25 June 1938, he had notably represented the Third Reich in the negotiations with Mussolini aimed at establishing the legal framework of the fascist "New Europe." That project also planned to abolish borders and create large traffic routes that would inspire a European feeling and favor free trade...

This conscientious law professor was later enrolled as a lieutenant in the Wehrmacht on the Atlantic front, where he was taken prisoner by the Americans. They reeducated him to their service, as they did a good number of his fellow Germans, during his internment at the Fort Getty "democratic reeducation camp." It was Jean Monnet who later recommended him to Chancellor Konrad Adenauer.

In the postwar context, one can understand these ideological choices. The most reasonable conservative spheres of the time were fiercely anti-parliamentarian. The Third Republic, with its chronic instability and successive scandals, had, after all, led France to its defeat. The German people, hypnotized by Hitler, had voted him into power and led Germany to its ruin. To them, democracy was suspicious. The fear and hatred of communism, fueled by the apprehension of powerful European communist parties, and the shrewd American propaganda dished out since the beginning of the Cold War, succeeded in giving their hostile approach to the nation-states and to the free expression of the peoples its apparent legitimacy. But context cannot justify everything.

The Dismissal of Democracy or the Jean Monnet Method

To understand how this economic and technocratic stranglehold influenced the heart of the European institutions, let us briefly go back to what was called the Jean Monnet method.

The first phase consisted in creating organs with supranational competency and totally independent from the national governments but specializing in specific fields: the management of coal and steel (ECSC), the management of the atom (EURATOM), the management of a common market (EEC), etc. It is no coincidence, either, that these entities were inspired by the American autonomous agencies. After all, Monnet had worked in close relationship with the United States governments for a long time after World War I. And after 1945, through the Ford Foundation and the American Committee for a Unified Europe, the US had supported the Action Committee for the United States of Europe presided over by Jean Monnet.

If Jean Monnet had always ensured his independence and refused any direct financial support, the same was not true for many other promoters of European integration, as evidenced by the official, declassified CIA documents recovered in particular by *The Telegraph* of London in September 2000.[10] Joseph Retinger, president of the European Movement, French Minister Robert Schuman and Belgian Prime Minister Paul-Henri Spaak are also mentioned in these documents updated by Georgetown University researcher, Joshua Paul.[11] As from 1950 and again at the request of Washington, Monnet outlined the creation of a European military force, including a rearmed Germany. Dean Acheson, who was the American Secretary of State at the time, had explicitly demanded the immediate reconstitution of a German army: "I want Germans in uniform by autumn 1951!" he told Jean Monnet at a NATO meeting in September 1950. Administrating this force would have been left to the European Defense Community (EDC). But the French refused the project that provided for placing the force directly under American command via a burgeoning NATO, and the idea was buried until French President Emmanuel Macron relaunched the idea of a European force of intervention in July 2018.

We know today to what extent this period marked a lasting shift by Europe towards the American social-cultural, economic, political and legal standards. Jean Monnet was the main vector, in close collaboration with his bosom friend John Foster Dulles,

---

10 Ambrose Evans-Pritchard, "Euro-federalists financed by US spy chiefs," *The Telegraph*, 19 September 2000. And also by the same author, "The European Union always was a CIA project, as Brexiteers discover," *The Telegraph*, 27 April 2016. See also the disclosures of Constantin Melnik, in charge of security and intelligence under the French Prime Minister (1959–1962).

11 The subsidizing by the American intelligence agencies at the end of the forties and in the fifties of the founders of the European Community and of the European Movement is well documented. See especially Richard J. Aldrich, "OSS-CIA and European Unity: The American Committee on United Europe," in University of Nottingham, *Diplomacy & Statecraft*, vol. 8, N° 1, March 1997, pp. 184–227; Laurence Zuckerman, "How the CIA Played Dirty Tricks with Culture," *The New York Times*, 18 March 2000. And also Frances Stonor Saunders, *Qui mène la danse ? La CIA et la guerre froide culturelle*, Paris, Denoël, 2003.

The European Technocratic Dictatorship

Secretary of State of the Eisenhower administration (1953–59) and former chargé d'affaires to the Third Reich in his capacity as a lawyer. What is more, his brother Allen, the first CIA boss, was a great recycler of Nazi officers during the Cold War.

The second phase consisted in transferring the national sectoral expertise to these supranational entities. At first, there was no question of infringing on sovereign competencies (the army, currency, taxes, etc.). But today this process of transfer is well under way. The European Central Bank, which excludes any political control, handles currency, the budgets are supervised at the European level, and defense is well under way in accordance with the obligations stemming from the North Atlantic Treaty for the Member States. These provisions were enshrined in the Treaty of Lisbon in 2009.

The third and last phase translates into granting the right to legislate with no possibility of democratic supervision. Jurisdictional supervision was entrusted to an autonomous supranational court. In the absence of a constitution that alone could have restricted its power, this court is able to impose the effective and permanent primacy of the European statutes over any national law. This is how the European Court of Justice (ECJ) gradually appropriated the constitutional function.

A Permanent Judiciary Coup d'État

Thanks to Jean Monnet, the ECJ has the right to validate and legitimize the standard-setting activity of the Union's different organs. To achieve this, all it took was the capacity to determine the scope of its competency, in other words, the extent of its power to decide for itself what comes under the sphere of the European law under its jurisdiction. This is how the co-opted judges constitutionalized Europe while circumventing its peoples.

The ECJ was therefore the instrument that sapped the national sovereignties. As early as 1963 it posed the principle of the direct application of European standards, i.e., the capacity for the elected and non-elected European institutions to produce legislation imposed directly on the Member States. This was accomplished without the national democratic representatives having their say and without their peoples having the slightest notion of what was happening. A year later, and still without consulting the European peoples, it consecrated the principle of the "absolute primacy of European law"[12] over preceding and even subsequent national laws, including any contrary national constitutional law.

What was the scope of this genuine judiciary coup d'état? To understand it, one need only recall that Europe was constructed legally by the signing of successive international treaties (about fifty in all). In order to be effective with regard to the Member States, each treaty, with some exceptions, had to be ratified by its national parliamentary bodies. It then had to overcome a double democratic catch: 1) the ratification must be voted on, and is therefore the object of a public debate; 2) the content of the treaty must conform to the constitutions of the states, hierarchically above the laws and the treaties.

By taking that position, the founders of Europe and their heirs were able to save the democratic appearance of their construction. They explained that the ratification procedure was based on very conventional delegations enshrined in the perfectly regular treaties, which were in turn respectful of national political procedures—except that the principles of direct effect and primacy of European law are, as we have seen, purely jurisprudential creations and were never included in any treaty. Yet they totally emptied the democratic double security lock mentioned above of its contents. Thanks to that, there is no longer any need for ratification laws, no need for constitutional conformity.

As for the antagonistic national texts, they were declared null, even if they were the expression of a sovereign, popular will. Domestic judiciary systems were automatically transformed into ECJ auxiliaries, for they have to apply European law directly and disregard domestic law. The 28 supranational European judges thus annihilated the principle and the mechanisms of the sovereignty of the people. The fact that such a tour de force succeeded so

---

12 Van Gend en Loos, ruling of 5 February 1963 and *Costa vs. Enel*, ruling of 15 July 1964.

quickly and so smoothly illustrates the tactical intelligence of Jean Monnet's team—especially as the judges, appointed directly by the politicians, have no responsibility towards the Member States. The fact that they continue to be appointed by the consensus of the Council, upon direct proposition by the national governments, makes it all the more disconcerting.

Europe seems to have thoroughly forgotten Montesquieu's reflection in his *Considerations on the Causes of the Greatness of the Romans*: "There is no greater tyranny than that which is perpetrated under the shield of the law and in the name of justice."

Backed by their American patrons at the time, Monnet and his team thus created a mechanism that gradually and irreversibly formed a recess in the members' sovereign competencies to the benefit of the supranational institutions and their myriad organs and committees.

An Obscure Legislative Circuit

Some observers continue to give a banal image of European power sharing by pointing out that Europe has an executive body (the Commission), a representation of the Member States (the Council), and a representation of the people (the Parliament), although this is a far cry from reality. The European governing institutions' construction site, open for sixty-two years now, has still not created *the separation* of the three legislative, executive and judiciary powers. Above all, it closes the door to any political responsibility to the people.

Let us begin with the European Commission.

In accordance with the model imagined by Jean Monnet, the European Commissioners are totally independent of their national governments; they enjoy diplomatic immunity and are virtually irrevocable during their term of office. As they are highly paid, this plays an important part in their strong solidarity as a group, leading them to progressively develop a feeling of omnipotence.

This is very likely what made Mario Monti, former European Commissioner (1995–2004) and later head of the Italian government, state that of course he appreciated democracy, but so long as government was not "in conflict with the fluctuation of the voters' moods," and that his passion for Europe was mainly due to the fact that it was sufficiently "far removed from electoral constraints." With these words, Mario Monti toed the ideological line of Europe's founding fathers, Walter Hallstein, Pierre Uri and Paul Reuter…

And yet, the spectrum of the Commission's constraining decisions regulating the publics of its component states is vast. There are tens of thousands of them. The Commission can also delegate its competencies to the agencies that work under its exclusive supervision. Today, they number about fifty and manage a budget of two billion Euros, employing over 6,000 people—with no justification for their laws and regulations owed to the public!

So we have here a largely irresponsible, non-elected supranational institution that concocts regulations binding in 28 States, and has the power to decide on issues that are then dealt with by the Council and the European Parliament that meet behind closed doors. Just how legitimate is that? The experts unanimously affirm this tautology: The Commission draws its legitimacy from its ability to dispense the law. Walter Hallstein phrased it very well: "The European Economic Community is a remarkable legal phenomenon. It is a creation of the law; it is a source of law; and it is a legal system." So we have come full circle. This is how a purely rational management of social relationships was implemented, with a view to proscribing the all-too-human, inconstant and uncertain play of democratic policies. The institutions respect their own rules, thus substituting the people's vote of confidence. This form of organization has a name: autocracy. It exudes in the reading of every regulation produced by the European Union, in a self-referential circuit that is inaudible for the people. German philosopher Jürgen Habermas, although deeply Europhile, did not hesitate to describe the European system as a "post-democratic autocracy."[13]

---

13 Jürgen Habermas, *La Constitution de l'Europe,* Paris, Gallimard, coll. "NRF/Essais," 2012.

The European Technocratic Dictatorship

The rest of the study of the legislative process is not any more reassuring. The Commission has a monopoly on legislative initiatives, although in fact it has no political popular mandate. The investiture of its members by the Parliament is symbolic. According to the ordinary European legislative procedure, the Commission transmits its draft texts (guidelines, regulations, decisions, etc.) to the Parliament that can impart its desired amendments to the Council. The Council often resembles a sort of senatorial assembly, an upper house in charge of defending the interests of the Member States because it is made up of their representatives. But this is far from the case insofar as the Council is not composed of elected members but of 28 ministers who are stationed in their native lands (one per state). They meet according to their policy areas and depending on the issues on the agenda. Few Europeans are aware of the fact that each time one of their fellow citizens is appointed as a minister in their national government, he/she automatically becomes a member of the Council and by the same token, a European minister-legislator for the issues dependent on its court of justice. In other words, a member of the national executive is automatically and without a vote invested with a major supranational role, given that the legislative powers of the Council supersede those of the European Parliament.

It is indeed the Council and not the Parliament that adopts the texts voted on in the ordinary procedure. As for the special legislative procedures, the Parliament's role is limited solely to voting en bloc without amendment (currency derogation), veto (amendments to treaties, new adhesions), or consultation (competition law, international agreements). This procedure gives the lobbies complete discretion to voice their standpoints far from prying eyes.

As Ségolène Royal plainly states regarding the glyphosate issue, Monsanto lobbyists were able to directly approach the Commission's President Jean-Claude Juncker requesting him to intervene discreetly with France against the banning of the toxic product. The ban was nonetheless maintained before being lifted by President Macron's government a few months later.[14]

Laws Drafted by Non-elected Officials

Even in ordinary legislative procedures, notes Arnaud Dotézac, the Council, along with the Commission, also has the right of direct interference in the activities of the Parliament from the start, i.e., the preliminary reading of the texts in parliamentary committee. Indeed, the Council's special advisers, including specially delegated diplomats accompanied by representatives of the Commission, often contribute to the drafting of legislative texts along with the elected officials. In this procedure known as "the trilogues," which is in principle informal, the Council and the Commission co-produce a text that everyone approves even before the Parliament holds its first plenary sitting vote. The bills thus drawn up constitute the basic work of the European deputies and are adopted, as is, one after the other, with no public debate. We can see that the separation between the legislative and executive bodies is therefore not respected, that the role of the Parliament as a forum is diverted—not to say emptied of its substance—and that the texts that are subsequently enacted by vote come from agreements reached in the Special Commission instead of being voted on after review by the Parliament as a whole—the only body that is competent to adopt the final text after debate.

What do diplomats have to do with legal drafting? Their arrival on the Council's activity scene dates back to the beginnings of the ECSC in 1953. It had endowed the ministers-legislators with a Coordination Committee to make their work easier. Generally unknown to the public, the Treaty of Rome had formalized the Committee in 1957 as the Permanent Representatives Committee (Coreper), while its members were promoted to the rank of ambassador with a permanent office in Brussels. They are the ones who in practice negotiate and draft the texts.

---

14 Ségolène Royal, *Ce que je peux enfin vous dire* (*What I Can Finally Tell You*), Paris, Fayard, 2018, pp. 20–21.

The European Technocratic Dictatorship

That said, we should note that the Council has not only a legislative function in the EU. It also coordinates the major orientations of the Member States' economic policies, approves the EU annual budget (while the Parliament can only disapprove it), and can even decide on the allocation of European aid in certain cases. In charge of foreign relations, it is the Council that signs the international agreements between the European Union and third countries and that defines the foreign and defense policy carried out by the European External Action Service (EEAS) directed by the High Representative for Foreign Affairs (Catherine Ashton until 2014, Federica Mogherini and Josep Borrel since then). It is also responsible for coordinating cooperation between the courts and the police forces of the Member States. Finally, the Council exercises an executive function that it usually delegates to the Commission for the implementation of the European Rules.

Thanks to the Council's power delegations, the Commission legislates directly. However, to avoid the risk of having it gain too much influence, a system known as *comitology* (committee procedures) was invented as early as 1966. Comitology is neither a science relative to working as a group, nor a syntax error, nor even a humorous quip on the part of European officials. Even if the Treaty of Lisbon changed the term, comitology remains the system that enables Member States to make the European texts compatible with their domestic realities. Hundreds of *ad hoc* committees, composed of national officials and Commission representatives, hone, plane, hash and rehash the texts to be implemented in the Member States.

What does this very brief overview of the mechanisms of the extremely complex circuit of European legislation tell us? We have seen that the absolute supremacy granted to European law absorbs the sovereignty of the Member States to the benefit of the European institutions. The principle of the superiority of the national constitutions, that normally represent the highest expression of popular sovereignty, was dissolved long ago in a legal system conceived and managed by experts with no political responsibility and covered by their diplomatic immunity.

Officials who produce legislation on their own generating a system that is literally autocratic thus replace the democratic and sovereign people. The values underpinning the European project stem from an ideology that disregards the democratic model and is maneuvered by an exterior and higher power acting in its own strategic interests. This model has not changed in seventy years.

The Democratic Gap

Such an antidemocratic process led to what the critics, right-wing and left-wing alike, call the "democratic deficit," a term that exceedingly horrifies Europeanists such as Jean Quatremer, who considers such critics as nothing more than "buggers."[15]

It was British academic David Marquand who coined the term in 1979. At the time he underlined how weak popular representation was in the European Economic Community because the Common Assembly, created in 1957, had had to wait for over twenty years (until 1979) before being elected by universal suffrage. Even so, it served merely as a consulting agency. It was not until the conclusion of the Maastricht Treaty (1992), nearly forty years after the founding treaties, that the European deputies were granted the right to co-decision with the Council of the European Union (the former EEC Council of Ministers), as indicated above.

Long scorned as a position held by the extreme right wing and the Eurosceptics, the democratic deficit has fortunately become a major concern over the past few years. It has been studied in many works, including that of Antoine Vauchez,[16] while the appeals and

---

15 Jean Quatremer, *Les Salauds de l'Europe. Guide à l'usage des eurosceptiques* (*The Buggers of Europe. A Guide for the Eurosceptics*), Paris, Calmann-Lévy, 2017. To the author's credit, he also attacks the States and the opportunist Europeanist politicians who transmogrified the European project, including Manuel Barroso, former President of the European Commission, who left lock, stock and barrel for the American bank Goldman Sachs at the end of his term.

16 Antoine Vauchez, *Démocratiser l'Europe* (*Democratizing Europe*), Paris, Seuil, 2014. See also Stéphanie Hennette, Thomas Piketty, Guillaume Sacriste and Antoine Vauchez, *Pour un traité de démocratisation de l'Europe* (*For a Treaty to Democratize Europe*), Paris, Seuil, 2017.

manifestos for the democratization of Europe are on the rise.[17]

This tendency to impose decisions from higher up and confront people with *faits accomplis* is particularly significant in the way international economic treaties are worked out. The European Union has become a master in the art of concocting these knowledgeable and contorted mixtures of economics and law, arbitrated without the slightest transparency and written in an incomprehensible language using terminology that delights legal advisors and attorneys reviewing it further on. The Multilateral Agreement on Investment (MAI) negotiated in secret between 1995 and 1997 by the twenty-nine members of the Organization for Economic Co-operation and Development (OECD) is a model of its kind.

It proposed further liberalizing trade to the detriment of culture, the environment, and salaried employment, and was finally dropped after being vigorously denounced by civil society. But its most disastrous dispositions—such as the right of multinationals to sue governments and that of companies to hold governments liable for any hindrance to their activity due to demonstrations or strikes—gradually made their way into international public law. This was experienced first-hand by Argentina when it was condemned by the American courts to pay back the undue interest on its debt.[18]

The TAFTA treaties (Transatlantic Free Trade Agreement) and TISA (Trade in Services Agreement) between the European Union and North America follow the same process. Proposed by the Obama administration and the European Commission, the TISA is covered by a United States copyright that makes it illegal to publish and diffuse it! Kept in a vault of the European Parliament,

---

17 "Nous les peuples européens… (We, European citizens…)," Manifesto for the democratization of Europe, 6 February 2016 on the initiative of the Democracy in Europe Movement 2015 launched by Yannis Varoufakis following the Greek crisis of 2015. And the Manifesto for the democratization of Europe of 12 December 2018 signed by a group of 120 intellectuals including Thomas Piketty and Massimo d'Alema.

18 In particular, see https://www.washingtonpost.com/news/business/wp/2016/03/29/how-one-hedge-fund-made-2-billion-from-argentinas-economic-collapse/

it was made known to the public only thanks to WikiLeaks in 2014 and 2016.[19]

Its implementation would have forbidden the States to enact any domestic legislation regarding employment, technologies and local products while at the same time protecting corporations from taxation. The public enterprises would also have fallen under this restraint, which would have had the effect of privatizing them without explicitly enacting that.

Every time that someone makes a move to oppose these treaties, the same Thatcherite argument is dished out: "*TINA, There Is No Alternative*" to what the markets demand. Once they are signed and ratified, there is no turning back: *pacta sunt servanda*. The international treaties are declared to supersede domestic law and must be executed even if they go against national law, practice and interest.

Countless authors who remain staunch Europeans have nevertheless emphasized the dangers of the democratic deficit engendered by this dictatorship over the economy and legal standards. Political scientist Zaki Laïdi thus warns against the folly of wanting to incorporate the whole world order into a constitutional shackle (or straightjacket) and impose the law by force, which is what happened when the constitutional treaty was refused by the French people in 2014 and then introduced all the same via the skillfully made-up Lisbon Treaty in 2009.[20] As he points out, a law, as well-intended as it may be, makes sense in the eyes of the community only when it serves the community.

---

19 The TISA was finally suspended after President Donald Trump refused to ratify it. It was replaced with the CETA (Comprehensive Economic and Trade Agreement) between Canada and the European Union that came into force on 21st September 2017, although to this day it has not been ratified by any of the national parliaments.

20 Zaki Laïdi, *La Norme sans la force. L'énigme de la puissance européenne* (*Norms without Force. The Enigma of European Power*), Paris, Presses de Sciences Po, 2008; "La fin du moment démocratique? Un défi pour l'Europe" ("The End of the Democratic Moment? A Challenge for Europe"), Centre d'études européennes (Center for European Studies), 2007.

Law is not a general, abstract principle detached from the community or a sort of extra-territorial legal UFO. The aim of a law is first political because it serves above all to maintain and consolidate the social order for which it was conceived. According to Zaki Laïdi, ethics without politics, that is to say, ethics that are not deeply rooted in and for a concrete society, serve only to mask very real despotism. Yet what does the European Union do if not create laws in the name of European "values" while ignoring politics, namely public debate and consultations with the citizenry?

Other left-wing authors like French philosopher Étienne Balibar and German writer Hans Magnus Enzensberger, also severely questioned this economistic and normative democratic deviation by the European Union.[21] Aware of Europe's incapability to address the new redistribution of capital and power, Étienne Balibar notes that its financial system is completely out of control insofar as the European Central Bank acts solely according to financial interests by delegitimizing the European Commission. After the 2008 financial crisis and during the Greek crisis of 2015, the governments and heads of state stepped forward as the exclusive holders of popular sovereignty and the rights of the peoples to dispose of themselves, while yet flouting their citizens' own viewpoint.

Étienne Balibar expresses it like this:

> Democracy was clipped at both ends simultaneously, and the political system as a whole took a step forward on the way to de-democratization. The democratic legitimacy crisis in Europe today is therefore twofold: the national States no longer have either the means or the will to defend or to renew the social contract; the authorities (or institutions) of the European Union are not predisposed to investigate the forms and the contents of a social

---

21 Étienne Balibar, *Europe, crise et fin?* (*Europe: Final Crisis?*), Lormont (Gironde, France), Le Bord de l'eau, 2016; Hans Magnus Enzensberger, *Le Doux monstre de Bruxelles ou l'Europe sous tutelle* (*This Tender and Loving Monster, Brussels or The Disenfranchisement of Europe*), Paris, Gallimard, 2011.

citizenship at the higher level—unless they are pressed to do so one day when they realize the political and moral dangers posed for Europe by the addition of a dictatorship exercised "from above" by the financial markets and the anti-elites discontent fed "from below" by the precariousness of living conditions, the contempt for work and the sacking of future prospects.

In this scenario, the ruptures announced, the promises made, the reforms envisaged never emerge. Indeed, they are drowned out or even ground down by community regulations and constraining international treaties like the TISA, or supposedly non-constraining but nonetheless normative agreements like the Global Compact for Migration negotiated at Marrakesh in 2018 under the auspices of the United Nations.[22]

In his short and very vivid essay, Hans Magnus Enzensberger does not wear kid gloves in critiquing Europe's—huge—shortcomings. It has an obsessional will to "communicate" while still hiding key figures (for example, the amounts of the member state contributions) and uses obscure language: "Even the Treaty of Lisbon, this constitution ersatz that serves the Union as a legal foundation, is characterized by the fact that to read it, even the most favorably disposed European citizen faces insurmountable difficulties. It is like a barbed wire fence."

An Ersatz Constitution

Europe's constitution covers 200 pages, as opposed to 22 for the American Constitution… Just like the famous Community acquis that nobody has ever read and that climbed from 85,000 pages in 1984 to 150,000 pages today! Or the Union's *Official Journal* that weighed a ton in 2005 and amounted to 62 million words in 2010. Not to forget the famous community regulation 1677/88 on

---

22 Adopted on 19 December 2018, the Global Compact for Safe, Orderly and Regular Migration or the Marrakech Migration Pact, is a UN convention aiming to cover all the dimensions of international migration. Falling under the category of soft law, it is not legally binding but is nevertheless considered by some specialists as potentially engendering obligations on the longer term.

cucurbits stipulating that to fall under the "extra" category, cucumbers "should present a curve not exceeding a maximum height of 10 mm at the arch for a length of 10cm."

As for democracy being overwhelmed by tons of paperwork and directives, we can quote the study by Austrian author Robert Menasse, who is nonetheless pro-European:

> Yet in the EU, the separation of powers is abolished. (...) The Commission is the institution where democratic legitimization is finally dispelled: it is where a non-elected apparatus that no vote can defeat and that did away with the separation of powers operates... As for political democracy, this Parliament-Council-Commission triad produces a black hole where what we understood as democracy vanished.[23]

We can admit that this "preference for the norm," which is the hallmark of the European Union, was not only negative, as Zaki Laïdi emphasized so well in his excellent work on Europe as a normative power. By preferring soft power to American-style hard power, Laïdi contends, Europe sought to construct a system resting on the elaboration of shared norms rather than on force. Better still, by its overflowing normative activity and its economic weight, it succeeded in gently imposing its norms on the rest of the world. Europe set the pace for sustainable development, human rights, democracy, and fundamental social rights, and advanced the principle of regulating the international system through legal rather than military channels. Its ambition to promote "global public goods" transcending the sovereignties via the major treaties such as the COPs on the environment, women or society is highly commendable. Duly noted. Without contesting Europe's contribution to world order and a better functioning of human societies, the fact remains that these positive effects are the result of less positive intentions, and that too often they mask a functioning that is in fact anything but transparent and

---

23 Hans Magnus Enzensberger, *op. cit.,* pp. 14, 15, 23 and 60.

democratic. Sometimes a dictatorship produces happy results, but even so, it remains a dictatorship. Europe, as we have shown, chose the path of "soft" economic and legal dictatorship—but a dictatorship all the same. This transformation of rules of law into a supranational, omnipotent Superstate Law, even if it sometimes produces favorable results, can only lead on the long term to a political and institutional disaster.

Again, there is no question of reproving Jean Monnet. On the contrary, we admire his pragmatic genius based on his sharp business acumen and recognize the fact that he worked wonders. Neither can we begrudge the founding fathers of the European Community for having chosen that option when the closely related EDC (European Defence Community) and EPC (European Political Community) failed. They are not entirely responsible for the failure of political Europe.[24]

Monnet's famous "method" or federal functionalist approach as it was later called, that gave preference to sectoral integration (coal, steel, atom, free trade, agriculture, etc.) rather than to a vast constitutional founding project, turned out to be very effective—perhaps too effective. With the West turning to neo-liberalism under the influence of Ronald Reagan, Margaret Thatcher and Jacques Delors in the 1980s, the primacy of the economy was reinforced all the more to the expense of all the checks and balances that could have rebalanced it.

Concretely, the option of an all-economic, all-legal and zero-political method for constructing and administrating a unified Europe also had its advantages. The European economy—and especially the German economy!—have prevailed in creating

---

24 The European Defence Community was supposed to have been directed by civilian bodies. The commission in charge of forming them had drawn up a constitution of a federalist and parliamentary type with a bicameral Parliament composed of a House of the Peoples elected by universal suffrage and a Senate appointed by the national parliaments, an effective Government of the Community, an Executive Council, a Court of Justice, and an Economic and Social Council. But the refusal of the French national assembly to ratify the EDC in 1954 overturned the project.

wealth and maintaining an honorable level of competitiveness even if China is quickly catching up.

But in looking back on the seven decades that have elapsed since the first rough drafts for a European community were outlined, it has become impossible to deny the fact that this trajectory has also generated contradictions with potentially explosive repercussions.

The first of these contradictions is ideological. In banning direct political representation from its governing bodies, the Council and the Commission, and by refusing its Parliament the right of parliamentary initiative, the very condition for an autonomous legislative power, the European Union is in total contradiction with the democratic ideal it promotes. How can it pretend to defend democracy *urbi et orbi* and hunt down and denounce the "illiberal" regimes and parties that are cropping up everywhere when it does not itself put into practice—at least not properly—the rules of democracy?

This very hypocritical attitude of "do what I say, not what I do" is contested by the Europeanists, who repeatedly point out that the governors of the Union are appointed by people who indeed have been elected. Only the fans, however, swallow this casuistry: in actual fact, the European Union has no democratic credibility or legitimacy. This ideological contradiction is widely ignored and not even mentioned in the media and the official speeches, but it undermines Europe as surely as underground water.

The Betrayal of the Social Model

Not surprisingly, the second major contradiction is political. Politics cannot change its spots! By adhering to the American neoliberalism of the 1980s and in opening up to globalization and full free trade with the zeal of new converts at the end of the 1980s, Europe simultaneously dismantled those very dimensions that had made up its uniqueness, its strength, and its identity, namely its social and political model. Germany had been built on what was known as "Rhineland capitalism," a good dose of capitalism mixed with a generous portion of social welfare measures, workers' cooperatives, and collective bargaining.

During the "Glorious Thirties," France and Germany for their part, had constructed a brand new social security system, the famous welfare state. It was this very social system of which the English were so proud that had kept the Labour government, concerned with safeguarding the English workers' social benefits, from adhering to the Treaty of Rome in 1957… United by the need to reconstruct the deeply indebted economies devastated by the war, everyone agreed to tax the rich and ensure a more equitable distribution of wealth.

But after the oil crisis of the seventies, the debt incurred by the Vietnam War and Richard Nixon's suspension of the dollar-to-gold convertibility, the scales were reversed on the pretext—not unfounded, we must admit—of ending the rigidity of the welfare state. Thus Margaret Thatcher, in crushing the miners' strike in the early 1980s, became the Trojan horse of European liberalism.

Very soon the neoliberal machine got carried away. With the fall of the Soviet bloc in 1991, economic liberalization and privatization sped up. Border taxes and other trade barriers vanished, emphasis was placed on exports, and trade exploded. The tax locks placed on the very rich were broken, one after the other. Optimization, tax havens and the tax shields aimed at protecting the very wealthy became widespread. At the same time, the unions, indispensable safeguards, were marginalized or reduced to a bare minimum. Remember American President Bill Clinton's famous slogan, "It's the economy, stupid!" addressed to his rival George Bush during the 1972 electoral campaign to show his superiority when it came to economics.

Over the past thirty years, practically all the political parties of the western countries, save for a few far left movements, have thus adopted the neoliberal slogan and program: less governmental intervention. The declarations of employers' associations as well as the political parties and parliaments in their speeches have made an enemy out of the state. In their eyes, it has become the obstacle to elaborating business plans, the gravedigger of individual initiative and the castrator of managers. The EU hastened to apply this strategy to its national states, while avoiding it in its own administration that has turned into a bureaucracy as powerful as it is opaque, ridded of any need to be accountable to anyone.

In no time, the political establishment as a whole, especially the left-wing parties, converted to the new neoliberal religion in support of the liberalist progression. The social will of the Mauroy government in the two early years of President François Mitterand's office, ended with an unconditional surrender as early as 1983 for not having been able to effectively control the country's capital flight. The other social-democratic parties followed. The Germans had already given in with Helmut Schmidt and would later continue with the Hartz reforms under Chancellor Gerhard Schröder that finished off the German social gains, while the American Democrats behind Bill Clinton and British Labour under Tony Blair were turning into ultraliberal falcons.

Since then, the great majority of parties represented in the European states' domestic parliaments address only a small group of their citizens: the middle and upper classes. The social-democratic left has a marked preference for civil servants and teachers; the Green Party focuses on the Vegan urban bumps and scratches and the societal minorities; the centrists appeal to the artisans, the SMEs and independent professions; while the liberals are at the service of the financial oligarchy, the very wealthy, and the multinational company owners.

The Left Betrays the Underprivileged Classes

The fall of the communist parties, the fact that the leftist parties betrayed their electorate and that the underprivileged classes were left to their fate logically produced two troubling phenomena. First, there was a general depoliticization for want of truly structural debates and clear policy issues, as most of the parties were saying more or less the same thing and defending the same interests with a few, minor semantic nuances. This episode of eroding political debate was a natural, extra add-on to the depoliticization of law and the proliferation of regulations imposed by the Court of Justice, described earlier.[25]

This depoliticization is reflected in the comprehensive electoral absenteeism that is becoming more and more alarming. In the last legislative elections in France, absenteeism reached 25% in the second round and 34% if we count the blank or invalid ballots. Is this not also a sign of defiance with respect to what was on offer in domestic politics?

The other logical result of this rejection by the working classes is the extraordinary rise to power of the so-called "populist" parties since the end of the 1990s. Almost all of these parties share an anti-European or Euro-skeptical attitude. Whether it is the British UKIP which prompted Brexit, the Rassemblement national in France, the Vlaams Belang in Belgium, the Lega in Italy, the AfD in Germany, the Austrian FPö, Switzerland's UDC, Vladimir Jirinovski's LDPR in Russia, the Swedish Democrats or the Danish Popular Party, all are wary of Brussels when they are not outright strongly denouncing the transgressions of the European Union.

In Eastern Europe, the situation is somewhat different. Because of their history and their long subjection to the German, Austro-Hungarian and Russian Empires and then to the communist dictatorship, many of these countries hoisted national-conservative parties into power. These parties, although not hostile to the European Union as such, refuse nonetheless to conform to its societal and migratory "diktats." Such is the case of Hungary, Poland, Slovakia, and to a lesser extent, the Czech Republic, Romania and Bulgaria. For reasons that the Western Europeans find hard to understand but that are obvious for anyone who knows Eastern Europe, these countries have never—or rarely—been able to freely express their national identity. Their national expression has almost always been bridled. Barely exaggerating,

---

25 On this matter see Luuk van Middelaar, *Quand l'Europe improvise. Dix ans de crises politiques* (in English: *Alarums and Excursions. Improvising Politics on the European Stage,* New York: Agenda Publishing, 2019), Paris, Gallimard, 2018, p. 19.

one could say that they went directly from the communist empire to the supranational empire of Brussels without passing through the national square.

The former Russian dissidents well understood this unrest. The feeling of having been spoliated of part of their history was still sharp. Solzhenitsyn, and especially Alexander Zinoviev with his masterful study on the western supra-society, as well as Vladimir Bukovsky in his book, *The European Union, a New USSR?*,[26] all brilliantly analyzed the phenomenon that was totally incomprehensible for the intellectuals of Western Europe.

Rightly or wrongly, many Eastern Europeans saw in the European Union a means of acceding to freedom and a higher standard of living. But some of them also had the impression of going from one form of totalitarianism to another, perhaps less brutal, but that tended to repress their legitimate ambition to national and cultural recognition.

In any case, the national-conservative parties that they brought to power contest Brussels, even if in a different way and for other reasons than those of the West European populist parties.

At any rate, they all come together on one point: opposition to migration. Angela Merkel's slogan *"Wir schaffen das!"* ("We can make it!"), hailed by the European establishment as a paragon of virtue, provoked an anti-immigrants outcry throughout central Europe. The acceptance of a million predominantly Muslim immigrants by Germany in 2015 did not get through for a very simple reason, even if it did not affect the European elite: already weakened by the flow of immigrants from within Europe—the "Polish plumber" syndrome—the lower classes found themselves in direct competition with the immigrants, not only for jobs but also salary-wise, as the lowering of wages was made possible

---

26 Alexander Solzhenitsyn, *Nos pluralistes* (*Our Pluralists*), Paris, Fayard, 1998; Alexander Zinoviev, *La Suprasociété globale et la Russie* (*The Global Super Society and Russia*), Lausanne, L'Âge d'Homme, 2000, and, by the same author: *L'Occidentisme. Essai sur le triomphe d'une idéologie* (*Westernism. Essay on the triumph of an ideology*) Paris, Plon, 1985; Vladimir Bukovsky, *L'Union européenne, une nouvelle URSS?* (*The European Union, a New USSR?*), Monaco, Éditions du Rocher, 2005.

by the importation of cheap labor. This did not, in the least bit, threaten the jobs and salaries of the upper-class lawyers, doctors, professors, engineers, entrepreneurs and politicians, who were protected by their diplomas, their supposed competence and a hidden corporatism, a *de facto numerus clausus* like those of the notaries, the barristers or the doctors.

This injustice did not escape the working classes who had no other choice but to fall into the arms of the populists, the only party that would listen to them and take their grievances into consideration. The fear that massive foreign immigration would moreover threaten their culture, their language, their religion and their traditions did the rest. The privileged elites, of course, who spoke several languages, were genuine believers in cosmopolitism and gave not the slightest importance to their national or cultural roots, considered this an ungrounded fear. QED.

To conclude this round table of populisms, let us discuss left-wing populism, which is more widespread in southern Europe, especially in Greece, Spain and France. But apart from Jean-Luc Mélenchon's "France insoumise" ("Unsubmissive" or "Rebellious France"), the left-wing populists are rapidly becoming *salonfähig* (socially acceptable), as the Germans say. Podemos turned dyed-in-the-wool social-democratic and is very Europhile, like Syriza in Greece since Prime Minister Alexis Tsipras resigned under German pressure in 2015. As for the Italian Five Star Movement, it stands alone on this list because even if it claims to be Europhile in spite of its alliance with the anti-European Lega of Matteo Salvini, it is also anti-system.

This tour of European populisms would be incomplete without including the French episode. The European and French establishment revels in denouncing Marine Le Pen's extreme right-wing populism and the extreme left-wing populism of Jean-Luc Mélenchon. But it declines to include, with good reason, Emmanuel Macron's high-class "populism" despite the fact that the young, charismatic French president pulverized the classic parties to get elected by breach, in a way, to the presidency of the Republic, and despite the fact that it is the very definition of populism to short-circuit the parties, the constituent bodies, and the intermediary bodies to claim to be directly representative of the people so as to come to power.

While the Europeanists nevertheless unanimously hailed Macron's populist charade as a masterstroke and a blessing for Europe, barely eighteen months after his triumph, Macron was contested—and how!—by the Yellow Jackets, the most powerful French insurrectionary movement of these past years. The populism of the elite was overtaken by the populism of the little people rebelling on the roundabouts, a fine tragedy indeed!

To date, the reaction of the political and intellectual European elite to this popular breaking wave has been contemptuous and full of invective. The more rational intellectuals like Thomas Piketty, Chantal Delsol, Emmanuel Todd, Michel Onfray, Christophe Guilly and Bertrant Badie have sincerely tried to propose more sophisticated and less arrogant political evaluation grids.[27] But the politicians have remained deaf. In Brussels, they look the other way, waiting for the tempest to subside. They wait, hoping that the wave will break before the next European elections. Guy Verhofstadt, the spokesperson of the liberal right in the European Parliament, cannot find words harsh enough to criticize these movements, even if otherwise his analysis of the drift of institutional Europe is

---

27 Thomas Piketty, *Peut-on sauver l'Europe? Chroniques* (*Can Europe be Saved? Chronicles*) 2004–2012, Paris, Les Liens qui libèrent, 2012 and by the same author: *Le Capital au XXIe siècle* (*Capital in the 20th Century*), Paris, Seuil, 2013; Chantal Delsol, *L'Identité de l'Europe* (*The Identity of Europe*), Paris, PUF, 2013 and by the same author: *Le Populisme et les demeurés de l'Histoire* (*Populism and History's Forgotten*) Monaco, Éditions du Rocher, 2015; Emmanuel Todd, "Le protectionnisme oppose des populistes lucides à un establishment aveugle" (Protectionism opposes rational populists to a blind establishment), a conversation with Alexandre Devecchio, in *Le Figaro Vox,* 16 March 2018; Emmanuel Todd, *Après la démocratie* (*After Democracy*), Paris, Gallimard, 2008; Christophe Guilluy, *La France périphérique: Comment on a sacrifié les classes populaires* (*Peripheral France. How the working classes were sacrificed*), Paris, Flammarion, 2014, and by the same author: *No Society. La fin de la classe moyenne occidentale* (*No Society. The end of the western middle class*), Paris, Flammarion, 2018; Bertrand Badie, *Un monde sans souveraineté* (*A World without Sovereignty*), Paris, Fayard, 1999 and by the same author: *Vers un monde néo-national?* (*Towards a neo-national world?*), Paris, CNRS Éditions, 2017.

rational.[28] Between the "illiberal" democracy popular in Eastern Europe and the democracy without democrats of the European supranational bodies, we do not know which is worse.

Because it is blind or caste-conscious or unable to question and reconsider its actions, the European nomenklatura refuses to heed the outraged working classes' call for help. And without the proper political instruments and democratic channels to express themselves before the higher levels of the Union, the latter do not stand a chance of being heard.

The peoples' revenge might well surprise them one day...

Third Contradiction: Unbearable Social Inequalities

Indeed, the most serious, the most dangerous of these contradictions is the social one. It is the result of increasing inequalities over the past twenty-five years. During the 20th century, income inequalities diminished in a great number of developed countries between 1939 and 1960. Thomas Piketty and Emmanuel Saez attributed this decrease to the effects of the progressive income tax.[29] The Great Depression, followed by the destructions of World War II and the period of severe inflation that went with it, wound up seriously affecting the large fortunes.

This decrease in inequalities in turn generated a decrease in income inequalities while the salary inequalities remained stable. Income taxes, that had rapidly become very progressive from 1945 and up until the 1980s, prevented large fortunes from being rebuilt.

---

28 Guy Verhofstadt, *Le Mal européen* (*Europe's Ills*), preface by Daniel Cohn-Bendit, Paris, Plon, 2016.

29 Thomas Piketty and Emmanuel Saez, "The Evolution of Top Incomes: A Historical and International Perspective," in *American Economic Review,* "Papers and Proceedings," 96(2), 2006, p. 202; Michel Aglietta and Laurent Berrebi, *Désordres dans le capitalisme mondial* (*Disorders in global capitalism*), Paris, Odile Jacob, 2007; Thomas Piketty, *L'Économie des inégalités* (*The Economy of Inequalities*), Paris, La Découverte, 2007. Thomas Piketty's interview in the monthly *Alternatives économiques* (*Economic Alternatives*), N° 276, January 2009, pp. 52–54, provides a synthesis of this type of study.

The European Technocratic Dictatorship

For the past thirty years, however, economic inequalities have been on the rise again in the Anglo-Saxon countries, with continental Europe following on their heels. The high salaries have cracked the ceilings while the wealth inequalities exacerbate the income inequalities. The increase in salary inequalities rests on two major economic trends: the lowest salary incomes are stagnating while the very high salaries escalate the salary pyramid. With large employers' income much higher (180 times in Switzerland and 295 times in the US) than that of their employees, the gaps within companies have become disgusting. Between 1989 and 2000, a CEO's total pay increased by 342% in the United States, while the median hourly wage only increased by 5.8%.

In Europe, this lowest incomes stagnation engenders increasing employment and unemployment insecurity even as dismissed managers are granted exorbitant golden parachutes. Such rank injustice creates deep resentment, especially in the suburbs and peripheral zones facing poor infrastructure that is ignored by the government authorities.

Let us briefly go over the causes of the increase in social inequalities advanced by university economists, most of whom, we should note, are paid by private funds on top of their teaching salary. First, there is the effect of technological progress that seems to favor productivity and therefore pay level (but why should it only benefit the higher salaries?). Second, there is the globalization effect whereby the working poor of the poor countries compete with those of the rich countries, thus creating pressure to lower the latter's income. Lastly, for the past thirty years the balance of power between capital and labor has shifted to the detriment of labor. This is due to the decline of the working class, of syndicalism and of the employees' power of negotiation that magnifies the power of the managers, who reap the capital gains produced for their sole profit.

To justify these growing inequalities, the liberal economists, who make up 90% of the academic discipline and hold 90% of the Nobel Prizes in Economics (awarded by the Bank of Sweden independently of the Nobel Academy), put forth the "trickle-down" theory or the idea that the wealth of the rich spills over onto the poor. Nothing could be less certain, as the theory has never actually been confirmed. The praise of philanthropy and the private foundations by the media and the universities is not reassuring enough. Their good deeds remain slight and have little to do with the euergetism of ancient times, considered a social obligation in its day.

The Spiral of Salary Stagnation and Debt

What matters here is the built-up tension caused by the growing inequalities that the EU does not—and has no desire to—heed. These tensions will end up exploding one day. We should remember that the Roman Republic collapsed after an endless civil war that ravaged Rome because the oligarchic Senate had refused to redistribute the land and reform the agricultural laws to address the needs of the poorest citizens!

The earliest Mesopotamian societies and ancient Greece alike understood that to preserve prosperity and the freedom of enterprise, the debtors had to be protected. The democratic Greek regimes prohibited enslavement for debt. By principle, the small farmers' debts were periodically cancelled. This was all the more necessary as in every society that practices uncontrolled interest-bearing loans, debtors are unfailingly doomed to become poorer, then to be deprived of their goods before being reduced to slavery by their creditors, who correspondingly accumulate enormous properties and become oligarchic parasites. According to American economic historian Michael Hudson,[30] this social polarization tendency—a result of the ruthless nature of the refusal to cancel debts—is the original and incurable curse on our western society.

---

30 Michael Hudson, *Lending, Foreclosure and Redemption from Bronze Age Finance to the Jubilee Year*, Dresde, ISLET Verlag, 2018; by the same author: *Debt and Economic Renewal in the Ancient Near East* (with Marc van de Mieroop), Baltimore, CDL Press, 2002; *Trade, Development and Foreign Debt. A History of Theories of Convergences in the International Economy*, ISLET Press, 2009.

Such periodical social upgrading is all the more necessary because the financial elites have always focused on centralizing control in their own hands and managing the economy in a predatory and extractive way. The supposed freedom of the rich is granted at the expense of governmental authority and society in general. The freedom of some is in opposition to the freedom of all...

Today, the spiral of debt is less threatening to the small farmers—who are on the road to pauperization and have been progressively disappearing anyway since the Industrial Revolution—than to the salaried employees and the small and medium enterprises who have become the indentured sub-contractors of the new oligarchic enterprises (the multinationals). The same holds true for nations, as reflected in the experiences of Greece in 2015 and Italy in 2018 where a power struggle arose regarding the budget, although their deficit was below the regulatory 3% limit.

The growing debt of both households and enterprises cumulatively increases the interest on loan repayment. While economic growth follows an S curve at best, the debtors, unless protected by a central authority, simply see their debts regularly increase and wind up being permanently insolvent. In many Western countries, household debts are running extremely high. Debt forgiveness concerns resetting the counters to enable the economy and society to start off anew on a sound footing: an unimaginable perspective today, according to Hudson. Look at Germany's intransigence over the idea, not even of cancelling but merely or restructuring the Greek debt. As for the debts of private households, they run up against the same wall. The economic crisis of 2008 showed that the banks, having thoughtlessly loaned to buyers of housing units and having just been saved by the taxpayers, nevertheless did not hesitate to hunt down insolvent debtors, going so far as to evict them from their homes...

Today, the power of the lenders over the borrowers has led to their financially dominating the economy. The gap between the thin oligarchic elite of the very wealthy and the large masses of the poor is growing wider. Society is being polarized and internal contradictions, amplified. Europe today is far more vulnerable in the face of inequalities than the United States, as we witnessed with the revolt of the Yellow Jackets.

The day is perhaps not far off when this anger will erupt because we did not know how—or even want—to prevent it in time. History shows that in that case there are only two possible alternatives, and both are disastrous: the decline of the republic and its transformation into a repressive totalitarian regime; or the brutal destruction of the system by a violent revolution followed by a long period of anarchy...

Since the end of the 1980s, the ultraliberal discourse has reigned supreme, invading everything: the economy, of course, but also politics, thinking, everyday life, and even people's private life, to the extent that it gnaws like a cancer or erodes like the sand of desert storms. Everything has become quantifiable, negotiable, buyable, monetizable, privatizable.

We remember that capitalism began in 17th-century England with the land grabbing of public common lands, the privatization of the commons by the aristocracy and the large landowners. For several decades now, water, a common good that was once free, is tending to become merchandise in the hands of private monopolies. And soon air itself will follow suit. There is little doubt that in one or two generations, when it will have been polluted by the very people who will appropriate it, air will become a rare resource that will be bargained and cashed in on. Carbon trading could be considered a first symptom of this trend, even if for a good purpose.

The problem with the ultraliberal economy is that it undermines the very idea of the public good, the public space, and the common good for humankind as a whole. Ultra-liberalism, far from promoting sound competition, has become an absolute, total and therefore totalitarian ideology.

For what does the digital economy amount to if not privatizing communication channels, language, words, and the human image; monetizing waves and the infravisible to the benefit of a few giant companies that, at the height of hypocrisy, pass them off as free while monetizing what had been inherently free until then: direct oral and written communication, and the physical communication between individuals. As Marx would say, the schemes of capital are incommensurate!

The Fourth Industrial Revolution (or Industry 4.0) is also Rousseau 4.0. The famous phrase from his *Discourse on the Origin and Basis of Inequality Among Men* is no longer, "The first man who, having enclosed a piece of ground, bethought himself of saying, 'This is mine,' and found people simple enough to believe him, was the real founder of civil society," but rather: "The first man who, having put water in a bottle, air in a capsule and words, images and sounds in a Smartphone, and who will dare to say, 'This is mine,' that man will be the real founder of global society…"

It is time that the European Union left standard ideology behind and put the politician back in his rightful place by tackling social unrest at the roots: restructuring or partially cancelling the debt of the overly-indebted States and households; taxing the Silicon Valley giants (Google, Amazon, Facebook, Apple, Microsoft) and the multinationals; taxing financial transactions (Tobin tax) and traffic payments that could replace the VAT; and withdraw the privileges granted to the large fortunes.

CHAPTER 6

AMERICAN TRUSTEESHIP, RUSSIAN EXCLUSION, GERMAN HEGEMONY

It is not yet a loss, but it is striking that three weeks after Brexit, not one European statesman has articulated a vision of Europe's future. They are the continent that built the international world. And no one has stood up with the vision of Churchill. They're talking about tactical matters while they're in the process of giving up the essence of what they've struggled for and what they've represented throughout history.

HENRY KISSINGER[1]

It is not Europe that made peace, but peace that made Europe.

JEAN-LOUIS BOURLANGES[2]

There can be no political personality of Europe if Europe has no personality in terms of its defense which has always been the basis of politics... NATO is not Europe's defense. It is the defense of Europe by the Americans.

GENERAL DE GAULLE[3]

---

1 "World Chaos and World Order, Conversations with Jeffrey Goldberg ," *The Atlantic*, 2016.

2 President of the *Fondation du Centre*, former European deputy, 2012.

3 [3] 17 July 1961, cited by Pierre Maillard, *De Gaulle et l'Europe entre la nation et Maastricht (De Gaulle and Europe between the nation and Maastricht)*, Paris, Tallandier, 1995.

American Trusteeship, Russian Exclusion, German Hegemony

We have just seen how the strategy of integration through economics and standards carried out to the detriment of politics gave rise to potentially explosive contradictions and internal tensions for Europe's future. We shall now concentrate on the geopolitical imbalances that weigh on its destiny.

By constantly eluding the issue of its sovereignty and its independence, Europe has indeed shut itself up in a doctrine of servitude that keeps it from fully playing its role on the world stage. It missed a great opportunity when the Soviet Union collapsed in 1991. Europe is expected to fulfill a pacifying, humanistic, ecological, balancing mission or even to arbitrate in the United States vs. China and Russia conflict. In giving up its independence and yielding its sovereignty, it runs the long-term risk of disappearing as a cradle of autonomous civilization, just as ancient Greece was absorbed by the Roman Empire, and the Holy (German) Empire was dissolved by Napoleon.

In the spring of 1945, just after Germany's surrender, the state of affairs was still wide open in Europe. The Yalta Conference, held in February, had traced the postwar contours of Europe with no major ruptures in the Allied camp. But ailing President Roosevelt died and was replaced by Harry Truman, who was much more hostile towards communism. This rapidly and radically changed the situation. At the Potsdam Conference in July, the tone was less conciliating. The United States informed Stalin that it had just tested the atomic bomb it was to use against Japan a few days later. The balance of power was hence greatly modified in its favor, exacerbating Stalin's apprehension.

Many historians consider this new scientific and military twist as the true start of the Cold War. General MacArthur took advantage of the strategic upper hand gained at Hiroshima and Nagasaki to obtain Japan's immediate surrender and avoid its joint occupation with the Soviet Union, as had been stipulated at Potsdam.

Stalin, who was already skeptical, stiffened. He had not forgotten the wars waged by the British Empire and France against Russia in the 19th century, the Crimean War of 1853, the support granted to the Caucasian rebels, and the British Great Game in

Central Asia; and certainly not that British, French and American troops were sent to combat Bolshevism in 1919–1920. He felt all the more deceived because the Soviet Union had lost 26 million men on the battlefields and undergone severe destruction. The American determination to reconstruct Germany without making it pay any substantial reparation upset him to no end.

Yet on the European continent, everything was open to discussion. There were two opposing tendencies. One, after the ravages of the world wars and the desire for peace, strongly militated for a united, pacified Europe inspired by the ideas upheld in the 1920s by Richard Coudenhove-Kalergi and Aristide Briand, and the principles defined by the French Resistance.

This show of goodwill was embodied in 1947 and 1948 in the Treaties of Dunkirk and Brussels that aimed above all to place restrictions on Germany and were not openly directed against the Soviet Union. Signed by France, the United Kingdom and Benelux, the Treaty of Brussels (or Brussels Pact) provided for military, economic, social and cultural cooperation between the five countries under the auspices of a common defense organization commanded by Field Marshal Montgomery and assisted by General de Lattre de Tassigny.

The same year, the Hague Conference, convened by the federalist European movements under the honorary chairmanship of Winston Churchill, assembled 750 delegates and laid the foundations for a European confederation. The congress adopted the "Message to Europeans" drawn up and read out by the Swiss federalist, Denis de Rougemont: "Together […] we can tomorrow build the greatest political formation and the greatest economic unit our age has seen. Never will the history of the world have known so powerful a gathering of free men. Never will war, fear and misery have been checked by a more formidable foe."[4]

Rougemont called in particular for abolishing the restrictions on the movement of goods, currency convertibility, resource programming, labor mobility, economic policies coordination,

---

4 Denis de Rougemont, *Message to Europeans*, The Hague, 10 May 1948 (www.cvce.eu).

and promoting full employment. He also advocated a European Assembly elected by universal suffrage and a united Europe open to Germany, he also championed the adoption of a Charter guaranteeing basic rights, the creation of a Supreme Court, and a European child, youth and culture center.

The Cold War Divides Europe

But already in late 1945, the climate began to change and take a more combative turn, encouraged notably by the United States. In early 1946, George Kennan, then deputy head of the American Mission in Moscow, sent a "Long Telegram" to Washington in which he reported Soviet Russia's permanent feeling of insecurity as well as its Komintern dangerous expansionist ideology. He proposed the vigorous application of counterforce against the Soviet Union. Early in 1947, Harry Truman used this message as a basis to launch his containment policy to curb the Soviet Union. Kennan then formalized it in a well-known article published in *Foreign Affairs* magazine.[5] Later, he would go back on his statement.[6]

Preceding that, on 5 March 1946 in the United States, Churchill had made his great speech in which he denounced the "iron curtain descending across Eastern Europe" for the first time. Thus began the Cold War, a term coined by George Orwell at the end of 1945 before being popularized after 1947 by Bernard Baruch, adviser to President Truman, and journalist Walter Lippmann.

Stalin did not take long to retaliate. The coalition governments of Eastern Europe were quickly replaced by hardcore communist regimes. In March 1948, the "Prague coup" set up a communist

---

5 Mr. X [George F. Kennan], "The Sources of Soviet Conflict," *Foreign Affairs*, 25, N° 4, 1947, pp. 566–582.

6 "My views on containment were distorted by those who understood and carried them out solely as a military concept: I believe that is what led us to 40 years of the useless, horribly expensive process that the Cold War turned out to be," he confided shortly before his death in 2005. He was against the war in Kosovo and NATO's eastward enlargement after 1991 describing it as a "strategic blunder of potentially epic proportions," Robert Skidelsky, "Kennan's revenge : remembering the reasons for the Cold War," in *The Guardian*, 23 April 2014 (amp.theguardian. com).

power in Czechoslovakia. The same year, the Soviet Union refused the economic reconstruction plan for Europe proposed by General George Marshall, American Secretary of State and later Secretary of Defense, that the Western Europeans had adopted in Paris in September 1947.

Still in 1948, the Soviets decreed the Berlin Blockade in response to Western maneuvers to recreate a new German state endowed with a new currency, the Deutschmark, in their occupation zone. The following year, the North Atlantic Treaty Organization (NATO) was signed on 4 April 1949, replacing the Treaty of Brussels, which had never been applied despite its innovative approach. A year later, the Korean War was launched, while the war in Indochina, waged by France against the troops of Ho Chi Minh, grew in intensity.

In this repeated highly tense context in which Stalin's paranoia rivaled with the anti-communist hysteria and the beginnings of McCarthyism in the United States, Robert Schuman, prompted by Jean Monnet, revealed his project for a European Coal and Steel Community. The project was immediately enhanced with a military facet. On Council President René Pléven's incentive, France proposed creating, "for the common defense, a European army attached to the political institutions of a united Europe placed under the responsibility of a European Defense minister, under the authority of a European assembly, with a common military budget and the participation of German contingencies."

But, as its promoter had to admit, in actual fact, the project depended on the United States: "This European army will be placed under the orders of a superior command of the Atlantic forces in Europe." The Pléven plan was modified to the benefit of the deceptively titled European Defence Community (EDC), adopted again in 1952, with Jean Monnet at the wheel. The concept had been touched up but the substance was the same. The EDC Commissariat was not intended to set up a common defense policy, but simply organize a supranational military administration subordinate to NATO and therefore, to Washington. Thus, it was NATO's commander-in-chief who was to decide on the weapons necessary for the strategy to be determined by the Alliance, which amounted to putting it under United States orders and purchasing American arms. Any exportation of military material was prohibited except under the express authorization of the NATO commander. This, in turn, amounted to placing the French armaments industry—the only major one on the continent—under US supervision.

Firmly contested by the left wing and the Gaullists, the EDC was abandoned following its rejection by the French National Assembly in August 1954. The campaign had given rise to heated debates between the "cedists and anticedists" as well as to very heavy American pressure, with Secretary of State John Foster Dulles insinuating the threat of an "agonizing reappraisal" of American aid in case of refusal.

The word got around that some articles of the treaty had been drawn up directly by American diplomats, to which General de Gaulle commented that the treaty attributed "to the Atlantic commander-in-chief with regard to the destiny of France, practically discretionary rights such that, in any case, at any time, in any country, no government had ever conceded to any of its generals."

The failure of both the EDC and the ensuing Western European Union showed that the western European states were unable to conceive a defense system without the United States. One of Jean Monnet's main co-workers, Robert Marjolin, later confessed in his Memoirs: "The incapacity of Europe to unite is the result of a decision made implicitly by the Europeans at the end of World War II, namely leaving their defense to the Americans."[7]

Military Subjection, Economic Absequience

If we have recalled the unfolding of these events that led to forty years of Cold War—that George Kennan moreover deeply regretted—it is to show how closely the military issue was linked to the first phase of Europe's construction. In actual fact, it even

---

[7] Robert Marjolin, *Le Travail d'une vie. Mémoires 1911–1986,* Paris, Robert Laffont, 1986. (In English: *Architect of European Unity: Memoirs 1911–1986,* translated by W. Hall, Weidenfeld & Nicolson, 1989).

preceded it to the extent that economic and political Europe seemed subordinated to it. The men who created the military alliance projects in close consultation with the United States were the very ones who drew up the economic and legal integration projects.

This willingness to let the United States ensure Europe's defense and economic recovery weighed heavily on the concept of modern Europe. There is, *a priori,* no question of rejecting the United States or distrusting them: they were obviously necessary allies, and the principle of this alliance was contested neither by de Gaulle nor Minister of Defense Jules Moch, who represented the "sovereignist" socialists of the time. The fact remains that the alliance rested on dependency rather than equality and therefore alienated European sovereignty.

Henceforward, Europe's defense was entrusted to NATO, which grew increasingly powerful over the decades. So it is no accident that admission to NATO, both chronologically and hierarchically, always preceded admission by candidate states to the European Community. And it is no coincidence that both institutions, military and economic, left France to establish their headquarters in Brussels, just a few kilometers away from one another.[8]

In the American mind, Europe's military subordination went hand in hand with converting it to liberal capitalism, the United States' official economic religion. The very purpose of the Marshall Plan was to parade American economic success in the face of Soviet Communism while securing access to Europe to the American economy. The capital necessary for reconstruction had first to be used to purchase American goods.

Glowing and prosperous in 1945, American industry had come out of the war greatly reinforced, totally unscathed, and operating at full capacity. At worst, it feared closed borders that would have prevented it from exporting its products; hence the United States' readiness to control Europe's economic revival and

---

[8] They moved because of General de Gaulle's reluctance when he returned to power in 1958.

counteract the slightest return to protectionism. Likewise, and in agreement on this point with the Soviets, the Americans strongly advocated rapid decolonization that had the double advantage of placing them up front and allowing *made in USA* products to freely access the colonial markets formerly controlled by the European metropoles. Interestingly enough, a century and a half earlier, Talleyrand had already forewarned of the danger. Exiled to the United States at the end of the 18th century, he had observed well before Tocqueville that:

> …as for America, Europe has to keep her eyes open at all times and never offer the slightest pretext for recrimination or retaliation…
>
> America is expanding every day. She will grow into a colossal power, and inevitably, there will come a time when the latest discoveries in communications will place her face to face with Europe, and she will want to have a say in and put her hand to our affairs. The governments of the Old Continent, therefore, must apply political prudence and remain alert to avoid the slightest pretext for any such intervention. The day America sets foot in Europe, peace and security will be lastingly banned.[9]

De Gaulle and the most perspicacious observers of European construction had pointed out the risk of confiding Europe's defense to an overly powerful friend. For a long time, such procedure has been the object of studies and criticism. In 1977, for instance, left-wing journalist Claude Bourdet, a former deportee and founder of *France Observateur*, (the ancestor of *L'Obs*, a prominent French general information magazine), had already denounced the transformation of Europe in "*L'Europe truquée*" (*Truncated Europe)*, as "a super-state closed in on itself, dominated by Federal Germany and infrangibly tied to American interests."

---

9 Michel Poniatowski, *Talleyrand aux États-Unis, 1794-1796 (Talleyrand in the United States 1794–1796)*, Paris, Librairie académique Perrin, 1976, p. 493.

"Every step taken forward towards crystallizing it into a supranational system will only supply the West-German and American leaders and dominating classes with the weapons necessary to sabotage a possible leftist experiment. European integration, Atlantic alliance, French nuclear defense: behind these three myths lie the powerful interests that are a threat to the popular movement and social rights," so he believed... Forty years have gone by since then and on this issue, prove him entirely right.[10]

The Europeans Acquiesce to Vassalization

The third major taboo in European construction after the democratic deficit and neo-liberalism is indeed NATO. Although economic cooperation was always coupled with military cooperation, the latter was almost invariably mentioned separately, as if the two were distinct and had nothing to do with each other. The same holds true for the reign of the experts, advisors, academic specialization, and journalistic cherry-picking of facts, where each sector falls under the control of diverse specialists. Decoupling conceals the military dimension behind the economic aspect.

NATO's growing influence over the decades and its impact on European construction as a whole are nevertheless essential components of the European equation. But if we want to understand why present-day Europe cannot function properly and might break apart one day, we have to bring this dark side out into the open and discuss it in the public square. The abandonment of European sovereignty and the vassalization of Europe by the United States are issues of public interest.

Let us reaffirm that American domination does not emanate from some American perversity. It is the logical result of the power differential that existed between the United States and Europe as they emerged from thirty years of the European civil war. It is also the fruit of the French and English calls for help to the United States in 1917, 1941 and at the beginning of the Cold War.

---

10 Claude Bourdet, *L'Europe truquée. Supranationalité, Pacte atlantique, force de frappe (Europe Truncated. Supranationality, Atlantic Alliance, Power)*, Paris, Seghers, 1977.

American Trusteeship, Russian Exclusion, German Hegemony

Likewise, the first request to enlarge NATO (normally limited to the North Atlantic as described by its name) did not arise from any American ambition but rather from France, who wanted to integrate into NATO the debris of its Indochinese and North African colonial empire. As for the United States stranglehold on the military structure (the effective military command of the Alliance troops and control of the nuclear shield and weapons), it could have been avoided if the Europeans had really wanted to and had complied with General de Gaulle's wishes. A shared or balanced military command would have been possible, such as had been stipulated between France and Great Britain in the Treaties of Dunkirk and Brussels.

Each of the European divisions was a boon for the United States. The Europeans' great fear—like that of the states of Ancient Greece—had always been that one member among them would overtake the others. France had been obsessed by Germany for a long time and in no way wanted Germany to recover its dominating power. Since 1815 Great Britain had been haunted by Russia, considering it a threat to its imperial projects in Asia. As for vanquished Germany and Italy, they wanted to regain their sovereignty at any cost—but not as great as the heavy price of 1918... These are the highly Machiavellian considerations that weighed on the genesis of NATO and the European Community, far more than the romantic enthusiasm for a pacific and democratic Europe. Leaving the Soviet threat aside, the Schuman Plan and the ECSC had been drawn up as much to pool and coordinate coal and steel production as to neutralize Germany. It was a way of delivering a final blow to any German designs on military domination.

The military alliance pursued the same objective, namely allowing Germany to rearm by forcing its troops to serve a common alliance. As no European country was in a position to claim command of the steering wheel, given that Great Britain's priority was to rearrange the rest of its empire within the Commonwealth and maintain its strategy as the United States' privileged ally, the command of the alliance naturally went to the United States,[11]

---

11 Until the early sixties, Great Britain had preferred to develop its relations

which was a good thing, as they had never considered any other option possible.

Once it had taken over, the United States, as expected, imposed its views on the allies, who had rapidly become ingratiating. Only Gaullist France contested US hegemony and measured what the trusteeship meant for Europe in terms of losing its independence, its sovereignty, and therefore its capacity to shoulder its own destiny and have its say in world affairs. The only episodes of European insubordination in seventy years were Charles de Gaulle's decision to pull out of NATO's integrated military command structure in 1966 and play the traditional card of the East-West Blocs balance as it stood during the last phase of the Cold War, and later, France and Germany's refusal to join the American crusade on Iraq in 2003. With these minor exceptions, the Alliance has always maintained its usual format and hierarchy. And in 2009, Nicolas Sarkozy, like the prodigal son, scurried to return to the fold.

The Total Flop of Gorbachev's Common European Home

That said, American military hegemony was and still is a source of dysfunction for Europe. The first important thing that can be held against the Americans is probably their refusal to even consider Mikhail Gorbachev's proposal to create a Common European Home. The opportunity was historical, and Europe missed it. After the collapse of the Soviet Union at the beginning of the nineties, there were two options: either dissolving NATO, which had lost its purpose, or admitting Russia into NATO. Launched in 1985, the concept of Russian-European reconciliation took shape in the course of 1986. It aimed at creating a true partnership with Western Europe and sharing its same freedoms,

---

with its former empire, including the United States, rather than with Europe. We know how Churchill felt: "If Britain must choose between Europe and the open sea, she must always choose the open sea." As for the United States of Europe that he nevertheless envisaged, it was fine for the Europeans but not for Britain: "With it, but not in it." This British refusal to participate in Europe and its defense played a significant part in Europe's falling back on NATO under the American aegis.

human rights and political pluralism. This Russian *return to Europe* was intended to allow Germany to reunify, which would have been possible within a framework of mutual cooperation.

The project aroused the interest of several western leaders, especially François Mitterrand, who sought to give it a concrete substance and advocated signing treaties on disarmament and security as well as on economic, scientific and technological cooperation. For François Mitterrand, the Common Home project supported by concrete action offered the chance to build a Great Europe. He considered that pan-European unity was possible without compromising Western European integration or the deepening of the Franco-German partnership.

In late 1989, Mitterrand presented his project for a European Confederation designed to ultimately favor a pan-European union in which a renovated USSR, won over to the ideals of democracy and rule of law, would naturally find its place. But the rapid decomposition of East Germany and Chancellor Helmut Kohl's US-supported readiness to reunify Germany, jeopardized the plan. In July 1990, Gorbachev was forced to give up his projected Common European Home while receiving nothing in return. As for the Confederation project, it also failed, having met with the hostility of the former popular democracies and harsh criticism by American diplomacy, which was little inclined to accept the birth of a Greater Europe in which it would have no part.[12]

During the discussions on the reunification of Germany, Mikhail Gorbachev nevertheless received oral, though not written, guarantees. He was promised that the East German territory would remain demilitarized after the Soviet troops had left and that the former Eastern Bloc countries would not join NATO. The American Ambassador in Moscow, Jack Matlock, confirmed these pledges several times.

On the European side, the interpretation of the Two Plus Four Agreement on the reunification of Germany was controversial.

---

12 Marie-Pierre Rey, "Gorbachev et la 'Maison commune européenne,' une opportunité manquée?" (*Gorbachev and the 'Common European Home,' a Missed Opportunity?*), Institut François Mitterrand, note of 12 March 2007.

Some alleged that no promise of the kind had been made while others, like former German Foreign Affairs Minister Hans-Dietrich Genscher, maintained that the promise had indeed been made to the USSR and its president.[13] This prompted some to declare that it could not have been kept after the USSR imploded... As for the Russians, Yevgeny Primakov states in his Memoirs that certain leaders, like Secretary of State James Baker, President Mitterrand, Chancellor Kohl and Prime Minister John Major had also undertaken not to enlarge NATO eastwards so as to preserve European stability.

In any event, exactly the opposite occurred. In 1997, when NATO had already confirmed its eastward expansion, the Founding Act on Mutual Relations, Cooperation and Security between NATO and the Russian Federation was finally signed in Paris, while the NATO-Russia Council was established in 2002. Meanwhile, in 1999, Poland, Hungary and the Czech Republic joined NATO, followed by Bulgaria, the three Baltic States, Romania, Slovakia and Slovenia in 2004, Albania and Croatia in 2009, and Montenegro in 2017. Finally, North Macedonia (formerly the Republic of Macedonia before the 2018 Prespa Agreement with Greece to change its name) joined in 2020, while Bosnia and Georgia are aspiring members and Ukraine has been knocking on the door since the Maidan "revolution" in February 2014.

NATO's progression towards the Russian borders created considerable strain with Moscow, aggravated by the US insistence to install missile shield bases in Romania, the Czech Republic and Poland, supposedly to ward off any prospective Iranian ballistic attack... The studies carried out by the leading American think tanks, and the analysis of anti-Russian former senator John

---

13 Jack Matlock, US Ambassador to the USSR (1987–1991): "We gave categorical assurances to Gorbachev back when the Soviet Union existed, that if a united Germany was able to stay in NATO, NATO would not be moved eastwards," cited in M. McGwire, "NATO Expansion: A Policy Error of Historic Importance," *Review of International Studies*, vol. 24, n° 1, 1998, pp. 23–42, and in *International Affairs*, vol. 84, N° 6, 2008, note 12. Uwe Klussmann, Mathias Scheppp and Klaus Wiegrefe, "Nato's Eastward Expansion: Did the West Break Its Promise to Moscow?" *Der Spiegel*, Internet Website, 26 November 2009.

McCain's fiery speeches, shed a special light on NATO's role as a divisive factor between Europe and Russia. Not to mention the publications of Zbigniew Brzezinski, former Advisor to President Jimmy Carter, who, as early as 1997, wrote in black and white that, "the aim of the United States is to preserve our hegemony over the world that only global improvement and stabilization can guarantee. And to do so, we have to crush the Russian power by dividing it into three different countries and cutting it off from Europe by pushing Ukraine into the western orbit."[14] The program was masterfully carried out in 2014 with the support given to the nationalist demonstrators by Vice-President Joe Biden, John McCain, and Assistant Secretary of State for European Affairs Victoria "Fuck the EU" Nuland.[15]

Anti-Russian Propaganda Campaigns

As from 1999 and the Second Chechen War, Russia was persistently criticized by the Western powers, Europe and the United States. In 2003, following Russia's opposition to the war in Iraq and the cession of the Iraqi oil industry to Texan groups, reproval went up a notch, to reach its peak in the summer of 2008 with the attack on South Ossetia by the Georgian army on the night the Olympic Games were being inaugurated in Beijing. Criticism transmuted into information war and spiteful propaganda campaigns in 2014 in support of the Maidan events along with the blackmail of Ukraine by the EU and the United States to make it give up its economic partnership with Russia and move closer to the West.

---

14 Zbigniew Brzezinski, *Le Grand Échiquier (The Grand Chessboard)*, Paris, Hachette, 1997. See also Nils Andersson, André Bellon, Gabriel Galice, Anne-Cécile Robert, "L'Union européenne entre dogmes et doutes. Contribution à quatre mains" (The European Union between dogmas and doubts. A four-fold contribution), *Recherches internationales*, N° 104, July–September 2015, pp. 2–19.

15 "Regime Change in Kiev. Victoria Nuland Admits: US has Invested 5 Billion USDs in the Development of Ukrainian 'Democratic Institutions,'" Video Washington National Press Club, 13 December 2013.

Since the beginning of the century, the tendency to build Russia up as the West's designated enemy has only grown stronger.[16] The economic sanctions adopted by the United States and the EU since 2014 have intensified the antipathy even more and seem to exclude all hope for any sort of reconciliation between Europe and Russia. For this, NATO is primarily responsible, constantly organizing, along with the Baltic States, Sweden and Poland, military maneuvers at Russia's doorstep to "counter the Russian menace."

Thus, through a toxic game of measures and counter-measures, Russia, a European country for the past three centuries, one that on two accounts played a significant role in liberating Europe from the tyranny of Napoleon and Hitler, finds itself isolated from the rest of the continent, rejected and cast towards Asia and China in the name of its supposed Eurasianism. This dangerous, if not suicidal, game is far from over. Through its culture, science, Christian roots, geography and economy, Russia is European, yet it is no longer a part of a Europe that used to boast, when convenient, of its borders extending from Portugal to the Urals, or from Vancouver to Vladivostock as suggested by Margaret Thatcher…

For Europe, there is the enormous paradox of cutting itself off from a country that shares a common territory, in order to serve the interests of a power with which it has close relations but lies 5,000 kilometers across the ocean. This almost ontological amputation weighs and will continue weighing on its destiny as long as it lasts, however unjustifiable it may be. The choice, that runs counter to nature, is even stranger as no new serious attempt to terminate it has been made since Mitterrand's initiative. And yet the EU has opened accession negotiations with Turkey, a power whose culture, religion and population are not really European, but whose eligibility rests on the fact that it is a member of NATO and was allied with Great Britain in the 19th century and Germany in 1914–18.

---

16 In this regard, see Guy Mettan, *Creating Russophobia, op. cit.*, for a detailed account of the build-up of anti-Russian discourse in the European media and establishments.

American Trusteeship, Russian Exclusion, German Hegemony

If the question of whether Turkey could or should join the EU is legitimate, then why shouldn't Russia? Its mass, its geography, its history and its population are comparable to those of Turkey. With its 143 million inhabitants, Russia is as populated as Germany and France put together. If its economy is half as large, its immense resources, on the contrary, would be an asset to Europe, which sorely needs them. Allied with Russia, Europe could quickly recover from its backwardness, catch up with China and become the world's leading power. And that is perhaps where we have to look for the real reason behind maintaining NATO and Russia's non-integration. A true economic, cultural and scientific partnership with Russia would mean the end of American hegemony in Europe and probably in the world. It would upset too many military interests, force the enemies of the day in Poland, the Baltic States and Sweden into radical considerations, and overshadow Germany, France and Great Britain.

The Western Europeans gave in to the anti-Russian blackmail of the former popular democracies of Eastern Europe[17] as well as to American pressure far too easily, rendering the entire European edifice wobbly because its very foundations are not properly secured. One can understand that Eastern Europe, driven into a gaping security void following the Soviet collapse, sought reassurance from the West and within NATO. However, like in republican regimes, the military sphere should have been subordinate to the civilian. In principle, it is the civilians who command the military and not the other way around.

---

17 We can note, for instance, Milan Kundera's contribution to essentializing the hereditary Russian enemy in his article "The Stolen West or the Tragedy of Central Europe" (in the magazine *Débat*, 1983/5, N° 27, pp. 3–23) in which he reproaches Europe with having abandoned the countries of Eastern Europe, who held the same values as the West, to Russian barbarism. Thirty years later, it appears that these countries completely disowned their cultures and their democratic aspirations to embrace the "cannibal capitalism sustained principally by the archaisms and the irrational fears of the masses," as a Romanian observer noted in the Swiss newspaper *Le Temps* (Ruxandra Stoicescu, "L'Occident kidnappé et la trahison de l'Europe—The Stolen West and Europe's Treason), blogs. letemps.ch, 2016).

In Europe, the military interests prevailed over the civilian to the detriment of the common good and the republican order.[18] It didn't take long for the countries of Eastern Europe to understand that they could join NATO and get around any stumbling blocks that might be proposed by the European Union. Like Georgia and Ukraine, they rushed to knock on the United States' door, one that opened gladly to welcome them in—sometimes even upon invitation—and generously distributed their subsidies. So it is not surprising that their joining NATO preceded their joining the Union, as though it were a prerequisite. In principle, joining NATO should have come after joining the EU and should have been negotiated as a principle among others. So there is growing confusion as to Europe's sovereignty and independence, making it seem as though getting into the European Union requires US approval.

The Hypocritical Battle against Nationalism

This strategic dependence conveyed by NATO also highlights Europe's contradictions regarding nationalities and nationalism. Europe prides itself on having put an end to the fratricidal wars that ravaged the continent, and that was indeed its greatest achievement. The EU takes special credit for having expunged the French-German and German-Polish resentments, making this ideological battle against war-provoking nationalisms its motto or its self-proclaimed *raison d'être*. The facts today, however, reveal a very ambiguous discourse that varies according to the prevailing interests. At any rate, it is not consistent with recent events, where

---

18 Regarding NATO and the consequences of its diverse operations on Europe, see Daniele Ganser, *Les Guerres illégales de l'OTAN. Une chronique de Cuba jusqu'à la Syrie (Nato's illegal wars. A chronicle from Cuba to Syria)*, translated from German by Daniel Bénac and Jonas Lismont, Plogastel-Saint-Germain (Finistère, France), Éditions Demi-Lune, 2017 and by the same author: *Les Armées secrètes de l'OTAN. Réseaux Stay behind, Opération Gladio et Terrorisme en Europe)*, Plogastel-Saint-Germain (Finistère, France), Éditions Demi-Lune, 2007, (in English: *NATO's Secret Armies: Operation Gladio and Terrorism in Western Europe*, Routledge, 2005).

again we see that the values professed, overtly contradict in-the-field action.

The case of former Yugoslavia is the best example. When the Eastern Bloc fell apart at the beginning of 1990, tensions mounted. They were already considerably heightened in the various provinces of the Yugoslavian Federation, especially in Slovenia and Croatia, former possessions of Austria-Hungary and close to the Germanic Catholic or Protestant world. By the summer of 1990, the Slovenian and Croatian authorities took several measures towards gaining their independence: referenda, election of the nationalist HDZ party in Croatia, a new constitution that downgraded the stature of the Serbs in Croatia from "constituent nation" to "national minority." Serbia and Montenegro opposed these attempts by supporting the Serbian minorities and mobilizing the federal army when the two republics proclaimed their independence on 25 June 1991.[19]

We shall not go into the whole story of the break-up of Yugoslavia at this point. But it is worth noting that Europe did little to prevent the implosion of the Yugoslavian Federation, although the state had the international community's legal recognition and was an important member of the United Nations. As a leader of the non-aligned countries, it had been a stabilizing factor in the Balkans for forty years.

Contrariwise, the evident activism of certain European states in favor of the Slovenian and Croatian nationalist claims, especially via their numerous diasporas, was one of the aggravating factors of the war. The Vatican's support of the Catholic Croatians and Germany's forthright solidarity with its former protégés (we should recall that Croatia had closely collaborated with Nazi Germany during World War II) were notably highly influential.

What is more, as their secession had long been under preparation, the Slovenian and Croatian authorities had already taken steps in 1990 to secure the financial, human and technical support of their diasporas, strongly present in Germany and Austria. In

---

19 Michel Parenti, *Tuer une nation. L'assassinat de la Yougoslavie (To Kill a Nation. Yugoslavia Assassinated)*, Paris, Belga, 2014.

Slovenia, a secret alternative command structure (MSNZ) of territorial forces had even been established seven months before the outbreak of the war, and was intended to intervene in June 1991 with the unilateral proclamation of independence. This is how, despite France's reticence, Germany was the first state followed by along with Iceland, Sweden and Italy (also a former occupying power) to recognize independent Croatia in December 1991, despite their communist recent past, while the European Community as a whole recognized the two new States on 15 January 1992.

The Yugoslavian conflict, as we know, was to take a particularly dramatic turn in Bosnia-Herzegovina, following its declaration of independence on 3 March 1992 supported by a favorable referendum, albeit boycotted by the Serbian minority (one-third of the population). Bosnia was immediately recognized by the European Union on 5 April, while the Serbian blockade on Sarajevo was to begin the next day. There ensued three years of war and ethnic cleansing that took 100,000 lives until the Dayton Accords ended the bloodshed in 1995.

Franjo Tudjman's Croatian army, trained by a private American mercenaries' undertaking (Military Professional Resources Inc.), took advantage of the NATO bombings against the Serbian forces to occupy Krajina, leading to the ethnic cleansing of Krajina and the flight of 200,000 Serbian refugees. Fifteen years later, the International Criminal Tribunal for former Yugoslavia condemned the Serbian leaders but acquitted the Croatians, while the Muslim Bosniak camps continued to deny the implication of Islamic jihadist fighters in spite of the facts and their affiliation with the terrorist al-Qaeda movement.[20]

---

20 Gordan Malic, "Terrorisme. En Bosnie, sur les traces d'Al-Qaida (Terrorism. In Bosnia, in the steps of Al-Qaida)," published on 17 May 2011 by *Jutarnji List*, Zagreb and again by *Courrier international* (www.courrierinternational.com). See also Jürgen Elsässer, *La RFA dans la guerre au Kosovo. Chronique d'une manipulation (The FRG in the Kosovo War. Chronicle of a Manipulation)*, Paris, L'Harmattan, 2003 and by the same author: *Comment le djihad est arrivé en Europe (How the Jihad Arrived in Europe)*, Vevey (Switzerland), Éditions Xenia, 2006.

The Illegal Bombing of Serbia and the Kosovo War

The conflict resumed four years later in Kosovo. This time, NATO was directly in command, in violation of the United Nations Charter.

On 23 September 1998, the United Nations Security Council voted resolution 1199 calling for the implementation of the arms embargo, ceasing all security forces action, authorizing the European Community's verification mission, facilitating the safe return of refugees, and establishing a calendar for resuming talks between the belligerents in what was still a Serbian province. On 13 October, NATO addressed an ultimatum to the Serbian side, demanding the retreat of its forces and the opening of negotiations with the Albanian side. So it was NATO that took the initiative in spite of articles 16 and 17 of resolution 1199 stating that the Security Council was in charge of in-the-field monitoring. But there were divergences. The Russian party announced its intention of placing its veto on a new resolution that would support armed intervention against the Serbian side.

The American neoconservatives mobilized so that NATO would take the upper hand over the UN, and on 30 January 1999, the NATO Council authorized its Secretary General to engage in military actions. On 10 June, after the bombing campaign, the Security Council voted resolution 1244 that stipulated sending an international civilian and military force to Kosovo under the auspices of the United Nations.

Following the tensions and harassment of the 1980s, a conflict in the field broke out in 1996 with the creation of the Kosovo Liberation Army (KLA) that initiated a campaign of violence, including the assassination of Serbian leaders, policemen and border guards as well as Albanians collaborating with Belgrade. The Serbs retaliated with drastic police and military countermeasures. The turning point occurred in March 1997, when the Albanian government collapsed due to failed pyramidal financial operations: arsenals were sacked and the arms fell into the hands of the KLA.

In the course of 1998, there were further allegations of intercommunity massacres. The American NGO Human Rights Watch asserted that the Serbian forces had expelled hundreds of thousands of Albanians from Kosovo. Rumors concerning a large-scale ethnic cleansing plan in Kosovo ("Operation Horseshoe" as it was called, actually forged by the German Ministry of Defense) were circulating in the Western media along with photos of an alleged massacre perpetrated in the village of Račak. All of these rumors turned out to be unfounded—fake news before coining of that meme!—but only after having served as a pretext for NATO military intervention.

In the spring of 1999, Serbian President Slobodan Miloševic accepted OSCE (Organization for Security and Co-operation in Europe) and European Community observers but refused the NATO envoys on the grounds that they were not impartial. NATO used this refusal as a pretext to launch an air bombing campaign (Operation Allied Forces) on 24 March 1999. General Wesley Clark directed the operations from the Supreme Headquarters Allied Powers in Europe. The strike was meant to be symbolic and last three or four days to bring Belgrade back to the negotiations table, as had been the case for Bosnia-Herzegovina. But the bombings wound up lasting seventy-eight days, during which no less than 58,574 air strikes were made, including the "accidental" bombing of the Serbian army's general headquarters, the Chinese embassy and the Radio-Television studios in Belgrade on 23 April 1999, leaving 16 people dead and 16 wounded…

According to International Red Cross Committee estimates, in June 2000, 3,368 civilians (2,500 Albanians, 400 Serbs and 100 Roma) were reported still missing one year after the end of the conflict while 13,472 people had been killed between January 1998 and December 2000. The Federal Republic of Yugoslavia for its part, estimated between 1,200 and 5,700 casualties from NATO bombings. The figures are still contested to this day. In 2017 this suspension in international law prompted a Serbian group to file a claim before the courts of each country that had bombed Kosovo and four places in southern Serbia without legal authorization and in violation of articles 5 and 6 of the NATO statutes whereby the Organization is a defensive and not an offensive structure. The team hopes to gather proof that the use of cluster and depleted uranium bombs as well as the bombing of chemical and petrochemical plants had major health effects on the civilian population.

Kosovo Recognized in Defiance of the Law

That is how, in the middle of Europe, a series of deadly wars were carried out with the tacit complicity of the European Community, and in the case of Kosovo, with their green light. Is this not tantamount to a low betrayal of the values of peace, rule of law and democracy proclaimed by Europe?

It is also in violation of the rules of international law that in 2008 the Europeans recognized Kosovo's independence and flouted Serbian sovereignty in circumventing United Nations resolution 1244 that placed Kosovo under provisional UN administration, and not NATO or EU administration.

It was Micheline Calmy-Rey who launched the recognition procedure in New York in 2005. The Swiss Foreign Affairs Minister made a speech before the United Nations Security Council in support of the province's independence. She wanted to position Switzerland as the first state in the world to promote Kosovo independence, effectively acting as an agent for the United States and NATO in defiance of her own country's neutrality. In February 2007, former Finnish president Martti Ahtisaari, designated by Kofi Annan as the United Nations special envoy to negotiate the issue of status with the Albanians and the Serbs, relaunched the idea of giving Kosovo its independence under international supervision. The UN Security Council rejected Ahtissari's report because of the Russian veto. But the provisional authorities in Kosovo used the report to proclaim their independence unilaterally in June 2008. It was immediately recognized by the United States and their NATO European allies.[21] On 22 July 2010, the

---

21 The same maneuver was used in Venezuela in January 2019 when the United States and the majority of the European countries recognized self-proclaimed president Juan Guaido.

International Court of Justice ruled that it "agreed that the adoption of Kosovo's declaration of independence of 17 February 2008 was not in violation of international law," but nevertheless refused to recognize the territory as a state. This cautious position did not prevent the International Steering Group for Kosovo (ISG) comprised of the United States and 23 European countries to declare a few years later that, as its mandate had terminated, Kosovo would accede to "full sovereignty" in September 2012... On 3 January 2019, 105 out of the 193 member States of the United Nations had recognized Kosovo, with a dozen having changed their minds following Serbian action.

Several voices concerned with the law were raised in protest to this sad legal and historical precedent. Former French Minister Jean-Pierre Chevènement, for instance, considered the Kosovo example to be a "triple mistake": a historical mistake, as the country had never been independent; a legal mistake because the NATO war launched in 1999 had ignored the principles of international law; and a mistake against a united Europe.[22]

Today the situation has reached a stalemate. Hashim Thaçi, the former leader of the KLA movement and president of the Republic of Kosovo from 2016 to 2020, classified as a terrorist at the time by the United States, was accused of having committed war crimes and organs trafficking by the former Swiss attorney and investigator, Dick Marty. Finally, after many years of impunity, he was incarcerated in The Hague in November 2020, judged as a war criminal guilty of a criminal against humanity. It should be pointed out that Kosovo is now home to one of NATO's largest military bases in Europe. Camp Bondsteel—which spawns over 3,865 km^2—has been described as a "reduced model of Guantanamo" by another European Council investigator, Spanish deputy Antonio Gil-Robles. Strangely enough, the camp is closed

---

[22] Jean-Pierre Chevènement, "La reconnaissance du Kosovo, c'est une triple faute (*Recognizing Kosovo is a Triple Mistake*)," *Le Figaro*, 22 February 2008, published on the blog m.chevènement.fr

off to inspection by the Council of Europe's Committee for the Prevention of Torture.[23]

Gratefully there are Europeans who at times succeed in denouncing cases of abuse by other Europeans...

Hypocrisy Concerning the Right of Peoples to Self-determination

The way the Kosovo issue was dealt with is emblematic of the EU's hypocritical attitude towards the nation and nationalism. On the one hand, it looked on passively as Yugoslavia was partitioned and hastened to recognize the independence-minded States and the national governments they set up. It even prompted Kosovo to secede in violation of the rules of international law. On the other hand, the EU very heavily condemned Crimea's secession, albeit proclaimed in March 2014 by popular referendum, as it condemns Catalonia's ambitions of independence although they also were sanctioned by popular vote. So what makes sense? What were the criteria for deciding which nationalism or secession was "good" and deserved support, as in the case of Kosovo, and which nationalisms were "bad" and independences "illegal" requiring them to be countered, like in Crimea, Southern Ossetia, Abkhazia or Catalonia?

This moral schizophrenia and double standard policy are even more flagrant regarding Ukraine. Although the EU endlessly denounces the supposed fascism and the excesses of the ultra right-wing AfD in Germany, the *Rassemblement national* in France or the Italian Lega, it has nothing to say about the fact that the neo-Nazi far right has taken over some of the Ukrainian government power levers and parades down the streets of Kiev displaying the insignia and slogans of the former Ukrainian World War II collaborators. The Svoboda and Pravy Sektor parties as well as the Azov movement are nonetheless well known for having turned over certain ministries from the Parliament to the army, and openly display their anti-Semitism without arousing the slightest

---

23 Dick Marty, *Une certaine idée de la justice (A certain idea of justice)*, Lausanne, Éditions Favre, 2018.

indignation on the part of the Europeans or the United States.[24] While this was denied at the time the legitimate government was overthrown on 22 February 2014, the implications of the far right in the Ukrainian government seem to be better recognized in the leading media today. But it has still not been officially denounced by the European governments—for whom there is naturally no question of imposing economic sanctions...

Peace Within But Repeated Wars Without

This European subjugation to the United States via NATO is also the cause of many a war waged by Europe outside the continent. There again, Europe's image as a "peacemaker" takes a blow in public opinion outside Europe nonetheless. NATO indeed modified its doctrine to be able to intervene outside the strict perimeter of the North Atlantic. Today it regards itself as the world's police and guardian of the neoliberal order.

In the aftermath of the Gulf War in 1991, NATO began striking up strategic partnerships outside of Europe with a view to extending its security arm with a view to facing global threats outside its borders. In 2002, it took a decisive step towards intervening all over the world in case of any threat to its security, opening the door to engagements in Afghanistan and Iraq in the footsteps of the United States...

In 2004, the Istanbul Cooperation Initiative targeted the Persian Gulf countries. Partnerships were also enhanced with US allies like Australia, New Zealand, Japan and South Korea, who joined the Allied Intervention Force in Afghanistan and Iraq. On the European scene, NATO decided to create a 25,000-strong quick reaction force, the NRF or NATO Response Force, and to reinforce its command structures, still under United States authority. The Force was enabled to carry out all the Alliance's missions

---

24 Fabrice Deprez, "L'extrême droite s'agite en Ukraine" (*The Far Right Touches Off in Ukraine), La Croix*, 23 May 2018, (www.la-croix.com); Xavier D***, "État des lieux des néonazis au pouvoir à Kiev" (*The state of affairs of the neo-Nazis in power in Kiev)*, 2 March 2014, blogs.mediapart.fr.; and also Benoit Vitkine, "L'extrême droite accroît son influence en Ukraine" (*The Far Right increases its influence in Ukraine), Le Monde*, 25 June 2017.

ranging from rescue operations in case of natural disasters, to peacekeeping, to the most intense combat operations—with persistent finger-pointing at Russia as the major threat.

In the early years of the 2010s, geopolitical tensions heightened with Russia back in the lead on the international stage and China's rise to power. The Alliance again revised its strategy and defense programs, combining conventional, nuclear, and antimissile defense (the shield that Russia sees as a direct threat to its security) forces, and putting the emphasis on the proliferation of Nuclear, Biological and Chemical arms of massive destruction and ballistic missiles, cyber attacks and terrorism, maritime and air security and developing its partnership with the EU. All the while it meticulously pursued its enlargement with the accession of Montenegro and shortly afterwards, Macedonia, and discretely opened the door to Georgia and Ukraine, which were boisterously demanding admission.

A Europe Embarked on Alien Wars

This is how a large number of European countries found themselves drawn into the wars in Afghanistan and Iraq in 2001 and 2003, with the enthusiastic support of Britain's Prime Minister Tony Blair and Manuel Barroso, Prime Minister of Portugal and future president of the European Commission. More cautious, France and Germany refused to meddle in the Iraqi adventure, little convinced by the American intelligence services' demonstrations accusing Saddam Hussein of having built up an arsenal of weapons of mass destruction—the WMDs that had actually never existed, as the world would realize some time later!

But Afghanistan and Iraq were only appetizers! In 2011, in spite of the hundreds of thousands of civilian and military casualties in Afghanistan and Iraq, Europe was dragged into the civil war in Syria, going so far as to take the initiative of bombing Libya and ousting its leader, Muammar Gaddafi, who was threatening French interests in the Middle East and Africa (Gaddafi notably intended to create an independent African currency to replace the CFA franc). On the pretext of encouraging the "Arab Spring" and its appeal for democracy, Europe—especially France and Great Britain—along with the United States fanned protest movements against the secular Arab leaders (while taking care to spare the Sunni and Wahhabi religious regimes of the Gulf States). They supported the armed rebellions by propaganda fiercely attacking the legal government of Bashar al-Assad and by providing logistical support via Turkey and the petro-monarchies as well as by bombing Libya in 2011, then Syria in 2013 in retaliation for the chemical weapons attacks attributed to the Syrian regime (but never really proved).[25]

It is compelling to note that the support granted to the rebels—who very soon proved to be under the influence of terrorist groups such as Al-Qaeda and the "Islamic State of the Levant" (or Daesh)—was given in the name of democracy and human rights although their aid transited through the Gulf monarchies and Turkey, who were at the very bottom of the list of countries seen to care about human rights. It is no doubt inappropriate to bring up the fact that the women in Gaddafi's Libya and the Assad's Syria had always been much better off status-wise than in Saudi Arabia or the Gulf Emirates, and that the Al-Qaeda fighters, supported by the Westerners in Syria, claimed allegiance to Osama bin Laden, the United States' Public Enemy Number One...

Europe's duplicity, double talk and double standards regarding respecting democracy and human rights are obviously not to its credit. Its attitude is all the more shocking in that France, steeped in self-praise for having intervened in Mali to protect the population and its cultural patrimony from Islamic misdeeds, supports these very Islamists against the secular government in Syria by combatting a regime that displeases the fundamentalist Gulf monarchies. Yet both parties embrace the same ideology, belong to the same Salafi movement and were trained by the Wahhabi ulemas of the University of Medina. Who can make any sense out of this?

---

25 Dennis J. Bernstein, "Weapons Inspector Refutes US Syria Chemical Claims," *Consortium News*, April 27, 2018. Robert Parry, "A New Hole in Syria—Sarin Certainty," *Consortium News*, September 7, 2017.

American Trusteeship, Russian Exclusion, German Hegemony

Is there anyone to point out the fact that the mass migration so deeply destabilizing Europe today is the direct consequence of Europe's own destabilizing operations in Libya and Syria? Who remembers that before 2011 migrants did not die by the thousands in crossing the Mediterranean? And who recalls that in Ukraine, on 21st February 2014, the French, Polish and German ministers made President Yanukovych sign an agreement providing for free and democratic elections, and that the agreement was immediately torn up by nationalist demonstrators eager to take over? The day after they took power, the protestors passed a law that discriminated against the Russian language spoken by a sizeable component of the Ukrainian population and sparked the Odessa tragedy,[26] the secession of Crimea and the Donbass Russo-Ukrainian War.

And recently, NATO officials have even opened the door to a formal acceptance of Ukraine into the organization, creating a possible casus belli with Russia.[27]

Clearly there is no questioning Europe's concern for its self-defense. What we can question, however, is its incapacity to stand up to American pressure, its haste to engage in wars that are none of its business, its zeal in supporting new regimes that are not in its interests, and its knack for creating an enemy—Russia—within its own territory. It is time that Europe took back control over its security and its freedom to determine its future democratically. It is time for Europe to stand on its own two feet, East and West, and to realize that its territory extends as far as the Ural. Why not integrate Ukraine and Russia, while engaging with Turkey (which is partly European) and the Mediterranean countries in a second sphere of cooperation that would cover the economic and common security interests, and would find its place in a renewed European Home as François Mitterrand had hoped for?

Germany's Outsized Influence

---

26 The nationalist anti-Russian arson caused 32 deaths in the trade union building in Odessa on 10 May 2014.

27 https://www.strategic-culture.org/news/2021/02/12/nato-road-to-perdition-with-ukraine

The weight of American tutelage over Europe and Russia's exclusion from the continent have another damaging effect for Europe, namely accentuating Germany's hegemony within the European Union itself. The reunification of the country in 1991 produced an oversized state throwing the entire European construction off balance.

There is no question here of giving in to any sort of Germanophobia. We do not suspect that Germany wishes to revive its former pan-Germanic or hegemonic inclinations. There is no German conspiracy, no Germanic Machiavellianism. Yet we can see that what happens in any human society when one of its members grows bigger and more influential than the others, is taking place now with regard to Germany: the difference in size creates instability and gives rise to tensions. Germany and Europe are no exception to the rule. The space that Germany takes up, whether deliberate or not, is tending to grow out of proportion. The imbalance is even more significant now that Great Britain has left the Union. The fact that France continues to weaken, losing its economic means and no longer playing its strategic counter-balancing role after having rejoined NATO and aligning itself unconditionally with Anglo-Saxon policy since 2009, is of no help, either.

So the Germany issue, which along with discourse related to NATO is highly taboo in Europe, requires calm and composed consideration. In France, Jean-Pierre Chevènement—him again—and the "unbowed lefty," Jean-Luc Mélenchon, were booed by the pro-German media and politicians when they touched upon the subject.[28] The greatest criticism, moreover, is voiced in Germany, through literature, the cinema, the theater and sociology with authors such as Hans Magnus Enzensberger, Jürgen Habermas and the Austrian Peter Handke (whose pro-Serbian positions during

---

28 Jean-Luc Mélenchon, *Le Hareng de Bismarck (le poison allemand)*, *(Bismarck's Herring—The German Poison)*, Paris, Plon, 2015; Jean-Pierre Chevènement, *1914–2014, l'Europe sortie de l'histoire? (1914–2014 Has Europe left history?)*, Paris, Fayard, 2013.

the war in Yugoslavia smacked of heresy and led to his exclusion from the media and even from official programs).[29]

To quote Enzenberger, an author above suspicion and a fierce critic, lampooning "the colonies of surfers, the citadels of senior citizens and the secondary or tertiary residences" that, having liberated the Germans "from the factory and the office," offer a culture of psychiatric clinical and masochistic self-development obligations (*Mediocrity and Delusion*). In *Civil War*, he describes the human being as "the only primate to practice the large-scale murder of his fellow men methodically and enthusiastically. War is one of his principal inventions."

He underlines a decaying behavior specific to Germany and Western European countries. What he calls "a molecular civil war" imperceptibly spread out. "Little by little, waste piles up along the streets. Mounds of syringes and broken beer bottles litter the parks. Walls everywhere sport the monotonous graffiti conveying their autistic message: a message evoking a Me that no longer exists… Furniture is broken in the classrooms; the parks stink of urine and shit… Such are the minute declarations of war that the experienced city dweller knows how to interpret."

Not as literary and more politically positioned, Jean-Luc Mélenchon believes that today's threat to Europe is the "German poison."[30] The poison consists in diffusing and imposing on all the European countries an economic and political model created to satisfy the needs of the German society; needs born of the social structure and history of an aging country with a dramatically low

---

29 Hans Magnus Enzensberger, *Médiocrité et folie* (in English: *Mediocrity and Delusion*), Paris, Gallimard, 1991; by the same author: *La Grande Migration. Vues sur la guerre civile* (in English: *The Great Migration. Views on the Civil War*), Paris, Gallimard, 1994. And earlier, *L'Allemagne, l'Allemagne entre autres. Réflexions sur la politique* (in English: *Germany. Germany among Other Things*), Paris, Christian Bourgois, 1970; Jürgen Habermas, *Morale et communication. Conscience morale et activité communicationnelle* (in English: *The Theory of Communicative Action*), Paris, Cerf, 1986, in which he discusses the establishment of specific values as universal values.

30 François Coustal, "À propos du hareng de Bismarck (Regarding Bismarck's Herring)," blog of the association *ensemble* (https://www.ensemble-fdg.org/content/ propos-du-hareng-de-bismarck).

fertility rate, where the well-to-do retirees and annuitants make up the electoral base of the governing parties. The German economic policy therefore focuses on satisfying them, which explains the dogma of a strong euro safeguarded by the independent European Central Bank.

One of the many disastrous consequences of a basically externally oriented industry is the need to transport products exported over long distances to the far corners of Europe if not of the planet. "The German exportation model alone is the cause of a global ecological dead end," Mélenchon continues. Making it profitable, moreover, implied doing away with the old model of social protection, introducing successive labor market reforms, lowering retirement age, creating one-euro jobs... In a nutshell, Europe has become "a model of social mistreatment" symbolized by an automobile industry that willingly cheats on the carbon dioxide gas emissions of the diesel vehicles manufactured in its plants. Since aging Germany is in shortage of both manpower and brainpower, it resorts to large-scale outsourcing, especially in Eastern Europe, where the components of various industrial products are manufactured at low cost before being assembled back in Germany. Since its university system is not very effective, Germany also gaily indulges in brain draining. And having rehearsed with the GDR *Anschluß* experiment, the country is reverting to its long history of eastern expansion and has no problem with taking part in NATO military expeditions. Germany has so widely imposed its model throughout Europe that the European Union can be described as the "New German Empire," Mélenchon concludes.

The Reality of German Oversizing

Is this strong—to say the least—view of Germany by France's unbowed lefty in line with reality? Let us have a look at the facts, beginning with the economy. In 2017, for instance, Germany's gross domestic product totaled 3,677 trillion dollars, while France's GDP came to 2,853 trillion dollars. But above all, the German current account surpluses have been breaking records for years with almost 300 billion dollars in annual surplus, while France has a deficit of 15 billion dollars per year.

This differential is not getting any smaller and threatens not only the longevity of the Franco-German partnership but also Europe's stability as a whole by creating imbalances that would prove unbearable on the long term.

The continuous pumping of global liquidity, converted into savings to finance the pensions of German retirees, poses a structural problem. It explains the obsession of Germany and the European Central Bank with austerity policies aiming to protect capital and the revenues derived therefrom. This in turn explains the unconditional support of the euro as a strong currency, at the risk of ruining the countries that, for historical and geographical reasons, do not have the same industrial power, the same subcontracting network or the vast, cheap workforce of Eastern Europe. Countless books have been written on the euro and its disastrous effect on the Latin countries and Greece which can no longer fall back on the advantage of competitive devaluation to support their economies.[31] Sovereign China can undervalue its currency to maintain its competitiveness, and the United States has freely done so on many occasions, when it came to conquering new markets at the beginning of their industrial expansion and to maintaining their shares of the market today. The euro is to Germany

---

31 We can mention in particular Economics Nobel Prize laureate Paul Krugman who excoriates the single currency, *Sortez-nous de cette crise… maintenant! (Get us out of this crisis…now!)*, Paris, Flammarion, 2012. See also Philippe Coste, Paul Krugman, "L'euro est une construction bancale" (The euro is a shaky construction), in *L'Express,* 6 September 2012, to read on the website voxeurope.eu. See also, *Challenges,* "Les attaques contre l'euro du Prix Nobel d'économie Paul Krugman" (The attacks against the euro of Economics Nobel Prize laureate Paul Krugman), 27 September 2012 on www.challenges. fr. In France, Jacques Sapir, *Faut-il sortir de l'euro ? (Should we leave the euro?)*, Paris, Seuil, 2012. And by the same author: *L'Euro contre la France, l'Euro contre l'Europe (The euro against France, the euro against Europe)*, Paris, Le Cerf, 2016. And in a more reformist and Europeanist optic, Richard Werly and Thomas Piketty, "L'axe Schäuble-Merkel dresse les pays européens les uns contre les autres" (The Schäuble-Merkel axis causes the European countries to rise against one another), in *Le Temps,* 13 March 2017 (www.letemps.ch).

what the dollar is to the United States: an instrument of economic domination and power management.

For France, which was at the origin of creating the single currency, the outcome is tragic. It was indeed François Mitterrand who had advocated a shared currency in constraining Germany to abandon the Deutschmark and making it play the European game when it was reunified. But since then, thanks to its power escalation, it is Germany that has absorbed the euro and put France into orbit.

In reactivating its commercial, industrial and financial networks in Eastern Europe, moreover, Germany has built up a system of indebted partners thanks to its investments. The haunting problem of economic opportunities that had plunged Germany into world war in the last century was resolved peacefully in the 21st. By taking a look at the map of its economic network, one can see that thanks to the ingenuity of its latest chancellors, Germany has reached its war objectives without firing a single shot! Quite an achievement, even if some good souls may find this shocking.

At the political level, Germany remains discreet. But we can see that after the 1990s, it managed to modify the European treaties in its favor. Using its new demographic weight as an argument, it increased its number of deputies in the European Parliament to 96 while France was left with only 74, although from the start, France had made the equality of French and German representation a sine qua non for the European Community. Lastly, Germany openly questions France's seat on the United Nations Security Council, claiming that it should go to Europe (that is, Germany).[32]

Germany's Demographics Obsession

The second German problem that weighs on Europe is demographic. Today the German population is almost 83 million, 15 million more than France (68 million). Its fertility rate has fallen to 1.4 birth per woman over many years. If Germany is ahead of

---

32 Laurent Lagneau, "The German Vice-Chancellor feels that the permanent seat of France to the UN should go to the European Union," *Diplomatie*, 28 November 2018 (www.opex360.com).

Spain, Portugal and Poland, it is far behind France and Ireland, who were not far from the natural fertility rate (around 2 in 2010 and 1.9 and 1.75 birth per woman in 2019. The rate of natural renewal is 2.1). What is more, aging is accelerating as shown by the continuous increase in its mortality rate. According to the CIA World Factbook of beginning January 2019, Germany is at 12 deaths per 1,000 inhabitants (Switzerland is at 8 and France, at 9). Because of this progressive population aging and very weak birthrate, Germany has to import massive foreign labor, Turkish for the most part. Nearly three million Turks work in Germany. This benevolent attitude towards migrants owes very little to compassion or a humanitarian strain, as trumpeted by the good souls when Chancellor Angela Merkel opened the door to one million refugees from Syria and Afghanistan in 2015. It corresponds rather to a selfish, well-defined interest, one moreover enthusiastically lauded by employers. It is not necessarily a bad thing that the selfishness of some enables the providence of others, but it is very hypocritical to hail this strictly economic decision as a humanitarian gesture. For Germany, who could lose 15 million inhabitants between now and 2060 according to demographers, it is simply a question of survival.

Spain, Portugal and Italy are in the same situation. But their population is differently structured, and their economies have vast reserves of unemployed to count on. With its bulimic economy and decreasing population, Germany thus puts all of Europe under pressure to accept migration, masking its economic needs with morality. The debate is concealed in Western Europe, where NGOs and pro-migrant parties constantly bring up the moral issue, specifically, which takes the upper hand over the concerns of the popular classes. And yet, setting aside the problem of social and cultural integration posed by these waves of migrants and the pressure they exert on lowering salaries, one could ask if they do not actually tip the scales of Europe's economic imbalance even further in Germany's favor.

In Bulgaria, Romania and the Baltic States, the situation is even more dramatic. In Bulgaria, the exodus of two million inhabitants out of a population of seven million contributed to an "unbelievable demographic shrinkage," as noted by *The Economist*.[33] Romania, Latvia and Lithuania are close on its heels, and Albania is the most affected. It would be easy to blame the poor management of these countries or their populist reactions, but the trouble in fact lies deeper.

The third problem posed by Germany's hypertrophy is the risk of freezing Europe's evolution. Since its reunification, Europe's center of gravity has shifted eastwards. As we have seen, the movement was amplified by the accession of new countries from central and Eastern Europe, by Brexit, and by Germany's economic expansion. Europe, which had revolved around its Franco-German axis with no major collisions between north and south or east and west; between Latin sensitivity and Anglo-Saxon perception; between Scandinavia and the Mediterranean, was suddenly turned upside down. Its center of gravity now lies somewhere between Germany and Poland, with France, Italy and Benelux marginalized.

Yet France has always been the motor of Europe, along with Italy under De Gasperi and Altiero Spinelli, and Benelux under Paul-Henri Spaak and Johann Willem Beyen. The hopes inspired by Emmanuel Macron's election corroborate France's leading role in European dynamics. But the fact that the European geometry has so drastically changed will inevitably have an impact on Europe's future. This is perhaps because neither German nor European societies push for political innovation and audacity. The general tendency is towards conservatism or even regression.

So there has to be an awareness of this dependence on Germany followed by a peaceful public debate to find political solutions. Otherwise, Europe could well fall apart again. Who knows if once it is cornered, Germany might not be tempted to go it alone, like the British? In default of succeeding in imposing a Grexit or of expelling the countries that refuse to ply to its financial diktats,

---

33 Jacques Hubert-Rodier, "La Bulgarie menacée d'effondrement démographique," (Bulgaria threatened with demographic collapse), *Les Échos*, 14 January 2018.

Germany might stiffen. And who can tell what will happen now that Angela Merkel has taken her bow...

This leveling of Euro-German relations is all the more significant in that, at the political level, Germany also serves as an amplifier for United States subjection. We had already had a taste of this with President John Kennedy's famous speech in Berlin in 1963. His *"Ich bin ein Berliner!"* was not just a rhetorical device. Yet more troubling is the disclosure by the former boss of German military counter-espionage, General Gerd-Helmut Komossa, asserting that since the Basic Law for the Federal Republic of Germany came into effect in 1949, the German Chancellors have been obliged to pledge allegiance to the three former occupying powers of 1945.[34] The existence of these secret provisions, the *Kanzler Akte*, is contested. But it has been attested to by Egon Bahr, a staunch social democrat and former co-worker of Chancellor Willy Brandt:

> In the magazine *Die Zeit*, I described how freshly-elected Chancellor Willy Brandt was given three letters to sign for the ambassadors of the Western powers. In signing, he would confirm agreement with the legal restrictions of the Allied military governors regarding the ratification of the Basic Law of 12 May 1949. Holding inalienable rights as victors over all of Germany and with respect to Berlin, they had suspended the articles of the Basic Law, thereby annulling them because they considered it a restraint on their sovereignty. Willy Brandt was indignant. On the one hand, because the procedures implied that as the former mayor of Berlin, he did not know what these reserves

---

34 Gerd-Helmut Komossa, *Die deutsche Karte. Das verdeckte Spiel der geheimen Dienste. Ein Amtschef des MAD berichtet*, (in English: *The German Card*), Graz (Austria), Ares Verlag, 2007. And Egon Bahr, "Kanzlerakte. Lebenslüge der Bundesrepublik" (The Chancellor Act), in *Junge Freiheit*, 11 October 2011 (https://jungefreiheit.de/wissen/geschichte/2011/ lebensluege-der-bundesrepublik/). See also an article recently published in the Europeist newspaper *Süddeutsche Zeitung* (https://www.sueddeutsche. de/politik/usa-in-deutschland-freie-fahrt-fuer-spione-1.1819376!amp).

meant for the city from the time the Federal Republic was founded. On the other, because he had always referred to the democratic elections and was convinced that the mandate of Chancellor was above that of a mayor under Allied orders, and that his first duty was to honor his oath.

We should note in passing that similar provisions were made for Italy, another power conquered in World War II.[35]

The above testimony makes it hard to believe that the *Kanzler Akte* are the sheer fabrication of the far right or the Russian secret services! One can understand that they were drawn up in the climate of suspicion that reigned after the war and in fear of Germany's military resurgence and a possible Soviet aggression. Yet these provisions have never been abolished in spite of the fact that they imply Germany's subjection to the Allied powers and in particular, to the United States.

In commenting on the new Franco-German friendship treaty signed in January 2019 by President Emmanuel Macron and Chancellor Angela Merkel, former Foreign Affairs Minister Sigmar Gabriel recalled that the first Franco-German treaty had been modified in 1963 by the Bundestag under United States pressure by adding a preamble calling on France to cooperate with America and Great Britain, and thus eliminating any possible autonomous European defense.[36]

We can understand more easily why, in this context, Germany has always been considered as the relaying point of American power on the continent (with Great Britain serving as an aircraft carrier on the sea), and why the country has always remained very close to the United States at the military and geopolitical levels,

---

[35] Bruno Romano, "Geheimvertrag mit USA im Zwielicht Cavalese- Fall beweist Einschränkung der Souveränität" (The secret treaty with the USA in the twilight of the Cavalese case proves sovereignty restrictions), in *Neues Deutschland*, 15 March 1999, https://www.neues-deutschland.de/artikel/755184.geheimvertrag-mit-usa-im-zwielicht.html.

[36] Sigmar Gabriel, "L'amitié franco-allemande ne suffit pas" (Franco-German friendship is not enough), transl. from German by Martin Morel, *Le Temps*, 1 February 2019.

as we saw in Ukraine in 2014, when it was one of the spearheads of the sanctions on Russia. Today, Germany weighs so heavily in Europe that it is threatening the stability of the whole European edifice. When its economy is booming, as is currently the case, the other countries are compelled to take measures that are to its advantage. But should its economy fail for any reason—a rise in protectionism, exports drop, labor issues—it would pull all the others down with it…

"Rather a European Germany than a German Europe," said Thomas Mann in a speech delivered in Hamburg in 1953.[37] He had not foreseen that there would be both: a European Germany and a German Europe. But what will happen in the future if nothing is done about it? Will there come a day when Germany will no longer need the Union because it will have completely swallowed it up, as in the great era of the Holy Roman German Empire? Or, like the Macedonians, who had become so sure of themselves after Alexander's victories, will it unexpectedly fall off the wagon and be tempted to shake free of the American yoke at the risk of causing Europe to collapse? Or still yet to come, could the other Europeans, tired of this weighty hegemony, rebel against Germany?

More generally speaking, how long can a subjected Europe that is neither sovereign nor autonomous in its decision-making, has no defined borders, is in artificial conflict with Russia, has cohorts of migrants crossing through it in search of a better life, and has to keep its balance on wobbly scales tilted by Germany's hypertrophy, survive?

---

[37] Jean Quatremer, "L'Union n'est plus européenne mais allemande" (The Union is no longer European but German), in *Libération*, 10 September 2018, bruxelles.blogs.liberation.fr.

CHAPTER 7
EUROPE'S ABSURD FORM OF GOVERNANCE: BAD PLANNING OR INTENTIONAL?

> *The federations in history were forged through constraint by the victor or were born of the consent of the peoples. Let this consent be tested. Constitutions have never sufficed to create feelings. They may activate them, but too great a leap forward would risk the sudden failure of the entire enterprise.*
>
> RAYMOND ARON[1]

In the two preceding chapters, we studied the terms and the consequences of Europe's political and geopolitical deficits. The first leads to a fatal contradiction between the elites and the peoples. It deprives the European construction of the indispensable momentum and dynamism for achieving the political unity necessary to maintain Europe's place on the world stage, increasingly marked by the confrontation of the new Chinese and American "empires." The second deprives Europe of the faculty to define its own objectives by compelling it to choose options that are not in its interest. It moreover contributes to creating permanent instability both within and without its borders by artificially sustaining hotbeds of tension with its Russian, Arab and North African neighbors.

Pacified within, Europe is at war with its periphery (yesterday, the Balkans; today, Donbass, Crimea and Caucasia; the Middle East, Iraq and Afghanistan; Libya and Mali). This makes

---

1 Raymond Aron, "Ce que peut être la Fédération des Six" (What the Inner Six Federation can be), (4 December 1952), in *Les Articles du Figaro,* Paris, Bernard de Fallois, 1990.

it vulnerable to pressure and interference from the outside while jeopardizing its political integration. Europe, instigated by NATO, the Nordic countries, the Baltic States and Poland with United States support, vigorously waves the anti-Russian bogeyman. But the external threats are not credible enough (at least not for the moment) to arouse the heightened security fears on which they are so direly contended. As for the war on terrorism, it is too blurred and too full of compromises, especially with such disreputable allies as Saudi Arabia and the Syrian Islamist Jihadis, to have an aggregating support by the Europeans.

This state of affairs naturally leads to a third, institutional, deficit. The political power of Europe as a single entity—as a federal state—has been the missing link in the European construction from the founding Rome Treaty in 1957. Earlier, in the 1920s, the creation of a true federal state has been often mentioned. After WW2 and even after the Rome Treaty, the question has been raised. But like the Holy Grail, everyone is always talking about it, but nobody has ever seen it. Countless attempts for creating or reforming institutions have been made to address this lacuna. All have failed. Tons of books and millions of words have been written or said on the subject, but still there is no true European governance to be seen. Or rather the phantom of governance serves to mask the institutional deficiency by concealing it under a varnish of respectability and a nebula of management and cooperation organs that no doubt have their use but not one of which can claim to embody the executive and legislative power worthy of the institutions of a republican state.

Consequently, there is no European state, but several European states headed by a supranational, institutional quasi mishmash. For some, this is a relief, since an efficient state would go against the liberalist dogma. For others, it is a reason to be proud, for it emphasizes the originality of the European construction. But for a growing fringe of public opinion, it is an absolute nightmare, considering the fact that any federal European state would erode national cultures, politics and traditions even further. Various expressions have been coined to describe the uncertain and novel condition of such a state in modern history. We hear talk of a "federation of Nation-States" or of a UIPO (unidentified political object). The most optimistic believe in a confederation or a federation in the making, along the lines of Jacques Delors' bicycle theory whereby the European construction cannot stop without falling and will continue to progress by successive crises up to the federal Omega Point.

We believe that the choices made since 1945 are losing their positive effects and leading Europe to a dead end. Clearly the bicycle is not moving along. It is beginning to lose its parts (Great Britain, maybe Catalonia), and some passengers (the Visegrad Group and the Euro-skeptics) refuse to pedal. A growing number of spectators (the United States, NATO, Russia, China, the Southern countries, the Islamic extremists) pretend to applaud but at the same time sow nails on its path to keep it from moving forward or to make it change directions.

Europe has now been struck by the Greek syndrome. Although its methods of integration differ from those of the Ancient Greeks (that rested more on religious feasts and shared temple management), its sophisticated economic, cultural, and in some cases even military cooperation have enabled it to reach a very high level of integration. Yet with its remaining contradictions and divisions blocking the way, it is doomed to gradually disappear if it does not manage to step up to the next level.

Various theories and methods have been put forth to pull Europe out of this deadlock and improve its integration capacity. Former French Foreign Affairs Minister Hubert Védrine proposed organizing new Estates General in Europe to reestablish it on a new constitutional basis. But the procedure, already attempted in 2002–2003, was only moderately successful with the convention in charge of formulating a draft constitution for Europe. The (Neo) functionalists bank on the ginning effect triggered by sectoral cooperation (coal, steel, customs union, agriculture policy, currency, finance, budget, etc.) that is supposed to lead to a federalization policy through the mathematical increase in the ensuing degree of economic interdependence. The Intergovernmentalists are more confident in the United States as an integration actor, while the supporters of the Community method feel that initiatives come first from the supranational organs such as the Commission, the Parliament and the European Court of Justice.

A Whirlwind of Proposals to Amend European Governance

These theoretical contributions are more descriptive than program-based. They do not attack the underlying problem, which is political, and propose no strategies for pulling Europe out of its rut. To understand why the European machine is spinning like a top, creating the impression of permanent agitation without movement, giving off steam, grinding but no longer advancing, we must briefly recall a bit of history and the institutional state of play.

Let us begin with the European Union,[2] which is the main organization. We have seen that it was instituted in 1950 with the Schuman Declaration and the ECSC of 1952. In 1957 the Treaty of Rome established Euratom and the Common Market. In early 1958, a European Commission, a Council of Ministers, a Parliamentary Assembly (later known as the European Parliament), as well as a Court of Justice of the European Communities were set up. In June 1979, the system was completed by the appointment of deputies to the European Parliament, elected at the time by the national parliaments of the different Member States following direct universal suffrage by the European citizens.

In 1986, the Single European Act stipulated that the Single Market was to be put in place on 1 January 1993. The new act made it compulsory for the twelve Member States to create a Europe with no internal barriers by the aforementioned date (at the latest). No restriction whatsoever, whether regulatory or fiscal, was to delay the setting up of a genuine, domestic European market. Some 300 measures were taken to abolish the various physical, technical and fiscal obstacles to the free circulation of goods and people. On 2 February 1992, the Treaty of Maastricht

---

2 http://www.strasbourg-europe.eu/les-grandes-etapes-de-la-construction-europeenne.3375.fr.html

brought the European construction a new dimension. It instituted the European Union and added to the Community a vocation that was also political.

The House of Europe then rested on three pillars. The community pillar (including the European Community, the European Coal and Steel Community, and the European Atomic Energy Community) deals with issues that were transferred from the sovereignty of the Member States to that of the European institutions. The Common Foreign and Security Policy (CFSP) provides for intergovernmental cooperation procedures regarding foreign policy without the transfer of sovereignty. The pillar of cooperation in the fields of justice and internal affairs also provides for intergovernmental cooperation procedures vis-à-vis immigration, right of asylum, and the fight against organized crime, again with no transfer of sovereignty.

Another innovation of the Treaty of Maastricht was the creation of European citizenship. It granted the nationals of Member States European citizenship and therefore new rights such as the right to live and travel freely in the countries of the European Union, the right to vote and stand for European and municipal elections by their state of residence, the right of recourse to a European ombudsperson in the event of a dispute, etc.

Lastly, in providing for the creation of a single currency managed by the European Central Bank by 1 January 1999, the Treaty of Maastricht finalized the establishment of an Economic and Monetary Union (EMU).

The "Maastricht criteria," or euro convergence criteria, were defined with a view to creating the euro and bringing the Member States' economic policies together. They are as follows: their public deficit should not exceed 3% of the GDP, and their debt, 60% of the GDP. The two criteria were reaffirmed in 1997 with the Treaty of Amsterdam by adopting the Stability and Growth Pact. The Pact made it mandatory to watch out at all times for any budgetary deficits; inflation was not to exceed more than 1.5% of the mean inflation rate of the three best performing Member States; the long-term interest rates were not to exceed more than 2% of those of the three best performing Member States; the countries had to respect the normal fluctuation margins of their exchange rates provided for by the EMS's exchange-rate mechanism.

The European Union was entering a new phase, and 1993 marked a turning point in its enlargement when the Copenhagen European Council laid down the criteria that all candidate countries had to meet for admission. The "Copenhagen criteria" as they are called, addressed mainly the central and eastern European countries that had been seeking rapprochement with the European Community since the Berlin Wall fell in 1989. There are broadly speaking, three criteria political, economic, and Community. The political criterion requires that the state has stable institutions guaranteeing democracy, the primacy of the law, human rights and respect of minority groups. The economic criterion requires the candidate country to have a viable market economy capable of withstanding competitive pressure and the European internal (or single) market power. The Community legal framework built during the past sixty years helps to implement the rights and obligations of the community system, i.e., the body of common laws, rights and obligations adopted and constantly evolving throughout the European construction process. These include the founding Treaties of Rome as revised by the Single European Act, the Treaties of Maastricht, Amsterdam and Nice as well as all the rules and regulations adopted by the Union Council and all the rulings of the European Communities Court of Justice.

Once the admission criteria were defined, it was no longer a question of *if* but *when* the expansion of the European Union would take place. After the Copenhagen European Council, the countries of central Europe would officially submit their candidacy for admission to the European Union, with admission to take place eleven years later on 1 May 2004, when Cyprus and Malta also became members of the Union.

In addition, the Schengen agreements came into force in seven Member States: Germany, Belgium, Spain, France, Luxemburg, the Netherlands and Portugal. These allowed for travelers of all nationalities to cross their borders with no identity check. Since then, other nations have joined the Schengen Area. The agreements authorize the free movement of persons and harmonize border controls within the Area. They deal in particular with the short-stay entry and exiting of foreigners through a common visa policy; the right of asylum (determining which member state is responsible for the asylum application procedure); measures to fight cross-border drug trafficking; police cooperation (police chase) and mutual legal assistance.

On 2 October 1997, the Treaty of Amsterdam was signed, superseding the Treaty of Maastricht. The new agreement perfected the organization of intergovernmental cooperation between the European Union Member States. New fields were created within the community domain, namely police, justice and employment. The Treaty also incorporated a Social Policy Agreement, all the States being responsible for complying with the common rules adopted therein.

According to the official wording, the Treaty of Amsterdam created "an area of freedom, security and justice" within the European Union. The Convention implementing the Schengen Agreement signed in 1990 by thirteen Member States (Germany, Austria, Belgium, Denmark, Spain, Finland, France, Greece, Italy, Luxemburg, the Netherlands, Portugal and Sweden) provided for the free movement of persons by abolishing border checks and organized police cooperation between the signatory countries. This Convention was fully incorporated into the Treaty of Amsterdam and therefore applied to all the Member States of the European Union. Special conditions, nevertheless, were applied to Ireland and Denmark (and to the UK before Brexit). The signatories were called upon to reinforce their actions against terrorism, organized crime, pedophilia, drugs and arms trafficking, fraud and corruption within an intergovernmental framework.

For the first time, the Treaty of Amsterdam also introduced into the treaties the notion of "enhanced cooperation," a concept that enabled a limited number of Member States who were willing and able to advance further, to pursue the deepening of the European construction. It came into force on 1 May 1999 and also provided that an Intergovernmental Conference (IGC) be held "one year at least before the time European Union membership should reach twenty members."

The IGC opened on 14 February 2000 to end in Nice in December of the same year. The heads of state or government leaders agreed on a new treaty, the Treaty of Nice, during the Nice European Council held from 7 to 11 December 2000. It was signed on 26 February 2001 by the fifteen and aimed essentially to modify the institutional and decisional system of the European Union so as to enable enlargement to twenty-five. The Treaty of Nice came into force on 1 February 2003.

Yet with a Union of twenty-five members and new memberships to come, the Treaty of Nice proved to be insufficient. A Declaration on the Future of Europe annexed to the Treaty at the very moment it was drawn up, provided for a major European debate on the Union's future. The inaugural session of the Convention on the Future of Europe that was to deal with the matter opened on 28 February 2002. After sixteen months of work, all the participants agreed on a single text: a draft constitutional treaty.

In June 2004 the heads of state and government reached a unanimous agreement on the text of the treaty establishing a European constitution. It put forth a whole series of measures for a more transparent and efficient Union that would be close to its citizens. They included: classifying the competencies of the Union, simplifying the legal instruments, redefining the qualified majority in the Council but also installing a permanent president of the European Council, a Union Foreign Affairs minister, a reduced European Commission and introducing the right to citizens' initiative. The text, signed by the 25 Member States on 29 October 2004, was planned to come into force on 1 November 2006 after ratification by all the Member States according to the national procedures envisaged, namely referendum or parliamentary.

But the future was to decide otherwise. With the failure of the French and Dutch referenda in 2005, the pace of the ratification procedure of the constitutional treaty slackened and the European

Union went into a phase of deep reflection bearing on treaty reform processes and on its future. For two long years, Europe thus tried to find a solution to its internal reform problems, going from one government position to another, some of which were sometimes extremely divergent. Once the 27 heads of state or government had reached an agreement in October 2007, the Treaty of Lisbon was signed on 13 December 2007 and entered into force on 1 December 2009. A good many of the principles introduced in the text of the draft constitutional treaty were taken up in the new European treaty. They include a stable presidency of the European Council through the creation of the post of president, elected for a term of two and a half years by the heads of state and government of the 27 Member States; the creation of a High Representative of the European Union for Foreign Affairs and Security Policy, appointed by the European Council influenced by the national parliaments; the right of citizens' initiative; the new system for calculating the qualified majority, and so on.

Some points, however, were omitted: the reference to the Union symbols and to free and undistorted competition towards reaching the EU objectives; incorporating the Charter of Fundamental Rights into the body of the text itself even if the Charter acquires a binding value anyway...

After the Treaty of Lisbon, Belgian Herman van Rompuy was designated President of the European Council and British Catherine Ashton, High Representative for Foreign Affairs and Security Policy. In 2014 van Rompuy gave up his position to Polish Donald Tusk, while Ashton was replaced by Federica Mogherini from Italy.

Meanwhile, other countries, notably the Balkans, submitted their candidacy to the Union, while talks opened even with Turkey. But in 2010–2016, this expansionist movement was suddenly curbed at the economic level with the shock triggered by the global financial crisis of 2008. We cannot overlook the extraordinary proliferation of treaties that ensued and the incredible complexity of the substance of crisscrossed competencies and obligations that are now making up the European Community. Let us now get down to the underlying problems.

The Democracy Deficit

First of all, we saw that the Parliament still does not fulfill the requirements that constitute the essence of democratic representation, namely the right of legislative initiative, or the right to propose new bills.[3] In point of fact, it is the European Commission that holds this monopoly. The only thing the Parliament can do, in the hopes of bringing up a subject it wishes to discuss, is ask the Commission to kindly concoct a proposition; but the Commission can always refuse. If the members of a parliament cannot propose bills of law, this counteracts *de facto* the very notion that the European deputies represent their electors through a classic mandate, for they by no means have a say in their legislature's political agenda.

In addition, the European Parliament does not represent the European people as understood by the *demos* of *democracy*. And this is not because the Treaty of Rome had failed to take them into consideration—rather, it had precisely specified their Treaty representation as "the peoples of the States brought together in the Community" (art. 137). Then, with the Treaty of Lisbon (2009), there was talk of "citizens of the European Union." The Treaty of Maastricht had introduced the term in 1992 simply as an administrative signifier, but maintained representation "of the peoples of the States brought together in the Community."

Why was "peoples of the States" surreptitiously replaced by "citizens of the Union"? Was it just a semantic anecdote? Not really. The term "people" as employed in international law can refer to internal peoples within a multinational state, such as the Catalans within Spain, and has legal ramifications in particular as it might concern their right to internal self-determination or even secession. The notion of "people" is in fact further determined by several factors some of which can be very specific and therefore differ from one country to another. These include in particular

---

3 Arnaud Dotézac, *Le Déficit démocratique européen, op. cit.*

a country's social pact, its common origin on the more or less long term, its language, culture, religion and self-determination. Representing a people implies representing all of these parameters but also protecting them.

By the same token, the way the older treaties were formulated adhered to a political model that was more "confederal," in other words, that upheld interstate cooperation, preserving the national sovereignty of the Member States and the identity of their minorities which is precisely what the European project had always aimed to transcend from the moment it was created. In contrast, if parliamentary representatives are designated as "European citizens," this evokes a federal state, i.e., the bringing together of several States as one, provided they at least partially give up their sovereignty to the benefit of a central power that is granted a subsidiary but superior sovereignty, the lot on a unified territory defined by distinct borders. Such a model necessarily rests on a double national and federal loyalty of its citizens stemming from an acknowledged collective consciousness.

For all that, since Europe possesses neither its own legally delineated territory nor the federal borders that would constitute its exclusive sovereign space, it is not a state. Consequently, it cannot confer primary European citizenship and therefore there can be no "European people" as the German Constitutional Court of Karlsruhe had so remarkably recalled in its ruling of 2009 on the Treaty of Lisbon. According to the Court, the European Parliament is not a true parliament for it is not "an organ of representation of the unified European people, or a body of representation of the citizens of the Union," and it never will be as long as "no unified European people, that would constitute a source of legitimacy, is able to express its majority will through effective channels." In short, as there is no people, there can be no power of the people and therefore no parliamentary power. The opposite is also true: since there is not an effective European Parliament with a law-initiating power, there can be no European people worthy of the name! All this leads to the notion that the new designation, "citizen of the European Union," remains a very ambiguous legal qualification for it refers to a paradigm of political organization that does not exist.

The very discreet suppression of a reference to "peoples of (European) States" is thence eminently political in that it aims to weaken the feeling of national belonging and to abolish the corollary concept of nation state, yet without establishing a federal state. Such action symbolically confirms that the furtive, secret decision made without debate is characteristic of the European method of government. It is a reminder that 70 years after the ECSC and 64 years after the Treaty of Rome, the primary citizens of the Member States have not yet been openly asked whether or not they wish to establish a federal state or a genuine confederation. In fact, by way of democracy deficit, it should be recalled that the initial referenda concerning the widenings of the European Constitution between 2005 and 2009. The approval of the proposed texts have been rejected by the citizenry of various member countries. Netherland (61.54% of no on June 1, 2005) and France (54,67% of no on May 29, 2005) have pushed away the project of a new constitution. Denmark cancelled the popular vote after negative polls and decided to bypass the democratic choice through a simple parliamentary vote. This popular resistance has been denied again with the new Treaty of Lisbon which, in 2007, modified a little bit the former constitutional text (while keeping almost the same dispositions) and was later ratified without any popular vote. Only Irish citizens were called to the ballot boxes. Irish citizens rejected the Treaty in 2008, but were forced to adopt it through a second vote one year later…

It points out that the "Jean Monnet method," set up from the beginning to get around the sovereignty of the people in building Europe, is still going strong. Its foundational idea—compelling the Member States to go towards a federal system but without ever having recourse to a founding constitutional act that would imply the intervention of a sovereign people's conscious and real choice by a true vote—is still topical, while there is more and more evidence that it has led the European Union to a deadlock.

The Countless Layers of Europe's Thousandfold Institutionalization

The second problem of the EU comes from the piling up of countless organs supposed to pilot the Union even if it is not a state. This institutional interlacing is a first in history. It illustrates how such diverse supranational instances make it to the top. The Council of the European Union (or "Council") is the reunion of the 28 acting ministers. The Court of Justice (CJEU) is both the Supreme Court and the supreme legislator of the Union. There is also: the European Parliament with its 751 deputies; the European Commission with its 28 commissaries, one for each member; the European Central Bank (ECB), which is the EU's monetary institution located in Frankfurt.

There are, of course, other organs, perhaps less visible and not as significant on the institutional level, but nevertheless just as influential. For the connoisseurs, we can mention Coreper, a true little masterpiece of technocratic opacity. Made up of member-state diplomats assigned on secondment, it is an organ of the Council (supranational) and at the same time, a diplomatic organ of negotiation between colleagues appointed by the States (intergovernmental). The group meets every Tuesday and has the upper hand in inter-state negotiations without the European citizens ever having heard of it...

So this gives a good idea of the Union's institutional system, although it would be wrong to minimize Europe as merely the institutions of the Union. There are a host of other more or less related or independent institutions that take part in the national governance. The most important, of course, is NATO, which has the upper hand in all the military and security issues. On the institutional level, NATO depends on the 29 governments of the Member States represented by their Defense and Foreign Affairs ministers. Administered by the North Atlantic Council, its secretariat is headed by a Secretary General (currently the former Prime Minister of Norway Jens Stoltenberg). NATO headquarters are located in Brussels and employ around a thousand civil servants.

NATO also includes a Military Committee and an International Military Staff in charge of advising the two Strategic Commands, one of which is headed by an American officer who is also the Commander of the American Forces in Europe, and the other, by a French General residing on the military base in Norfolk, Virginia... We should also note that NATO has a parliamentary component as well, with an Assembly of 266 representatives of national parliaments and 53 representatives of associated countries, except Russia, excluded in 2014.

As for the European security organizations, we can tag on the Organization for Security and Co-operation in Europe (OSCE) to our list. Created in 1973, the OSCE is the only European organization with a more generalized vocation as it includes all of the European States plus the United States and Canada as well as the Caucasian and Central Asian countries. Its 320-member parliamentary assembly sits in Copenhagen. Quite ineffective, it basically fulfills in-the-field observation missions.

Other Intergovernmental Organizations in Europe

There are two more organizations we can mention on the economic level that are outside the Union: the OECD and EFTA. Born with the Marshall Plan in 1948 and therefore alongside the Cold War, the Organization for European Economic Cooperation (OEEC) that became the OECD in 1960, is in a way NATO's economic component. Based in Paris, in 2018 the OECD had 36 member countries whose 2,500 civil servants worked basically to promote the Anglo-Saxon economic agenda, namely every form of capitalism and the liberalization of commerce through free trade and competition, and to enhance labor innovation, competitiveness and flexibility. The OECD includes the group of free market countries in Europe and the rest of the world, from Japan and Korea to North America, Chile and Israel.

As for the European Free Trade Association (EFTA), it was also created in 1960 upon British instigation and for the same reasons. But it was to lose its influence very quickly due to the enlargement of the European Community, and of GATT and

WTO on the global scale. Its membership dwindled down to four (Iceland, Liechtenstein, Norway and Switzerland) and has very little weight on Europe. Its headquarters are in Geneva.

To wrap up this institutional panorama of contemporary Europe, we should mention the Council of Europe, created on 5 May 1949 by the Treaty of London, just one month after NATO. Its headquarters are in Strasbourg, and after some hesitation, the Council of Europe completely separated from the EU. It was established following Churchill's speeches at the University of Zurich in 1946 and The Hague Congress in 1948 and deals essentially with rule of law, culture and social issues. Its two main organs are the Committee of Ministers that sits at least once a year, and the Parliamentary Assembly that was, historically speaking, the first parliamentary assembly of the continent. Composed of 47 member states, 324 members and 324 substitutes elected or appointed by the national parliaments, it is dedicated to enquiry missions and drawing up recommendations. And it includes, inter alia, Turkey, Georgia, Ukraine and Russia.

Judicial power is vested in the European Court of Human Rights, the guardian of the European Convention for the Protection of Human Rights and Fundamental Freedoms. The ECHR acts as a European supreme court and plays an important role in this domain, for like the Council of Europe, its jurisdiction spans the European territory as a whole including the Caucasian countries (except Belarus, which is a candidate for membership).

A Wobbly Institutional Pudding

This panorama of the European institutions in their broadest sense, as lengthy as it may be, has the merit of showing the complexity but also the almost ontological difficulty in establishing effective and strong European governance. Indeed, there is no definition of or any consensus on the European borders. The EU itself is not clear on the matter: is the "useful" European territory limited to the euro zone, the Schengen Area, or to the territory of the 27 Member States? Nobody knows...

And what about expansion to include the other countries? Should Europe's borders coincide with NATO's to comply with the wish of the Atlanticists and the Americans? Could it be that the borders are left undetermined since the intent is to expand them? But then Europe would no longer be in Europe! That's already the case with the OECD zone, which also includes non-European countries. And expansion to where—the formerly colonized territories of the Middle East, whose refugee/immigrant flows are presently so hotly contested—as may indeed be the US plan for NATO, as proposed by Donald Trump?[4] Would they also then have freedom of movement within Europe?

The most pertinent territory for Europe is that represented in the Council of Europe. But then it would have to incorporate Turkey and Russia, which would outrage the Turkophobes and Russophobes alike... However desirable it may be on the spatial, historical and geopolitical front, this option is impossible on the political and practical front because of the mental revolution that it would entail. Europe would naturally have everything to gain, as Russia at least is such a part of its cultural, economic and territorial sphere. By integrating Russia, Europe would immediately recover its status of the leading world power and thus have a stabilizing influence on the global scale. But the deep-rooted hostility that this perspective arouses in some countries makes the exercise highly improbable.

With a bit of cynicism (or clear-sightedness), it seems reasonable to contend that these overlapping international cutouts were deliberately conceived to prevent the emergence of an efficient European government. By neutralizing the component States via multiple international instances that go beyond the geographic continental framework, Europe was deliberately layered with a galaxy of fragmented organizations to prevent it from reconstituting itself as speaking with a single voice, that of a world power that could contend the American hegemony. Instead Europe finds

---

4 https://www.politico.eu/article/nato-plus-me-donald-trump-proposes-nato-expansion-into-middle-east/.

itself tied up by its own institutions and hindered in taking a decisive leap towards a federal state.

With no border and no defined territory, there can be no sovereignty or independence. With no power hierarchy or constitution, no government is possible. Without a defined European people, there is no effective democracy. The Citizens' Assembly is but a cliché to designate a political society that has been anemic for decades. Whether it is dreaded (by the populists focused on securing the national identity of their respective states) or only allegedly desired (by the Europeanists who want a strong state, but have qualms about democracy), the transformation of Europe into a free, democratic and independent federal state is a pure utopia.

The Europeanists and Populists against Federal Europe

Besides its improbable structure, there are also political and psychological problems that inhibit achieving a European federal system. Most Europeanists are staunch liberals or even neoliberals and therefore support an economic doctrine that deeply dismantles society and destroys traditional social ties by promoting the free circulation of goods, capitals and especially workers, whether they come from within Europe or from abroad. It fosters the emergence of excessive individualism and defense of the continuously new self-proclaimed gender, racial or religious minorities—and even sexual and intersectional micro-minorities—whose demands push aside or shatter the existing traditional cultures, with the resultant agitation then being used to destabilize and undermine the existing historical cultures.

At the macro-social level, the proponents encourage the creation of supranational technocratic bodies that are opaque, abstract, cut off from reality, fundamentally anxiety-inducing and doubt-provoking because they have no limits or apparent control mechanisms. And all of this generates the identity crises milked by the "neo-national" populist conservatives and that in reality blocks the creation of a federal European state. For the liberals, the state is the enemy, so they set out to curb its damaging potential as much as possible. Nothing, in all fact, is as contrary to liberalism as a European Federal state. By its mere existence, it would have far more latitude to intervene in the economy than do the galaxy of institutions we now know. They are Europeanists in word but not in deed: the Europeanist liberal parties actually do not want strong European institutions.

As for the populists, they are the self-made prisoners of their own contradictions. They want to preserve the national identities, combating the principle of an open, multicultural society, and distrust—not without reason—the supranational governance that serves as a cover-up for the neoliberal plan. But all they have to offer the insecure social classes deeply weakened by liberalism is to cultivate their national preserve to the point of raising its barricades. They believe—and they are not totally wrong—that the nation is the last protecting dike against the global tsunami. But at the economic level, they all defend a liberal economy and capitalist free enterprise, from the Swiss UDC (People's Party) and the Italian Lega, to the French Rassemblement national (National Rally) and the Flemish Vlaams Belang. Some of them, like Donald Trump in the United States and Christoph Blocher in Switzerland, are billionaires and made their fortunes through the globalized economy. So while they may cannily put up a front with their fine speeches on patriotism and migration, the kind of economy they defend is completely opposed to their discourse.

This explains why these parties, so loud on their national stages, are mute on the European scene. They are careful not to specify what type of Europe they aspire to. After all, the Europe of nations could be a desirable project, albeit confederal rather than federal. But up until now, no populist party has succeeded in drawing up a credible European project, for they are incapable of articulating the national and European dimensions.

It is true that the parties' national cults frequently collide with those of their neighbors. In the nation-states that were often built to protect one people from another, this friction is inevitable, as we saw not long ago in the quarrel that opposed the leader of the Italian Lega and the president of the French Rassemblement national: Matteo Salvini's statement accusing France of "colonial crime in Africa"[5] came as a blow to Marine Le Pen, who is hostile to any postcolonial repentance or self-hatred of official France... Italy, given its own colonial history in Libya and Ethiopia was, of course, in no position to be pointing fingers.

"The *Internationale* of the nationalists" branded by their opponents is therefore not a feasible plan for tomorrow. If the populist parties want to take on their European ambitions, they are going to have to surpass their contradictions and develop their strategic vision and their capacity to reflect theoretically on the Europe they hope for.

Basically neither side is bent on a strong Europe. It is therefore a safe bet that short of a major international crisis, there is no will to take the qualitative leap towards a genuine and democratic European state that can act as a true force in the world, while benefiting its constituent peoples. The Europeanists stick to the community method that they value and will continue to pile on layers of governance at every major crisis.

Plausibly, against the backdrop of the euro crisis, a new institution to manage the European budget that would include a new *ad hoc* Parliamentary Assembly could be created. Or, to face the migrant and climate change crises, a new Council on Migration and a new Council of Ministers for the Environment with their assorted parliamentary forums could be established, along the lines of NATO for defense and the Council of Europe for human rights.

The skeptics, for their part, will continue to foster a strictly national approach towards addressing the global problems and bridging the most blatant social, financial and environmental gaps. This stalemate in the state of affairs, or "neither-nor" situation in which no side either wins or loses, can still last for some time. But sooner or later the bubble will burst and pave the way to either a violent revolution of a generalized Yellow Jackets' type, or to more or less absorption by consent into a larger and better

---

5 A remark which pretty funny from an Italian nationalist, knowing that Italy has been a colonial power in Africa's Libya, Somalia and Ethiopia and in Europe's Albania...

organized empire: the United States of America. Things could evolve either way on the long term.

That said, the European way of proceeding, which has the advantage of relying on verbal dialogue and confrontation rather than on physical constraint and state violence, contrasts favorably with the more vertical approaches of the other comparable powers, the United States, China and Russia.[6]

Russian Geography and Chinese Demography Require a Strong State

The above-mentioned three powers are in the midst of a global neo-imperialistic rebalancing. In their last special edition entitled *L'Atlas des empires (The Atlas of Empires), Le Monde* (a French daily newspaper) and *La Vie* (a weekly French Roman Catholic magazine) pose the question, "Where is the power today?" and whether empires are in the process of being dissolved or reconstructed.[7] The optimist technophiles explain that the Digital Revolution and the transnational enterprises are going to throw these old categories into history's garbage can. That is unlikely. If we scratch the surface, we can see that the multinationals and the globalized financial capital share a common cause with the new imperial strategies. Google, Apple, Facebook, Amazon, Microsoft (GAFAM), Tesla, Boeing and Goldman Sachs are the instruments

---

6 By its population and its economic weight, India is indisputably a member of this foursome, but not by its political functioning. Its internal operation comes close to that of Europe with its democratic system, its somewhat liberal economy, its oligarchic society and its organized disorganization. But its foreign policy differs completely in that it is true to its tradition of non-alignment and non-interference in third country affairs. It pursues no imperialistic policy on the pretext of sharing its neoliberal, free-trade, democratic or human-rightist values. As for Turkey, it follows the same neo-imperialist reshaping process as China, Russia and the United States. A former empire, its dream, with Recep Tayyip Erdogan, is to renew its prestigious past and—why not?—reinstate the caliphate that Daesh had claimed it would recreate in Syria. But for the time being at least, it is only a second-class power.

7 *L'Atlas des empires. Où est le pouvoir aujourd'hui* (*The Atlas of Empires. Where is the Power Today?*), special edition of *Le Monde/La Vie*, 2019.

of American hegemony just as Huawei, Alibaba and Tencent are for China.

To maintain or re-conquer its global hegemony, the United States has put its confidence in the capitalist development strategy of its private sector that has proven to be efficient. Likewise, China, in an endeavor to retrieve its position of number one world leader once held at the time of its most dynamic imperial dynasties, is reverting to its thousand-year tradition of command economy and a tight administrative framework in the hands of a caste of well-trained and hierarchically structured mandarins. Viewed carefully and free of any ideological prejudice, the Chinese system is not much different from the French system with its centralized republican monarchy, its economy à la Colbert, and its caste of mandarin-ENA graduates who monopolize the high positions in the public sector as well as in the big CAC 40 ("continuous assisted trading" French stock market benchmark index) companies.

As for Russia, the weakest of the "Four Great Powers," it is also out to restore its rank on the world stage, fully aware of its weaknesses and its frailties. It also knows that it is never as vulnerable as when it is weak. For ten years, at the end of the Soviet Union and beginning of the new liberal era with Gorbachev and Yeltsin, Russia thought it would come closer to the West and be admitted to the class on the same terms as the others. But that was a castle in the air! Russia very quickly had to get its feet back on the ground. It was not wanted and there was no question of giving to it any role, despite all the beautiful declarations on a West stretching "from Vancouver to Vladivosotck."

The economic and political trauma of the 1990s and the humiliation ensuing from Russia's rejection by the West in spite of Boris Yeltsin's repeated efforts towards reconciliation as well as those of Vladimir Putin during his first term of office, convinced the Russians that they could expect nothing from the United States, totally dominated by the Russophobe neo-conservatives like John McCain, or from the Europeans, incapable of having their own, independent Russian policy.

The surge of Russophobe propaganda, exacerbated by Donald Trump's election, actually masks a very prosaic truth, perfectly summed up by French historian Marlène Laruelle in a Swiss radio interview: far from being a menacing and imperialist dictatorship, Vladimir Putin's Russia is simply going through a phase of national assertion of the de Gaullist type.[8] It needs to reconstruct as an independent, sovereign nation recognized by the world, just as de Gaulle's France had to retrieve its lost honor after the military defeats of 1940, 1954 and 1962, and reconfirm its independence after losing its colonial empire in Indochina, Africa and Algeria. Russia, rejected by the West, is shifting towards China, as structurally speaking it straddles two ontologically Eurasian continents. Unless it finds itself with its back against a wall, it will never choose between one in opposition to the other.

At the institutional level that we are discussing here, however, it is interesting to note that the three countries all place their bets on a strong state. For Russia, things are very clear. To the Russian way of thinking, a weak state means chaos, distress, economic ruin, and foreign invasions (Teutonic, Mongol, Polish and Swedish yesterday, French in 1812, English in 1853, German in 1914 and 1941, Allied in 1919, NATO in the 1990s and of Ukraine since 2014). The reconstruction of a strong central state after the disaster of the 1990s explains President Putin's popularity. But notwithstanding the propaganda spread in the West and complacently relayed by Hillary Clinton when she compared Putin to Hitler during her electoral campaign in 2016, this in no way signifies the return in Russia to the tyranny of Stalin or Nicholas I.

Constantly threatened with anarchy because of its geography and its economic elites who are not always really very patriotic,

---

8 Marlène Laruelle, *La Quête d'une identité impériale. Le néo-eurasisme dans la Russie contemporaine* (*The Quest for an Imperial Identity. Neo-Eurasianism in Contemporary Russia*), Paris, Éditions Pétra, 2007; and by the same author: *Le Nouveau nationalisme russe. Des repères pour comprendre* (*The New Russian Nationalism. Markers for Understanding*), Paris, Éditions de l'Œuvre, 2010. See also Jean Radvanyi and Marlène Laruelle, *La Russie entre peurs et défis* (*Russia, between Fears and Challenges*), Paris, Armand Colin, 2018. On Western Russophobia, see Guy Mettan, *Creating Russophobia, op. cit.*

Russia can nevertheless count on an extraordinarily resilient people, ready and willing to make many sacrifices for their homeland. When the institutions function, as they do today with the reinforced federal system (the famous power vertical) that integrates the provinces, often very remote and of extremely unequal significance, and the peoples of very diverse cultures and religions without crushing them, Russia has once again become a country that has weight on the international stage.[9]

No one will contest the fact that China is a strong, even authoritarian, state. China faces the same problem as Russia, but for demographic rather than geographic reasons. While Russia has to oversee immense territories, China has to manage an immense mass of human beings within a limited usable space. Both China and Russia regard periods of weak government and anarchy as disastrous. For them, nothing is more creditable than "social harmony" backed by an enlightened government resting on a competent and honest ruling bureaucracy. This is how President Xi Jinping's control should be considered since he came to power. Conscious of the dangers that an economic slowdown and the transformation of an industrial export economy employing cheap, low-skilled labor into a consumer economy based on high-end services can entail on the one hand, and the social tensions generated by the explosion of capitalistic inequalities and an aging population on the other, the regime closes ranks with a purified communist party refocused on its fundamentals. Here again, notwithstanding some public protest that is always given wide coverage by the Western media, the regime can rely on vertical and efficient institutions: the party, the army, the schools, Parliament, the provincial governors, higher education, large companies, the Central Committee and the State Council are all in line. The lot, without the country becoming a huge re-education camp as sometimes described by

---

9 Jean de Gliniasty, *Géopolitique de la Russie. 40 fiches illustrées pour comprendre le monde* (*Russia's Geopolitics. 40 illustrated factsheets to understand the world*), Paris, Eyrolles/IRIS, 2018. The European stance about Russian economic size as "smaller than Spain or Italy" is clearly wrong if considering the GDP in terms of purchasing power parity.

the Western media: the Chinese continue to travel, study and work abroad without questioning the legitimacy of the state.

The Strengths of the United States: Its Institutions, Its Army and the US Dollar

What about the United States? During the recent years, United States has suffered two major setbacks, an economic one and a symbolic one. If US keeps its economic leadership in nominative terms (25.3 trillions of USD GDP in 2019) ahead of China (at 20.6 trillions), it has already lost its top place if calculated in terms of purchasing power parity (PPP).[10] According to the IMF, China has already surpassed the US in 2019 with a PPP of 25.3 vs. 20.5 trillions of USD. And the trend is largely unfavorable for the US.

And secondly, after the Trump's more or less chaotic presidency and the events of the Capitol on Januray 6, 2021, United States have known a severe hit to their leadership as a world emblem for democracy and moral values. The spectacle of both their parliamentary assembly halls besieged by an angry crowd has ruined their reputation abroad for many years, as well as the censorhip of an acting president and his millions of supporters by the big social networks such as Facebook, Twitter and others. Despite all the grievances which could be addressed to Trump, this in a clear aggression against the freedom of speech, seen from the non-western countries.

But despite these disorders, the United States has the additional great advantage of being able to rely on its foolproof institutions. The American Constitution, guarantor of the federal and democratic representation systems, is the United States' best asset, to which the dollar, the economy and the army owe their stability. The American Constitution has proven itself for almost two and a half centuries and has enabled the country to endure and come out stronger from all of its crises: the War of 1812 against Great Britain, the Mexican-American War of 1845–1848, the Civil War,

---

10 Oliver Reynolds, "The World's Top 5 Largest Economies in 2024," in *FocusEconomics: Economic Forecasts fron the World's Leading Economists,* February 16, 2021.

the World Wars. As for the institutions of the European States, they did not survive the ordeals of war (the revolutionary Republic, the first and second Napoleonic Empires, Fascist dictatorships), or internal crises (the Prussian, Austro-Hungarian, Russian and Italian monarchies, the Third and Fourth Republics...). Neither the defeat in Vietnam nor racial conflicts have challenged the standing of the constitution any more than the populist presidents like Andrew Jackson in the past or Donald Trump more recently. In point of fact, the dominant complaint with regard to the US Constitution concerns failure to abide by it, rather than the desire to replace it.

Inspired by the institutions of the Roman Republic to the extent of copying their very denominations (Senate, Capitol, White House architecture, and so on), the American Constitution is the perfect response to the needs of the modern imperial republic, as Raymond Aron had fittingly explained already in 1973.[11] It is as efficient on the vertical level as it is on the horizontal. It has the ability to coordinate the lower echelons (communes, counties, States) with the higher echelons (the federal and international levels) and to facilitate communication between the different strata of society (the elites and the citizens' people). It also provides for the coexistence of the various religions, cultures, minorities and social classes. As a society, the United States may be more violent than Europe, but this has never led to calling the structuring of its institutions into question.

This institutional stability and the faculty of the Constitution to adapt, thanks especially to the possibility of amendment, are unrivaled in modern history, except by Great Britain. Even Switzerland, renowned for its stability, did not adopt its federal system until 1848 or introduce direct democracy until the end of the 19th century. The American institutions therefore have the great advantage of ushering the country smoothly—with no risk of contesting its architecture in the Yellow Jackets style, even in

---

11 Raymond Aron, *La République impériale. Les États-Unis dans le monde 1945–1972* (*The Imperial Republic. The United States in the World 1945–1972*), Paris, Calmann-Lévy, 1973.

the worst riots—into the era of post-modernity, post-truth and post-democracy.

The second asset of the United States is its military capacity. The US is still, and by far, the first world military power, with a defense budget much bigger than any else and, added to the other NATO countries' budgets, is two or three times higher than Chinese and Russian ones (around 1 trillion vs. 250 billions of USD). With 800 military bases all around the globe and Navy Fleets on almost every sea, its military dominance is still undisputable, even if challenged by new Russian hypersonic weapons and the growing Chinese defense budget.

The third US trump card is assuredly its currency which serves as the international reserve currency for trade and financial exchanges, giving the United States the capacity to influence and exert pressure on every foreign country or corporation which it deems as breaching its unilaterally-imposed sanctions or as an unfair competitor. This gives it a very strong lever and a disproportionate means of pressure over all other powers, including China, as most particularly witnessed in its multitude of actions against Huawei.

At the international level, it is said the world is leaving the age of American hegemony to enter the era of multipolarity. The scholars and the optimists always have a tendency to invent new formulas and jargon to describe the new aspects of reality—or even older ones. I fear there are none. For the reality today, in spite of all that one may hear about the Industry 4.0, digitalization and robotization, is that we are entering a period of merciless competition. The planet is a finite space with limited resources.

So are the markets of the multinational companies. The climate is changing. The underdeveloped peoples and the emerging nations thirst for self-government. The old Western hegemony led by the United States is increasingly under pressure. In this context, the tensions and conflicts between peoples, religions, ethnic groups and social classes can only increase with time. Culture and information are growing power instruments and are more than ever part of the great struggle for global domination. In this regard, US is better armed than Europe to face the upcoming challenges.

Europe, a "Non-imperial" Empire?

This is how the transition period that we are entering, with the great powers refashioning in an imperial mode, should be understood. Based on its intrinsic strengths and weaknesses, the United States is in the process of leaving what Raymond Aron called "the imperial republic" to enter progressively into the age of a "new empire." This terminology is important, for the objectives, ambitions and resources of an imperial republic are very different from those of an empire.

This possible evolution did not escape the European elites. At a press conference held on 10 July 2007 in Strasbourg, former European Commission president José Manuel Barroso openly stated his commendation of the empire:

> Sometimes I like to compare the EU creation with the organization of empire. We have the dimension of empire, but there is a great difference. Empires were usually made with force, with a center imposing a diktat, a will on the others. And now we have what some authors call the first non-imperial empire. We have, by dimension, twenty-seven countries that fully decided to work together and to pool their sovereignty. I believe it is a great construction and we should be proud of it. At least, we in the Commission are proud of it.[12]

Unfortunately for Barroso, Europe is not at all a "non-imperial empire." It is imperialist as it concerns the wars it wages on its exterior, in Mali and Afghanistan for instance, but it is not an empire, for it is not sovereign in its decisions but rather dances to

---

12 "L'Observatoire de l'Europe, Libre forum des universitaires, journalistes, fonctionnaires pour un libre débat sur l'Europe"(The European Observatory. Free forum of university graduates, journalists, civil servants for a free debate on Europe) https://www.observatoiredeleurope.com/notes/Barroso-avoue-l-UE-est-comparable-a-un- empire_b678643.html).

the US tune, as witnessed by the decisions it takes against its own interest (no Nordstream 2, no China deal). Could it transform itself into a proxy empire in the pay of the US? Or is that oxymoron a feel-good self-deception belying its vassalization?

Or should Europe, rather than wanting to become a proxy empire, on the contrary, have the ambition to transform itself into a strong federal state that is free, democratic, sovereign, respectful of others, peaceful with its close neighbors such as Russia and, above all, fully independent from the US?

That's the great European existential dilemma.

PART IV
SCENARIOS FOR THE FUTURE: A DEMOCRATIC INDEPENDENT FEDERATION OR A PROVINCE OF THE EMPIRE?

CHAPTER 8

THE IMPERIAL SCENARIO: THE CHOICE OF INSIGNIFICANCE UNDER AMERICAN ASCENDANCY

> *For our major enemy is within us. [...]*
> *It lies in our incapacity to think ahead about our destiny and to assume our community of common destiny. Thus and so, the main enemy of the Greek States in the face of the Macedonian was their incapacity to understand and to unite.*
> EDGAR MORIN, *PENSER L'EUROPE*

To be or not to be? After this long analysis of the weaknesses of the European Union, the stagnation of continental integration and of cooperation with the EU's great neighbors such as Russia, Turkey and North Africa, here are the two main alternatives Europe is likely to face if it decides to come to grips with its future—or not.

1) The acceptance of inaction and denial. I call this the choice of insignificance. Here, business goes on as usual under the NATO umbrella and the US hegemonic grip. The European Union survives following the institutional model of a cooperative, a co-owners' association managed by old-style administrators who apply the rules dictated from Washington in the hope the security costs will be paid by US military forces and that our benevolent protector will not plunge us into war and obliteration.

2) The adoption of efficient and democratic European governance in order to restore a full European sovereignty. Europe does not settle for agitated entropy as it approaches the end of the dead end and waiting for the sky to fall. Instead, Europe moves forward to change its way of functioning and endow itself with effective federal institutions by focusing on the democratic method, paving the way towards a federal, free, democratic and sovereign Europe, which could be inspired by the historical experience and institutional model of Switzerland. This is our preferred option, even if not the most realistic… We'll examine it in the next chapter.

If, as I'm tending to think, Europe chooses not to be and prefers to avoid the difficulties and the potential turmoil of a democratic reset, then there is only one scenario for its future: the "business as usual" model and slow transformation into a second rank confederation of vassal states under the control of the US nascent Empire.

In order to understand why this scenario looks largely probable, we have to explain the transformation of the structure of the power within the US and how this process will affect the European destiny while condemning Europe to accept the US ascendancy.

The notion of the US as an empire is obviously not very new and has an extensive literature addressing it. But in our view, this term is not relevant, or to be more precise, is *not yet* relevant. In our mind, its transformation to an empire is only presently underway but not yet a fait accompli. The US is not yet an empire, in the full meaning of this word, but rather is still an "imperial republic," en route towards becoming an empire. What might be regarded as a nuance between the two political regimes is actually important because the two terms reflect differences in behavior. An imperial republic doesn't behave exactly like an empire.

Sci-Fi movies have already perceived and described this process of a republic decaying into an empire. Remember the US movie saga, *Starwars*, produced in Hollywood by George Lucas where the famous emperor without a face and his evil lieutenant,

The Imperial Scenario

Darth Vader were fighting for universal hegemony against an improbable coalition of rebels supported by the wise Jedi knights? The corrupted galaxy republic was divided by internal struggles for power and a ferocious competition for trade markets; its ambitious chancellor, Palpatin, exploiting the greed of the merchants of the powerful Federation of Commerce, had designed a plot for legally seizing supreme power and transforming the decaying Republic into an Empire ruled by an autocrat without face.

This metaphoric story describes exactly the transition from Republic to Empire that is now happening in our world—but not for the first time. To understand what is happening now, we have to look not only to recent history, to the Cold War paradigm which is no longer relevant, but deep into the past, to the lessons provided by humanity's long history, when the Roman Republic was decaying and transforming itself into a world empire between 202 and 27 BC.

In Chapter 3, we drew a parallel between the evolution of ancient Greece and showed how the fiery Greeks were finally conquered and subjugated by the Romans after decades of civil turmoil, political decay, social unrest caused by a great civil war, and the emergence of an oligarchic ruling class caused by the economic transformations and wealth accumulation resulting from colonial conquests.

But then, the more or less democratic Roman Republic, despite its strong political republican constitutional framework, at first declined to transform itself into the new type of political entity we call now the Roman empire. The Roman Republic had institutions strong enough to advance towards an imperial state, but not strong enough to resist the erosion of democracy brought about by the oligarchic forces within it, which were strengthened by the concentration of wealth which followed the colonial conquests of the Roman Republic.

After the second Punic war and the victory over Carthage and Hannibal in 202 BC, Rome become the foremost power in the western Mediterranean world. This victory was consolidated in 146 BC, when Rome completely destroyed Carthage and its

Graeco-Macedonian allies. Huge amounts of new territories submitted to its authority and were incorporated into the new-born Roman empire. In 133 BC, the realm of Pergamum was given to Rome after the death of its king. In just a few decades, Rome and Italy were transformed into a vast empire.

This new configuration completely transformed the Roman economy and its social structure, leading to the politics of the traditional Roman republic then transforming itself into an imperial republic. To make it short, the permanent state-of-war against the supposed enemies of Rome deeply transformed its society: the middle class—the peasant-soldier-citizen who cultivated his field, fought voluntarily for his liberty and voted freely in elections— was killed at war while the survivors were massively impoverished by years of military service and poor agricultural management. In the meantime, the upper class of nobles, the *nobilitas* and Senate ruling class, bought the small farms to low prices and accumulated huge fortunes. As they loaned their money to the Republic in order to finance the wars, the indebted state, unable to pay back the lenders, surrendered the public common fields to them, which were privatized at their sole profit.

Thanks to the wars of conquests, the upper class increased in importance. This evolution was amplified by the transformation of the economic structure, to the point that the social inequalities and tensions became unbearable for the lower Roman classes and other Latin people allied with Rome.

The traditional Italian economy, based on small farming, collapsed gradually under the pressure of the more competitive and productive big landowners (the latifundia) using a slave labour force, and thereby creating a mass of unemployed in the cities. The new "international" division of the labour between Italy and new markets and productive territories like Sicily, North Africa, Greece, Asia Minor contributed as well to destabilize the traditional economy. Wheat, olive oil and wines were from then on largely produced in Sicily, North Africa, Greece and later Egypt. In Rome, trading, shipping and big merchants were developing fast, as well as a new financial class of entrepreneurs, while Italy

The Imperial Scenario

and the Roman Italians of the low and middle classes were turned into clients of the wealthy ruling class.

This explains why Roman democracy declined step by step and how the oligarchy concentrated an ultra-potent economic and political power in its hands. The agricultural and democratic reforms initiated by the defenders of the people (the Gracques) were overturned by the oligarchical senatorial class while lower class citizens became embedded as client voters for the rich. This evolution led to the rise of populism, with the struggles for power within the oligarchy driving some leaders to make an alliance with the popular forces in order to seize power while others tried to monopolize it for the sole benefit of the oligarchy.

These struggles for power, wealth and benefits linked to the governance of the imperial colonies and the economic control of the subjugated provinces, slowly but surely corrupted the functioning of the democratic institutions of the Republic. Fights between "populists" and "oligarchs" became more and more deadly, while coups d'etat, social and civil wars, proscriptions of opponents, temporary dictatorships, slave revolts, kept increasing until Julius Caesar and finally Augustus were able to create a new autocratic state—a dynastical dictatorship, which re-established social order under its iron rule and generated what we now term the Roman Empire.

This is a very similar process to that now at work within the US imperial republic, following the twentieth century United States "victory" in the world wars against Germany and the Cold War against the Soviet Union.

Thanks to the divide between Europeans and the 1914 and 1939 wars in Europe, the United States of America was asked by some threatened European states to intervene in European affairs and to transform their former enemies—first Germany, then later Japan into vassals. But then the US transformed their former allies—i.e., Great Britain and France—into vassals as well. The two Europeans wars, like in the Roman-Carthagean history, were followed by a third one, the so-called Cold War, against the USSR. Then in 1991, echoing the last Roman war, the United

States became the winner of against the "Punic" Soviet challenger. Taking advantage of two hot and one cold wars, the American imperial Republic succeeded in becoming the hegemonic power on the planet in less than eight decades. What an outstanding performance—much of which was fortuitous!

The neo-conservatives and liberal democrats in Washington briefly thought that they had definitively won and imposed their liberal democracy views and free market ideology on the rest of the world. Such was the hope that Francis Fukuyama had fatuously expressed in his book *The End of History* proclaiming the triumph of liberal democratic values. Both Presidents Bush, President Bill Clinton and his defeated wife Hillary Clinton, as well as Barack Obama, were promoters of this imperial republican hegemonic conviction so abundantly described and ascribed to in all the studies released by the think tanks close to the neo-conservatives and the Pentagon: the Project for the New American Century, the Rand Corporation, the Brookings Institution, the Heritage Foundation, the Atlantic Council, the American Enterprise Institute and their relays in Europe (the German Marshall Fund, George Soros and the Open Society Foundations, NGOs active in human rights, and the color revolutions in the countries they considered to be hostile).

A New Era of Post-Truth and Post-Democracy

This new crony capitalism, or neo-liberalism, has been reigning from North to South and East to West without any real counterweight until re-emerging Russia and developing communist China started to oppose to it. This hegemony is now increasingly contested by Russia, Iran and/or China. Since the beginning of this century, the so-called emerging countries led by China and Russia are accelerating the transformation of the US power structure. In some fields, this transformation has speeded up over the past twenty years or so, dropping us into an unforeseeable era of post-modernity, post-truth and post-democracy.

On the political field, the US Republic is becoming an increasingly less democratic and pacified state. Is it still possible

The Imperial Scenario

to call a democracy a country in which it is possible to transfer presidential power from father to son, as per Presidents Bush the First and Second? Or from husband to wife as was attempted by President Clinton and the would-be President Clinton, his wife? Is it appropriate to call a state a democracy in which presidential elections can only be won by a multi-billionaire candidate—or senate seats by millionaires? During 2020 presidential elections, "democrat" Joe Biden was able to raise more money than the billionaire Donald Trump. With electoral costs like this, is it not a sign that the oligarchy will win the US presidency, whoever may be the candidate, Democrat or Republican?

The rise of populism and racial protestations represent a similar parallel. Globalization and its growing inequalities have exacerbated the social, racial and gender inequalities within the American republic. What has most irritated the liberal US Democrats about Donald Trump's election and presidency is the fact that he was able to make a successful alliance with the poorer lower classes such as from Midwestern states and traditional old oil business against the new wealthy class of Silicon Valley capitalists and the urban upper classes from the coastal states. The sudden shift in the power between the two parts of the oligarchy has been considered inadmissible by the so-called "Democrats" who had in the meantime betrayed the lower classes who had largely been their supporters until the end of the 20th Century. Their return to power thanks to Trump election was a real slap in the Democrats' faces. While Joe Biden's election has been a great relief for them it will not appease their greed for absolute power, reflected in new forms of censorship and hawkishness in foreign policy.

This aggressive struggle for world dominance is another reason why Trump has been so contested, indeed demonized, inside the US by the American imperial neoconservatives, and why American Russophobia was so heightened during his mandate and has even speeded up since Joe Biden's election. Trump gathered public support by calling for a big shift in American policy: the renunciation of the goals of the imperial republic, i.e. of American hegemony over the world, for a more pragmatic and convenient domination of a limited portion of it.

Trump shared the view that the United States must now focus on its core territory—its infrastructures are in disrepair while its lower social classes are in despair—while restricting its zone of influence, roughly speaking, to Europe, Latin America, Israel and Pacific vassal states like Japan, South Korea or Thailand (not counting the four remaining eyes of the Anglo-Saxon five-eyes group). It is this point which so hurt the neoconservatives like John McCain and the liberal democrats like the Clintons. They could not and do not accept this renunciation of world hegemony. That is the main reason why they cannot ever pardon Trump, who has broken their Game Boy.

After the self-destruction of the Soviet Union, the US liberal republic had enjoyed its decade of complete hegemony. The neoconservatives and liberal democrats in Washington briefly thought that they this was it! They had won the Cold War and imposed the liberal democracy and free market paradigm on the entire rest of the world, as Francis Fukuyama had written.

For them, Russia, the USSR successor, was a stone in their shoes and they looked for ways to break it. But as this effort was not successful, they then tried to dominate it or transform it by force—a process still ongoing today by way of economic sanctions, as well as by tricky soft power means—into a western liberal democracy and free market economy dominated by United States multinationals and ruled by representatives of a globalist oligarchy.

The European Union, dominated by the good will of Angela Merkel's Germany and a new anti-Gaullist, Sarkozist, Hollandist and Macronist France which hastened to join the NATO command and play the role of loyal supporters of US interests against their traditional enemies like Qaddafi's Libya and Assad's Syria, the European Union has been transformed into a proxy relay of the purported Western values of liberal democracy and a free market economy not only in Europe and Ukraine but also in the rest of the world, and especially in Africa and the Middle East.

The Impact of the US Imperial Republic on Europe

Here is where we are now—the transformation of the United States into an Imperial Republic—and what it means for the domestic US, for Europe, and globally:

- **The vassalization of allies and client states**. The domination goals on a more delimited territory signifies a stronger control of them. In fact (even if not in words), an empire doesn't recognize allies or friends, but only vassal states. That's what was on course in Latin America with the fight against South American leftist governments such as Venezuelan Maduro, Ecuadorian Correa, Bolivian Morales, Nicaraguan Ortega and Brazilian Lula and portends the full submission of the European Union to American policies. In Europe, this phenomenon has been less crude than in Latin America but it follows the same path. Thanks to NATO, European military power has been entirely put in American hands. And thanks to astute economic pressures and sanctions, as well as massive propaganda campaigns against the supposed enemies of "Western values," most of the European countries has been turned into vassals of the US.

- **The silent killing of democracy**. We are now entering a phase of post-democracy, and the establishment of an oligarchic state with democracy strictly limited to local levels, ie. municipalities and regional governments. When multiple and repeated crises arise and it is unable to control the tensions accumulating between the social classes, the system turns to authoritarianism at the upper level of power. The disturbing signs of a post-democratic evolution are becoming more evident in the Western world. Generalized mass surveillance (surveillance cameras, police custody, telephone tapping, spying on suspect internal populations, secret prisons and Special Courts) is on the rise. The social network and media are controlled by the states and the private monopolies in the hands of a few oligarchs; the police force is strengthened along with its doctrines of intervening during demonstrations; anti-fake news laws are passed, legal proceedings are filed against whistleblowers like Julian Assange and Edward Snowden, and human rights continues to be used as a tool for geopolitical purposes.

- **The belittling of the people by the elites.**[1] The growing influence of the oligarchies within the democratic societies through the progressive pauperization and crushing of the middle classes, which provided the social basis for democracy, have led to the proliferation of illiberal regimes of all persuasions, with Donald Trump's America in the lead. All of these measures are in the process of being implemented under the most diverse pretexts, including the defense of democracy against terrorism and the fight against fake news and Russian interference. With the tensions caused by globalization and the growing struggle for world hegemony, there is no reason for it all to stop.

- **In this less democratic world, true culture can only decay**. There is no more room for creativity, independence and breakthroughs. It can only use old patterns or trivial and socially insignificant novelties. Mass technocratic culture is predominant and impressive but true culture is severely limited and reduced to small circles of thinkers or artists who keep the lamp lit for limited audiences.

---

1 This phenomenon was identified for the first time in the United States by sociologist Christopher Lasch, who was close to the Frankfurt School, (*The Revolt of the Elites and the Betrayal of Democracy*), (*La Révolte des élites et la trahison de la démocratie*, Paris, Climats, 1999). The transformation of democracies into oligarchies, well defined by Aristotle with respect to the Greeks, appears through the increasing domination of the public debate by the intellectual and financial elites. The abhorrence of the people, the "plebeians," is widespread on the air and in the media. On this, see the statement by France's more-activist-than-philosopher Bernard-Henry Lévy in the newspaper *Le Temps* of 25 January 2015: "In Europe, the people must not be the only sovereign! […] If we keep repeating the people, the people, the people… we are heading straight for a civilization crisis."

The Imperial Scenario

- **An astute management of violence.** As an empire is less and less democratic and increasingly authoritarian, it faces the problem of managing violence. The strength of an empire relies on its capacity to ensure inner protection (security, defence) and a relative prosperity to its subjects. To achieve this, the empire has to exploit its periphery and to expel its internal violence to the outskirts of its core territories. Economic and security order is its motto and its survival kit, necessitating a massive intelligence surveillance apparatus. This special exportation of violence has been theorized by Muslim thinker Ibn Khaldun who tried to explain the successes and failures of the Muslim caliphs. Ibn Khaldun showed that the legitimacy of an empire relies on its capacity to bring prosperity and security to its population. To achieve this, it has to encourage internal exchanges of goods and services and to expel insecurity outside. In that perspective, the casual terrorist attacks and other "wars on terror" such as the one declared by former President Bush are appropriate tools to justify a perpetual "état d'urgence" (state of emergency) and a high level of police and defence expenditures in order to keep the inner populations under control. In other terms, an empire excludes wars of conquest but needs controlled "small" wars outside of its territory.

- **An empire, by definition, is not national.** A nation could give birth to an empire but as soon as a national republic transforms itself into an empire, it can no longer be a nation. An empire is constituted by an addition of the populations of different nations, with different religions, cultures and so on. An empire is cosmopolitan in essence, and by definition. It could be a melting pot or an open market for migrations, which oblige it to be authoritarian in order to manage domestic xenophobic reactions to same and to control the flows of immigrants at their borders. It must make a balance between the need for a cheap labour force brought about by migrants and demanded by the oligarchic capitalists in order to keep the domestic wages at very low rates, and the animosity created internally by the unending arrivals of legal or clandestine immigrants diluting local cultures, and seen to be taking jobs.

- **A new organization of labour with the creation of a new type of serfdom**. In the new imperial order, the economy tends to become more and more concentrated into the hands of a small group of entrepreneurs who are becoming richer and richer. Income equality and the middle classes are disappearing in order to be replaced by only two very unequal classes: the big owners and oligarchic class and the popular masses, now reduced into a vulnerable and "flexible" working class, or even an unemployed lumpenproletariat or plebian class like in the Roman Empire, when the lower classes were supported by public distribution of bread and grains.

- **The privatization of the state**. Public services and usual state responsibilities are step by step privatized or delegated to private hands as was the case under the Roman Empire or the French monarchy. Armies are privatized through the recruitment of so-called professional armies with volunteer soldiers. The citizen-soldier and mass conscription are disappearing. And soon, in the next decades, the fiscal services will also be privatized under the pretext of the greater efficiency of the private sector. In the Roman Empire as in the old European monarchic States, the IRS was not a public service but a private one.

The Differences between an Imperial Republic and an Empire

The biggest difference between an imperial republic and an empire is stability. Empires look for stability while imperial republics are turbulent and troubled, expansionist, looking for conquests, new territories, adventures, revolutions, propagandistic ideals to impose upon everybody else. Instability inside their

The Imperial Scenario

boarders and above all outside their boarders is an accepted way of life and their primary objective.

Imperial republics are always subjected to frustrations. Their aspirations for new conquests is never satisfied, while empires can admit their own limits, if they are not threatened inside their core territory. The conquest of new spaces is a condition of their existence, it doesn't matter what the prize is, down to cultural achievements, religious beliefs or physical territories. The democratic confrontation of social classes, personal power, political parties, cultural differences, and religious divides inside an imperial republic maintain the pot in a permanent boiling state: the cap can always blow up.

As exposed above, the Roman conquests have been accomplished by republican generals and oligarchs before the creation of the Empire, and not by emperors. The Roman Empire created by Augustus abandoned its mission to conquer new territories and to subsume new peoples in order to keep the existing status quo and was quite happy to administrate it and simply manage it within the boundaries established by the old Republic.

And again, to ensure stability, empires need to fulfil the two basic needs of people even more efficiently than republics. These basic needs are prosperity and security. In order to keep the people quiet and in a permanent state of moderate social temperature, an empire must be able to provide to its peoples a minimum standard of living and comfort. In Roman times, this capacity was named *panem and circenses*. In other terms, as long as they can provide bread and circus games, food and entertainment, the empires can survive for centuries without their legitimacy being in question.

Within the empire, the citizens are allowed to participate to local elections but not to the upper level. Democracy doesn't exist anymore in fact but only in words. As they are not allowed to participate to the governance of the empire, it is crucially important to keep alive a fictional but not effective democracy, as Emperor Augustus perfectly understood. They also must enjoy a reasonable level of personal safety. Domestic police must be strong and efficient: pirates, thieves, fraudulent speculators as well as social troublemakers or anti-establishment protesters must be publicly condemned, And, if too disturbing, crucified like Jesus Christ or Spartacus.

In that sense, Roman emperors were clever enough to kill two birds with one stone. As the former Christians in the roman Empire refused to honor the Emperor, they were given to lions in order to ensure at the same time a good spectacle for the joy and the edification of the masses. As peacebreakers of the social order of their time, they could, and had to, be punished with the support and applause of a large majority of people—until this majority was slowly reduced by the growth of Christianity. But it took three centuries until Constantine in 313 AD.

Same games exist today with those populations headed by figures such as the former Serbian President Milosevic, Saddam Hussein and later with Colonel Gaddafi, who were bombed, hanged and killed like in a TV show thanks to CNN cameras. President Assad was targeted for the same fate, but he was more resilient or luckier because he was rescued by an unexpected ally called Vladimir Putin. Will Kim Jong-Un or the Iranian leaders be the next to be sacrificed in the great circus of the American empire delivered for the edification of the global public, friends and enemies alike, with unanimous applause, by the Western media? As the show must go on, we can be sure that other candidates will arise and be felled.

As is well understood and occasionally admitted, in order to keep domestic peace, empires often need to wage wars outside their borders. In order to keep a low degree of violence inside the domestic area, empires have the necessity to expel their internal potential for violence outside their walls. That's the reason why an empire is never in peace with its neighbours for a long time. It must wage a war at least at each human generation, every 20 or 25 years, but not more. During the imperial republic time, the necessity to wage wars is much higher: if you look at the 230 years of American history, you can observe America has waged a war every 3–4 years.

The Imperial Scenario

A US-Driven Global Corporate Empire

Let us now examine what all of this is meaning for Europe and the Western world.

What are the main challenges of the present emerging empire? As drafted by former president Obama and underlined by the previous president, Trump, and now Biden, the main challenge is no longer the Middle East and terrorism nor is it Europe or even Russia: it is China. With a population of 1.4 billion people and a booming economy located in the heart of the Eurasian continent, China is clearly the next target of the empire.

The shift of the US focus from Europe to the Pacific area by Obama, Trump and now Joe Biden demonstrates this new concern as did the last electoral declarations of President Trump against China. But China is reacting skilfully, avoiding frontal fight, trying to build its "One Road, One Belt" project through the Eurasian continent and to defend free-trade policy with the support of the European Union. China is now too big to fail and the competition between both empires will require not only muscles but a lot of brain.

The only difference between the three US presidents is that Obama and Biden think that China and Russia form a common threat while Trump thought Russia is a separate problem as did Henry Kissinger in the 1970s, requiring the US to divide the two main powers of the Heartland against each other. Trump recognized also by his decision that US was no longer powerful enough to compete against a united Chinese-Russian front. In that sense, Trump was more prescient than the Democrats who are still locked into old Cold War ideology. Now that Joe Biden has referred to Russian President Putin as a "killer" who must be punished in a press meeting in March 2021, the anti-Russian stance and neoconservative aggressive policies will nonetheless remain strong for a long while in Washington.

At the economic level, the neo-imperial US state will look for a new way to organize labor by creating a new type of servitude. In the new, imperial, profoundly oligarchic order, the economy will be even more concentrated in the hands of a small group of entrepreneurs who get richer and richer. After the oil and gas economy and the Hollywood exports, the tools of this new economic dominance are now based on the new technologies of information and the digital economy developed by the Silicon Valley giants, Google, Amazon, Facebook, Apple, and Microsoft along with the projects of the new technology tycoon, Elon Musk. Their overall dominance has become one of the bigger threats for democracy, since they are able to impose their censorship on their platforms, and even censor a former US president. This trend, encouraged by the Democrat majority at the Congress under the pretext of protecting democracy against populism, is unprecedented in a democratic Republic. What was until now a public mandate and a competence of the state, i.e. the surveillance of the citizens and the regulation of free speech, has been de facto privatized by the technological giants—albeit under pressure from the government.

This new era of privatization is the last in a long list of the weakening of the public good. Public services and responsibilities have been consistently privatized since the Reaganomics and deregulated capitalism era of the 1980s. We have seen that this process is taking large leaps forward regarding security. The multiplication of private jails, private security companies, the use of private mercenaries in armed conflicts, the development of professional soldiers and cancellation of the conscript armies are all steps towards a complete privatization of the public security and national defense.

We can wager that in the decades to come, everything that was once free, like water or air, will have to be paid for and that even the tax services will be privatized on the pretext of greater efficiency provided by the private sector. This calls to mind the parable of the Publican in the Bible: at the time, the Publicans were the private agents in charge of levying the imperial Roman tax.

Last but not least, the increasing weight of the industrial-military complex since President Eisenhower's first statement about it in 1961, is another sign of the militarization of the state by private companies. The military and intelligence lobbies have become so powerful in the state structures and the political institutions such as the US Congress that it is now impossible to thwart them. The military expenses are still growing, as are the growing number of US military bases (around 800 on all continents, against only two for Russia and one in Djibouti for China...) or military alignments around the world, most recently the so-called Quad encompassing India, Japan and Australia. If it comes to war, Europe is surely the closest and most accessible target. It is already the victim of the American economic wars against Russia (no Nordstream 2) and China (no profitable trade deals). And assuredly, if indeed this is possible, if the US resorts to war against Russia, it will see that it is fought on European, not American, territory.

This economic and political development, which shows a close nesting between private business and state governance, is the most obvious sign of the mergence of what we can call the "corporate empire," a new form of political organization which mixes private and public interests, with people coming and going between the two spheres according to the circumstances and career opportunities, and increasingly divorced from specifically American national interests and that of the American people.

The US is no longer representative of a democracy or a true republic.

Serfdom? A Dubious Fate for Europe

Nothing new will happen for the European continent. The links between the two sides of the Atlantic Ocean are so closely interconnected, the military dependence vis à vis NATO, that the European elites are incapable of generating an independent foreign policy and create Europe's own path. But the many platforms of meetings and discussions where American and European elites have the opportunity to advocate on behalf of uniquely European interests, such as World Economic Forum, IMF, Bilderberg, Atlantic Council and so on, indicate that the European Union elites have not only no capacity but no desire to escape the US ascendancy.

Today, the European liberals and the populists, are so comfortably settled in their voluntary servitude and political insignificance that they have no desire to come out. They abjure the Julius Caesar syndrome ("I had rather be first in a village than second at Rome"), and seem to sweep away all hope of European regeneration. Is it too late? Has Europe really reached the terminal stage of the Greek degeneration syndrome under the rule of the emerging American corporate empire?

It seems Europe has not the will to struggle for another destiny. It may not even be aware that another is possible. But might the European peoples feel differently, as it is they who will bear the brunt, while the elites will enjoy the fruits? Might they pursue another option?

Let us outline one in the next chapter.

CHAPTER 9

THE SCENARIO OF INDEPENDENCE: A DEMOCRATIC RESET AND FULL SOVEREIGNTY

Even if I knew that tomorrow the world would go to pieces, I would still plant my apple tree.
MARTIN **LUTHER**

The days when we could totally rest on others are partially over. We Europeans have to take our destiny into our own hands once and for all.
ANGELA MERKEL[1]

Does Europe have a chance to escape American tutelage? Is it as relentless and irremediable as we presented it in the previous chapter? In other words: can Europe emancipate itself and regain its full sovereignty by becoming the free, independent and democratic power to which its ruling elites pretend to aspire?

All these questions can be answered in the affirmative, despite the circumstances and adverse developments we have described above. After all, the future is never written in advance and the unthinkable can always happen. History is not stingy with this kind of unforeseen reversals. Few, at the end of the last century, had anticipated such a rapid collapse of the Soviet Union or such a dramatic rise of China.

It is therefore not forbidden to think that this spineless and pusillanimous Europe, subservient to Atlantic interests that are

---

1 28 May 2017, at the G7 Summit in Taormina.

often not its own, can find the resources to rebuild itself and assert itself on the international scene.

Two Conditions for a European Recovery

This reset depends on two sets of factors, external as well as internal:

1) Europe's ability to fully apprehend the ramifications of the decline of American power and to mitigate American influence by other global engagements, and

2) Europe's ability to re-institutionalize itself to a democratic formation that would generate sufficient enthusiasm for the European project as to enable the European peoples to counter the narrow purviews of its elites in furtherance of true European freedom, interests, and wellbeing.

As long as American power was overall, hegemonic and undisputed, the revival and development of an independent Europe has been impossible. But this is no longer the case now that China has caught up with the United States economically and since the American international order is being challenged by new powers that proclaim a multipolar world in which they also intend to play their part. The growing tensions within the United States and its transformation into an authoritarian empire are a sign that their domination is no longer self-evident and that the use of coercion is becoming more and more necessary to preserve it.

The United States remains the world's leading global power but is now in an unfavorable competitive position against China, which is the rising power while the US is on a downward slope. Its absolute power continues to diminish. In 1960, the United States alone accounted for 40% of the world's gross domestic product. Today, that share has halved to less than 20%. However, as the British historian Paul Kennedy has very well analyzed, it is the evolution of the relative power of a country that must be taken into account in determining its possible trajectory and its ability to put pressure on subordinate allied states such as Europe and Japan.[2]

Paul Kennedy noted that the long-term power of a nation depends, first of all, on the size of its economy and its ability to finance its wars of conquest, to maintain its military spending and political alliances in peacetime, and to sustain long-term conflicts against rival powers. There is always a hiatus until economic power turns into political power. The United States had already achieved economic parity with Great Britain at the beginning of the 20th century, but it was necessary to reach the end of the 1940s and the victory of 1945 in order to be able to force the British empire to give it first place and succeed in imposing *pax americana* on the world at the expense of the *pax britannica*.

This shift means that the emerging power will likely have to wait decades before its economic power translates into political power. This is the case today for China, whose economy has just surpassed that of the United States in terms of purchasing power parity as we have seen, but whose political and military power, despite timid assertions that give rise to waves of criticism in the Western media, will take many years to be recognized and accepted.[3]

Relative Decline in the United States Opens Up New Opportunities

This relative decline in American power is masked by a redoubling of its military, diplomatic, economic and informational activism. Since nuclear weapons make it impossible to attack a

---

[2] Paul M. Kennedy, *The Rise and Fall of the Great Powers*, Random House, 1987.

[3] It should be noted here that China is showing great strategic prudence. Unlike William II's Imperial Germany, which was eager to see its economic power transformed into a political power on the world stage and recklessly rushed into the First World War, China is careful not to repeat the same mistake. While asserting itself militarily in its near historical space (Hong Kong, China Sea, Taiwan), it carefully avoids any direct external confrontation and shows great patience. It knows that time works for it and applies Sun-Tzu's principles: all China has to do is to excite her opponent and let it agitate in vain gesticulations until its time runs out.

competing nuclear power head-on, the battle for world domination takes many different forms and is played out on all terrains other than nuclear. So today we are witnessing a flood of so-called hybrid forms of warfare, including waves of propaganda and disinformation. The battle for control of the narrative has become a crucial issue, whether to retain it (United States), or to conquer or challenge US global leadership (China, Russia, Iran…).

This battle is fought on two fronts, defensive and offensive. First of all, each side must protect itself from the propaganda of the other and ensure the loyalty of its own citizens by controlling their access to information. This is what Shoshana Zuboff called surveillance capitalism, further highlighted by Julian Assange's revelations about the war crimes committed by the United States and those of Edward Snowden on the massive US espionage on its citizens—and even the phones of allied heads of state like Angela Merkel—by its intelligence agencies. It is a question of monitoring, controlling and guiding public opinion by preventing any alternative discourse from deploying freely. These surveillance operations have recently taken a totalitarian turn since they culminated in the censorship in January 2021 of a US president in charge, Donald Trump, whose accounts were deleted from social networks.

This violation of the First Amendment of the US Constitution is a historic, unprecedented attack on American freedom of expression, and therefore on attendant freedoms and democracy, by the very country that proclaims them upmost. Such restrictions on freedom are violently denounced by the mainstream media when they are attributed to China, whose dictatorship over its citizens as exemplified by its social credit policy the media relentlessly denounces while ignoring same when they are committed by so-called democratic governments.

On the offensive front, the US strategy consists in attacking its adversaries through massive disinformation campaigns aimed at discrediting them in their own public's opinion, as well as in Western public opinion. The means include the legitimization of aggressive postures, military spending, so-called humanitarian

The Scenario of Independence

interventions, unilateral economic sanctions, attempted putsches and regime changes. The US tends to exaggerate the threat of rival countries Russia, China, Iran, and to denounce—with often tampered "evidence"—their alleged human rights violations. Relentlessly, the "human rights violations" suffered by Hong Kong Democrats, the "genocide" of the Sinkiang Uighurs by the Chinese or the imprisonment of "opposition leader" Alexey Navalny in Russia occupy center stage in all news cycles.

Journalists, think tank experts, university professors, NGO leaders are mobilized tirelessly to denounce the crimes committed by the camp of Evil (while curiously silent when it comes to the crimes of their own camp...). Everything that justifies the costs of the struggle for global leadership (military spending, self-punitive economic sanctions) and the push to have them shared by the allies meets with their approval.

The Power of the American Narrative Is Losing Its Impact

But this massive propaganda spill is reaching its limits. It is less and less successful in hiding the vulnerabilities of American power and its increasing difficulty in imposing an order increasingly perceived as unfair and totalitarian, even though it has long been portrayed and even considered as liberating. Outside the Western world, the targeted states have put in place safeguards against Western cyberwarfare and disinformation and deployed their own news outlets such as Russia Today or CCTV to fight them in the West in turn. Throughout the West, doubts are growing about the merits of the official discourse disseminated by the elites and the mainstream media, as evidenced by the proliferation of movements such as the Yellow Jackets, the "conspiracists," the anti-vaccine skeptics, the QAnon movement and other separatisms.

The first doubts about American supremacy emerged after the September 11, 2001 attacks. This day can be seen as a major turning point in the perception of the decline of American hegemony by world public opinion. For the first time in its history, the United States was spectacularly struck at home by a team of terrorists who had come out of nowhere, without state support. This sudden vulnerability created a shock that the violence of the response (invasions of Afghanistan and Iraq) failed to erase. Other disturbing events came later, such as the storming of the Capitol on January 6, 2021 by a crowd of angry protesters. For a country that is the world's leading democracy and claims the right to impose its political model on other countries, these images have been calamitous and will be remembered despite the silence that surrounds them now—at least, in the media of other countries.

Similarly, we can mention the repeated lies that have been used to justify indefensible military interventions and wars of aggression. The 78-day bombing of Serbia and the deliberate attack on the Chinese embassy in Belgrade in 1999 by NATO forces led by Madeleine Albright and the Clinton Administration under the false pretext of preventing Kosovo from Serb massacres have not been forgotten by those who suffered them. The claims that Iraqi soldiers entered a Kuwaiti maternity hospital in 1990, throwing babies out of their incubators, was used to justify the Gulf War a few weeks later –also proved to be a crude lie. Similar lies followed concerning Saddam Hussein's so-called possession of weapons of mass destruction, which served as a pretext for the invasion of Iraq in 2003.

The invasion of Afghanistan in September 2001, despite the Taliban having agreed to extradite Osama bin Laden if given evidence of his involvement in the September 9/11 attacks, was similarly a sham. As for the destruction of Libya and the assassination of Muammar Gaddafi, the same logic of lies is obsessively pursued: Hillary Clinton and Barack Obama let NATO aircraft bomb Libya (even though the Security Council only allowed them to monitor the airspace) on the grounds that mass graves (which never existed) had been discovered and a column of tanks was ready to slaughter the civilian population (tanks that never existed, either). The intervention in Syria, a little later, followed the same false pattern to justify massive bombings against the Syrian legal government: the official propaganda poured out drops of false information about the rebels (presented as oppressed Syrians seeking democracy when they were in actuality fanatical groups such as Al Qaeda—earlier designated by the US as responsible for 9/11—whom the West was now supporting with weapons and intelligence) and purported chemical attacks whose provenance was disputed by OPCW whistleblowers.

These few examples show that all the wars that the Imperial Republic has waged in recent decades have been triggered on the basis of proven lies. Propagandists used to say that a thousand-times-repeated lie ends up enabling the purpose for which it was put forth. Perhaps they are right. But a regular multiplication of lies tends to erode the credibility of the one who propagates it.

The same applies to massive US interference in third-country elections. The hypocrisy of US accusations against Russia's meddling in the 2016 US elections in the face of repeated US interference in foreign democratic processes is evident to outsiders, even if remaining unexpressed in the media bullhorn, and therefore unconsidered by the great proportion of oblivious Americans. The Russian elections of 1996, as an instance, were distorted by the fraudulent support that the United States gave to Boris Yeltsin—and this was celebrated in *Time* magazine.[4] For good measure, keep in mind the coup in Ukraine in February 2014 to overthrow President Yanukovych, and the illegal seizure of power by the Bolivian right in 2019 following the electoral victory of Evo Morales in Bolivia.

The United States Knows How to Destroy, but Fails to Build Peace

These maneuvers, even if they are concealed by the mainstream Western media, seriously undermine the credibility of the United States as a democratic power and attached to human rights, both in the informed minorities of the Western world and outside the West.

---

4 Seth Connell, "Flashback: Time Magazine Brags About US Interfering in Russian Election," July 17, 2017. https://thefederalistpapers.org/us/time-magazine-interfered-russia.

Its inability to win peace also plays against the United States. While glorifying itself as having "won" the Cold War (according to George H. W. Bush) against a self-disbanding Soviet Union, America has never managed to win a war against determined adversaries. It has only managed to defeat weak adversaries (Grenada in 1983, Panama in 1989–1990), but proved unable to win difficult wars (the fiascos of Somalia, Lebanon, Afghanistan) let alone being able to win peace.

The United States has therefore provided proof that it knows how to destroy (Somalia, Iraq, Afghanistan, Libya, Syria) but that it could not build peace under any circumstances. Each military intervention has led to the lasting ruin of the countries concerned. As the Vietnam War had already shown,[5] the United States remained trapped in its Wild West mentality and the cowboys vs. Indians strategy. With its technical and tactical superiority, the US cavalry unleashes wars, shoots at everything that moves, massacres everyone, including women and children, and returns to its fort after setting fire to the enemy encampment. This pattern has not changed since the 19th century. Drone strikes and cruise missiles have simply replaced the Gatling machine gun.

Thus, after twenty years of war, Afghanistan will find itself in the same situation as it was in 2001, when it was ruled by the Taliban. By the end of 2019, spending on wars in Afghanistan, Iraq, Syria and Pakistan since 2001 had cost $6.4 trillion only to

---

5 By the end of the Vietnam War, Secretary of Defense Robert McNamara had already acknowledged that the United States had lost the war because it had failed to gain the trust of the Vietnamese people (nation-building). The United States is in fact a victim of its technological superiority. Its superiority helps US to win a war but prevents it from winning peace. In a foreign country, technical superiority quickly turns into arrogance. It traps the winner in his bubble and prevents him from understanding the reality of the field. The desire to impose democracy and human rights at all costs—if this is indeed the motive rather than the pretext—thus backfires on its promoters, who give the impression of overriding and denying national values and traditions. And the fact that the United States still installs representatives of the local oligarchy, a minority and already Americanized but often corrupt and hated by the people's base, still discredits them even more. In contrast, China does not seek to transform the countries with which it interacts. It adapts to their culture, religion, language, political system and works with democratic regimes as well as military dictatorships.

The Scenario of Independence

lead to a disastrous outcome.[6] Today, Syria is doomed to starve, as Iraq had been before it. Ditto for Venezuela and Cuba, victims of an unrelenting economic blockade. Libya is more than ever plagued by divisions, armed factional fighting, and state disintegration, just like Somalia has been since the 1993 intervention. In Georgia and Ukraine, support for anti-Russian regimes has not made significant improvements within that country, either in terms of democracy or economic development, despite the billions invested. Ukraine, plagued by corruption and poor governance, has become the poorest country in Europe since the Maidan revolution and its government is straining into an increasingly aggressive nationalism in the hope of retaining its remaining legitimacy.

These patent and persistent failures do not increase American power, either in the eyes of world public opinion or in the eyes of Europe.

There are many examples of actions and behaviors that increase allies' distrust of their great American protector and embolden its adversaries. President Obama's decision to make the major strategic pivot to Asia, amplified brutally by President Trump, also shocked Europeans. By focusing on China and appearing to abandon Europe, by increasing economic sanctions and customs retaliatory taxes not only against countries deemed hostile, such as Iran, Russia or China, but also against European companies, the United States has forced the Europeans to question the strength and viability of their American alliance. Confidence in NATO has collapsed as concerns have grown regarding the need to preserve the competitiveness of European economies in the face of customs taxes, economic sanctions and competition from digital giants, arms manufacturers, and the risks that now weigh on their energy supply.

In the area of defense, the decision of the United States not to renew the Intermediate-Range Nuclear Weapons Limitation Treaty (INF) with Russia and to install nuclear missiles in Poland and Romania is also likely to worry Europe. We remember that

---

6 Amanda M. Macias, "America has spent 6.4 trillion on wars in the Middle East and Asia since 2001, a new study says," *CNBC,* November 20, 2019.

in the 1980s, European citizens protested massively against the installation of American Pershing rockets in Germany, knowing that in the event of a nuclear conflict with Russia, they would have been the first to find themselves obliterated.

All these factors make Europeans more circumspect. To reassure them, the declaration of the new Biden Administration during the first months of its entry into office of its unconditional support given to Ukraine in its tussle against Russia will hardly reassure them. Europeans will continue to monitor US sanctions…while continuing to trade with Russia and China.

In Europe, the United States Is Content to Replay the Cold War

In Europe, beyond the usual protestations of friendship, the dominant impression is that the United States seeks to isolate China by simply replaying the Cold War to bring down the current Russian power as it had succeeded in bringing down Soviet power in 1990s. The fall of Ukraine into the American orbit in 2014 seemed to enshrine the success of this strategy inspired by Zbigniew Brzezinski and his neoconservative followers. You can see the maneuver. As evidenced by a recent Rand Corporation report, the goal is to push Russia into a military and strategic overextension too costly for it to sustain, in order to unbalance the current Russian government, which is seen as too focused on defending its national interests in Washington's eyes.[7] The denunciation of the INF Treaty and other military treaties was intended to revive the war of arms that had been fatal to the Soviet Union during the Ronald Reagan era.

Except that in the meantime, the Russians, and their Chinese allies, have learned the lesson of the Soviet failure. They do not intend to be ensnared in the same trap. On the contrary, they seek to turn it against its author. This is why Russia avoids debt and builds gold and foreign exchange reserves that put it beyond the reach of Western attempts at blockade and blackmail while

---

7 Rand Corporation, *Overextending and Unbalancing Russia. Assessing the Impact of Cost-Imposing Options*, Washington, 2019.

The Scenario of Independence

using US sanctions to strengthen its image with its own public opinion, adopting countersanctions against the United States and the European Union for developing new sectors of its economy. China does likewise.[8] They even reap some advantages from this economic attack, as it allows them to improve their own agricultural, industrial and military productivity. In 2016, for example, Russia overtook the United States as the world's largest wheat producer.

In general, the Russians and Chinese are seeking to break the economic and military blockade that the United States seeks to impose on them by locking down the *Rimland*, the maritime and coastal area that stretches from Scandinavia to Southeast Asia through the Middle East and through which the bulk of world merchandise trade and energy trade passes.[9]

Their strategy is to open loopholes in this blockade in order to render it inoperative. It was to break this encirclement that the Russians retaliated against Georgia's attack on South Ossetia in 2008 and intervened in Syria in 2015. For them, it was to protect the Caucasus from NATO presence and Western-backed and armed jihadist movements through the Gulf monarchies.

Ukraine's fall into the US orbit in 2014 was a major setback for Russia at a time when its Syrian ally was under siege by armed Islamist rebels financed and under the control of the West. By restoring the Syrian government sovereignty and consolidating

---

[8] In recent decades, economic sanctions have never succeeded in inducing the citizens to overthrow a government. Neither in Cuba, Venezuela, Russia, Iran or China. Even in Saddam Hussein's Iraq, the government collapsed because of the US military invasion but not because of the hard regime of sanctions.

[9] The Rimland theory, adopted by neoconservative thinkers, was first elaborated by British geopolitician Halford John MacKinder (https://www.thoughtco.com/what-is-mackinders-heartland-theory-4068393) and then developed by the US professor and thinker Nicholas Spykman in 1942 (*America's Strategy in World Politics. The United States and the Balance of Power*). It argues that the objective of a maritime power such as the United States is to control the maritime fringe that controls Heartland, the part of Eurasia that forms the demographic and economic center of gravity of the planet. The theory is summed up by the formula "Who controls the Rimland controls the Heartland, who controls the Heartland controls the World."

its military presence in the heart of the Middle Eastern rimland, Russia succeeded in breaking one link in the chain of American blockade that the United States had just completed, thanks to the Maidan "revolution." By establishing an unlikely but effective collaboration with Turkey, a NATO member, (construction of the Turkish Stream pipeline to bypass the US blockade against South Stream, sale of the S-400 anti-missile system, construction of a nuclear power plant in Turkey), Russia has even managed to widen this gap, bypassing the Ukrainian and Bulgarian blockage while securing a Caucasus still very unstable and permeable to Islamist activism funded by Qatar and Saudi Arabia.

Similarly, the recent resurgence of tension between China and India in the Himalayas reflects the Chinese endeavor to open up the Rimland via Pakistan. China wishes to build direct land transit routes over to the Indian Ocean without passing through the hostile Strait of Malacca heavily guarded by the US Navy. Pharaonic investments in motorways, railways and ports are planned.

In early 2021, the fight turned to Myanmar, which is at the heart of another tussle with the West, which has focused on the situation of the Rohingya Islamic minority and, since the February 2021 military coup, once again supported former Prime Minister Aung San Suu Kyi against a military power that the Chinese are forced to support, even unwillingly. Indeed, China must at all costs keep open this third breach in the South Asian rimland space.

Notably, the resurgence of Chinese efforts to counter Western-supported and promoted protests in Hong Kong and Sinkiang (the repression of democracy advocates and the genocide of the Uyghurs dominating Western news feeds)—and thereby counter the West—indicates a new Chinese willingness to oppose Western aims that seek to sabotage the legitimacy of the Chinese government in its own territories. For China, the question of Hong Kong and Uyghur separatism is vital. It is not negotiable.

Since the early 2000s the wars that ravaged the entire Middle East from Pakistan to Libya through Georgia and Ukraine bear witness to a remake of the "Great Game" that the British Empire

The Scenario of Independence

had conducted in the 19th century against Russia in order to secure the road to and control of India and to subjugate China.

The New Silk Roads Are a Game Changer

Nonetheless, despite appearances, the United States today finds itself in a much less favorable position than did the British in the 1830s–1840s. Firstly because, as we have seen, they are no longer an emerging power (unlike the British Empire in the 19th century) but a declining power. It is China that is in the position of the rising power. If faced with any military attack, China, like Russia for that matter, also has the advantage of confronting it from its own territory, unlike the United States, which has to fight fifteen or twenty thousand miles away from home. Despite their present technological, military and financial superiority, there will come a time when US military posturing shall become too costly and lead to financial and social difficulties at the very heart of the American empire, as we have seen already expressed in the wrath of those who voted for Donald Trump in 2016.[10]

The steady growth of the US military budget and the continued expansion of the number of its military bases abroad suggests that the risk of overextension and the costs of power projection now threaten the United States more than Russia or China. To be effective, Russia only needs to mass a few troops at its borders (as in the spring of 2021 near the Donbass border) while the United States must undertake costly troop movements to defend its interests in Ukraine. Similarly, Russia only needs to spend a few billion dollars to produce new deterrent weapons, such as hypersonic missiles, while the United States must invest thousands of billions of dollars to maintain its long-range military projection capability. The development of its latest aircraft, the F-35, alone cost more than a trillion dollars for a mixed result.

---

10 It's interesting to notice that the Pentagon is starting to be aware of this. A recent Pentagon wargame opposing Red Chinese forces to Blue American has shown that the US loses in every case because of an overextension and dispersion of forces : https://news.yahoo.com/were-going-to-lose-fast-us-air-force-held-a-war-game-that-started-with-a-chinese-biological-attack-170003936.html

It is on the economic front that the future will indeed play out. And in that respect, China does not necessarily lose. Launched in 2013, the Belt and Road initiative has already proven its practical effectiveness. While shipping routes remain subject to US Navy pressure and incidents such as the grounding of a container ship in the Suez Canal, the establishment of land routes across the Eurasian continent has already begun widely. China has been investing tens of billions a year since 2015 leading to an increase in transcontinental rail traffic of almost 100% yearly between 2017 and 2020. Thousands of freight trains are now crisscrossing Central Asia to Europe, while Russia is seeking to take advantage of climate change to open a new sea route in the Arctic.

These new channels of communication already have a huge impact on Europe. Although it is wary of China and tries to limit Chinese investment in its territory, Europe will find it difficult to resist. The attractiveness of Chinese markets is as vital to its companies as the European market is to Chinese businesses. Singaporean economist and geopolitician Kishore Mahubani, for example, believes that the United States is seriously underestimating China. Always the same superiority complex! Ten years from now, the Chinese market will be much larger than the US market, he says.[11]

Political preferences (or mistrusts) will not weigh heavily in the balance. The same goes for energy: despite intense US pressure to reverse the construction of the Nordstream II gas pipeline between Germany and Russia, it will be completed simply because Germany cannot do without it if it wants to maintain the competitiveness of its industry until the end of its energy transition.

---

11 Like Nobel prize winner Joseph Stiglitz and American columnist Martin Wolf, Mahubahni also believes that the United States is emerging from democracy to enter an unequal and authoritarian plutocratic regime, while China has succeeded in transforming its single party, the Communist Party, into a meritocracy capable of attracting and selecting the country's brightest minds. Its successful handling of the Covid-19 crisis, as Europe and the United States plunged into chaos, further exacerbated the gap between the West and China. See Kishore Mahubani, *Has China Won? The Chinese Challenge to American Primacy*, PublicAffairs, 2020.

The Scenario of Independence

If German companies were to buy more American liquefied gas, via longer and less secure routes than the pipeline with Russia, German industry and European competitiveness would be over. This, the Germans, have understood perfectly even if they are subservient to the United States and insensitive to China's political attractions. That is why, while maintaining aggressive rhetoric against Russia about the Donbass and the Skripal and Navalny affairs, they waiver when it comes to sacrificing their economy on the altar of transatlantic friendship.

China's Rise to Power Opens Up Opportunities for Europe

As we can see, the situation is changing in Europe. By its mass alone, China is shaking up Europe and slowly drawing it away from American influence, just as a planet attracts a satellite, however distant it may be. The rise of China opens up a new space for Europeans to maneuver. For the time being, the Cold War generation is still in power in Europe and anti-Russian revanchism is still very powerful while mistrust of China remains strong. But once the new generation, which has not experienced the Cold War, comes to power and realizes that these past resentments are not theirs and stand in the way of Europe's economic and political emancipation, everything can change quickly. There is a good chance that bids in the United States will become less attractive.

Notably, a taboo was broken in the spring of 2021 with the decision of several Eastern European countries formerly occupied by the Soviet Union to buy the Russian vaccine Sputnik V to fight the pandemic. For the first time since 1991, Hungary, Slovakia, the Czech Republic, Austria and even Bavaria turned their backs on Brussels and solicited Russia. France, Poland and the Baltic countries are doing all they can to prevent the recognition of the Russian vaccine by the European Medicines Agency. But whatever the final answer, a loophole has been opened. The possibility of establishing pragmatic cooperation with Russia is no longer taboo in Europe. Such a decision was unimaginable a year earlier.

The same pragmatism prompted Greece to sell the port of Athens to China and Hungary to reach an agreement with China to build Europe's largest Chinese campus in partnership with Shanghai's Fudan University, a $1.4 billion project. This is yet another sign that some Europeans have now understood that they can increase their flexibility without risk and that Europe's natural vocation would be to serve as a bridge—or as an arbiter—between the United States and the Russian-Chinese Eurasian bloc.

How Switzerland Could Inspire Europe

How to get rid of a friend who is too cumbersome? This is where the Swiss experience becomes interesting. We saw how, after Napoleon's defeat, the enlightened fringe of the Swiss elite had taken advantage of the circumstances to embark on a major national construction project. This project was to focus on the people and democracy rather than on the aristocracy and the oligarchy, which are self-interested, unpatriotic and fickle social classes. The Swiss elites agreed to cede power and wealth rather than concentrate them in their hands with the help of an external power. Nothing prevents Europe from doing the same today, using China's rise as a lever to peacefully counterbalance the weight of the United States and increase its strategic autonomy.

Two hundred years ago, when it faced the same kind of difficulties as today's Europe is facing with regard to the United States, China, Russia and the global challenges of climate change and the energy transition, tiny Switzerland managed to break away from the tutelage and interference of the great empires that surrounded it—France, Austria-Hungary and the German empire. With the support of Britain and Russia in 1815, it was able to create its own democratic and independent path and modernize a rural economy facing the challenges of industrialization. It was able to do so by playing on the rivalry of the three superpowers, each of which wanted to subjugate it. Switzerland took advantage of this rivalry to develop the democratic institutions that enabled it, in return, through popular votes, to consolidate its independence. As it concerns Europe today, the proportions differ, insofar as world affairs

The Scenario of Independence

are global and the size of the protagonists is much larger. But the conditions for developing this third pathway are the same.[12]

It will be objected that it is difficult for Europe to go against the tide and to bet on democracy when China has opted for an authoritarian regime based on an all-powerful state and a single party and the United States itself is undergoing an increasingly marked oligarchic and authoritarian transformation. But Swiss history shows that this context does not prevent a third country from making a democratic choice. Between 1815 and 1874, Switzerland made this choice when all the great powers surrounding it were monarchical or despotic. Despite their reluctance, neither monarchical France, imperial and reactionary Austria-Hungary, nor Despotic Russia and Prussia could prevent it.

In fact, the circumstances enabling such an action are even more favorable today than they were at the time for Switzerland. Since the United States continues to preach the democratic crusade and the defense of freedom and human rights, Europeans need only to take it at its word: building a democratic and sovereign independent European federal state would be an unimpeachable project, perfectly in tune with the official ideology of the West, constantly invoked but never applied.

Finally, it can be pointed out that Europe will soon be bordered by a third major emerging power: Africa. Africa has been growing in population for a few decades and its demography will be four to five times larger than that of Europe by the end of this century. The economy of several African countries is

---

[12] We are talking here about the creation of modern Switzerland in the 19th century, when it was largely subject to the domination of France (under the monarchy and during the time of Napoleon in particular) and Austria-Hungary (between 1815 and 1848). Contemporary Switzerland has largely compromised its independence and neutrality by seeking to bring itself closer to the European Union economically and to NATO at all costs in terms of defense and intelligence. Only its institutions of direct democracy have been preserved. It is thanks to popular pressure that the Swiss ruling elites have had to limit their globalist ambitions because the Swiss people still care about their political, economic and military independence. But attempts are regularly being made to limit or circumvent these rights (such as the Partnership for Peace with NATO that allows the Swiss Air Force to train in NATO member Norway without a popular mandate).

taking off. Although totally underestimated, this continent will be increasingly important in the decades to come. For Europe, Africa is both a threat because of the difference in living standards that generates unwanted migration flows and an opportunity by offering new markets, resources and productivity reservoirs close to home—thus helping to further expand Europe's strategic room and its freedom of political action by allowing it to escape the Sino-Russian-American antagonism.

Let us examine, through the Swiss example, how such a program could be carried out in Europe and what are the internal conditions for implementing it.

Seen from Brussels, Washington or Beijing, the Swiss "model" can make you smile. How could the tiny and insignificant Switzerland serve as an example to the great Europe? How could 8 million Swiss people inspire 500 million Europeans with their political system, which is so complicated and expensive? The answer will be that it is not a matter of comparing and copying and pasting Swiss institutions to create the future European federal state. It has to be considered as a case study and a method of work for defining principles of action.[13]

It is not to overestimate the importance of Switzerland to say that, despite all its defects, it has been able to establish an original, genuinely democratic and pretty effective federal system for resolving internal conflicts, whether religious, ethnic, cultural or social. This system is based on three pillars:

- a method of federal organization in which each state (canton) is equal to the others regardless of its size and population;
- a collegial government in which the main political sensitivities are represented and are obliged to cooperate; and
- a method of conflict resolution based on popular rights of initiative and referendum. Any minority can at any time

---

[13] We're not going to deny that size matters. But it plays only a marginal role. Let us also not forget that, in the world of tomorrow, faced with an Asia of five billion inhabitants and an Africa with two or three billion inhabitants, Europe will soon appear as numerically insignificant as did Switzerland compared to it, two centuries ago.

question a majority decision through a referendum or may propose a law through a popular initiative. These proposals rarely succeed in obtaining a popular majority, but, thanks to the national debate they provoke, they often manage to make changes to the legislation in their favor.

It is the invention and implementation of this system that needs to be examined in more detail, in order to understand how Europe could be built as an independent, sovereign and functional democratic federation. Europe, as we saw in the second part of this book, is already used to bargain and negotiate compromises. Thanks to this achievement and the new geopolitical context, it is no longer impossible for it to transform itself into a democratic, independent and sovereign federal state.

To Trust or Not to Trust the People, This Is the True Question

This leads to the question of whether or not the people can be trusted. Are the people capable of discernment? Do they have the capacity to recognize what is at stake? These are the big questions. Of course, the people can make mistakes and fall under the spell of the populist sirens. The newspapers are full of self-proclaimed experts who, behind the mask of false arguments concerning human rights, the efficacy of the market economy, the dangers of public deficits, etc., warn that one has to beware of the people in the name of their higher interest and to protect them from themselves, when actually, these experts are only out to defend their own interests, seen of those of respective elites. But this is all part of the typical democratic debate, with its false pretenses and misleading arguments permitting the emergence of countervailing truths.

Indeed, experience shows that in a federal system consolidated by instruments of direct democracy such as referenda and the right of initiative, the people are seldom wrong, and generally speaking, less often than are the elites. The people understand what is at stake perfectly well, even if the governing elites are not always pleased with the directions they attempt to pursue. In the people's debates, the general interest is preserved, and the notion of the common good is constantly considered, even on matters that are as anecdotal as letting the cows keep their horns, a current Swiss issue. This political jewel lies at the heart of political life without any party or social class being able to corner it.

In the long run, if mistakes are made, they self-correct. The Swiss abolished the death penalty, gave women the right to vote, joined the UN, invented humanitarian law and are as "progressive" as the other nations (or even more with regard to democratic rights, for instance), although it may sometimes take a long time for them to reach the desired goal.[14]

The great advantage of this perhaps complex system is that once the laws are adopted, they are durable because the people have endorsed them, either tacitly or by referendum. Progress is made slowly but surely, and there are no locks or blocks that a slow abrasive process or political digestion could break. Trust is a shared, two-way process: it is easier to trust someone who trusts you back.

But before looking more closely into how the system works, let us see how and why the Swiss system emerged and took the form that it did. This will give us a few hints on the genesis of the federal system and the basic guidelines to achieve it within a conglomerate of states that, as opposed to the United States, has been multilingual, multi-confessional, and multicultural for generations.

Contrary to common perception, the history of the construction of Swiss federalism was a turbulent process. While it was long in the making, it was marred by sometimes-bloody conflicts, often-fierce political struggles, experimentation and failures. It

---

14 The case of the universal basic income or the age of retirement are good examples of this way of doing. The problem of age of retirement and public pension fund is regularly submitted to popular votes until a solution will find a narrow margin of voters. The case of the universal basic income is still in discussion. A first initiative has been rejected by a popular vote in 2016. But a second initiative will be launched in 2021 in order to gather the 100,000 signatures necessary for a second popular vote…

The Scenario of Independence

also resulted from outside pressure. In this respect, it is no different from the European unification process, which was the fruit of two fratricidal world wars and arose from the determination of the powerful victors, the United States and the Soviet Union, to impose the unification of the continent in their own interests after their victory in 1945.

Nothing could be farther from the truth than to believe that all of this happened with gladness and joy. Each step was marked by sharp tensions and fierce struggles between the federalists and the anti-federalists on the one hand, and the conservatives and the liberals, or progressive radicals, on the other.[15] Like in the United States at the end of the 18th century and Europe today, the fronts were divided between the advocates of free-trade industrial development, the defenders of the traditional economy and tax barriers, the patricians and conservatives who were opposed to increased democratic rights, the radical modernizers, the socialists and the enlightened bourgeois with them, the Catholic defenders of the Church and the clergy, and the uncompromising anti-clericals who staunchly upheld the *Kulturkampf* and secularism.

The Security Dimension and The Role of the Army

During the Restoration and Regeneration period, Switzerland also had to shed the weighty tutelage of Metternich's Austria that had followed up the French protectorate by constantly meddling in internal and external affairs. Again in 1848 and the years

---

15 It is important to note that in Swiss terminology, the federalists were those who supported sovereignty at the cantonal level (today's "populists"), while the centralists, who advocated a stronger and more centralized federal state were in the "anti-federalist" camp. The opposite is true in the American tradition (the Federalists of the *Federalist Papers* of 1787 defended the Federal Constitution, in other words, strong federalism), and in European practice, where the federalists also advocate a strong and centralized union. Another confusion factor is the term "Swiss Confederation," adopted in 1815. It can be misleading because Switzerland is indeed a federation and not a confederation. This semantic confusion, which was not totally involuntary, reflects the heated debates that took place on the subject. Another example is that of Augustus, who, to keep up the appearances of the Roman Republic, had taken care to maintain all the institutions and passed himself off merely as a modest servant of the Senate and the Roman people and not as an all-powerful *imperator*.

that followed, Switzerland found itself isolated in a Europe that had once again become ultra-reactionary after the failure of the European spring of that epoch. The construction of federalism therefore went hand in hand with recovering full and complete sovereignty. One could not be done without the other.

This parallelism was evident for Alexis de Tocqueville. A shrewd observer of democracy, he believed that the questions of security and sovereignty—the primary symbols of which are defense and the army—are closely connected. Article 8 of the Federal Pact of 1815 stipulated that the Diet was to take all the measures necessary for the internal and external security of Switzerland. "This allows it to do everything," Tocqueville noted, adding that, "the strongest of the federal governments did not have any greater prerogatives."[16]

The question of forming the federal army that was to replace the cantonal contingents (budget, command, armament, uniforms, training) gave rise to fifty years of epic discussions and strongly recalls the debates on the EDC in 1954 or on the European army today, where the camps are divided according to the allegiances of some to foreign powers or the attachment of others to the cantonal traditions.

This gestation period in which restoration gradually gave way to regeneration and the oligarchy gave way to democracy is important, for it calls to mind Europe's unification phase from the 1950s until today. In Switzerland there was also a "functionalist" method based on the progress made in unifying various sectors, such as the postal service, weights and measures, currency, and customs fees, and an intergovernmental method based on the concordats drawn up between the cantons.

How Switzerland Addressed the Threat of Separatism

There were also several attempts at secession (Glaris and Schwytz, the separation of Upper and Lower Valais in 1839, the

---

[16] Georges Andrey, "La quête d'un État national 1798–1848" (The Quest for a National State 1798–1848), in *Nouvelle histoire de la Suisse et des Suisses*, vol. II, 1983.

The Scenario of Independence

subordination of the principality/canton of Neuchâtel to the King of Prussia in 1850), just as in Catalonia, Flanders and Northern Italy today, or the successful Czech Republic and Slovakia in 1992. The threat of separatism is permanent if the democratic federal institutions are not well working, as it was the case in the former Habsburg Empire or as it is the case in the Spain/Catalonia nowadays.

What made the difference in Switzerland is that a political party and the social basis behind the movement for a strong federation ended up winning, thanks to patience and appropriate democratic process. A strong will of negotiation, and a spirit of compromise as well as a renunciation of the axiom, "The winner takes all" are required. It's essential that the ethnic or cultural majority keeps those principles in mind and is convinced that an ethnic or a cultural minority is equal in rights, whatever could be the differences in terms of numbers, as in a federal state: tiny Rhode Island has the same rights as California, even if they have not the same economic and demographic weight. In Switzerland, the tiny Romantsch community (100,000 people) or the Italian community (450,000 people) are equal in rights with the 6 million German community.

This party and this basis had been created little by little, first in the cantons then at the "supra-cantonal" level and were anchored in the trust that democracy would prosper rather than mistrusting it and ruling it out. There were setbacks and regressions. Some cantons took advantage of the instruments of direct democracy to briefly restore the death penalty. Others, like Zurich, Lucerne and Valais, temporarily set up ultra-conservative, authoritarian regimes. But isn't this the case in some Eastern countries today? Despite these disturbances, the ship sailed onward and finally reached its destination safe and sound thanks to, and not against, the energy of its citizens who were increasingly won over to the idea.[17] In other words, appetite comes with eating. As for democracy, if you don't use it, you lose it, as the saying goes.

---

17 This should reassure the technocrats and intellectuals who distrust the people and wonder what would happen if passengers were asked to vote on who

After federalism was established in 1848, direct democracy was not actually set up overnight, either. First, veto rights were introduced whereby only the opponents of a bill had a voice. In relation to the number of registered voters, this amounted to counting the abstainers as acceptors in the name of the principle that "silence is consent," an unquestionable means of validating the bill if the question was turned around so as to prompt an "aye." It is only gradually that for initiative and referendum the number of ayes and nays were counted to determine the result.

Lastly, a vast, painstaking internal reconstruction was necessary. Prior to the French Revolution, the Swiss Confederation was composed of thirteen States reigning over vassal territories (for example, Berne, the most powerful canton, dominated what was to become the sovereign canton of Vaud in 1803) or maintaining alliances (Berne was allied to Geneva, an independent republic). Other territories were still common bailiwicks co-managed by certain Member States (in Aargau and Ticino). The French regime put an end to these disparities and thereby favored the expansion of federalism that implied equality between the Member States.

This meant making painful sacrifices for the most powerful cantons (Berne, Zurich, Fribourg). They had to accept losing not only vast territories but also major privileges. Regarding international diplomacy, for instance, they were no longer able to negotiate directly with foreign sovereigns, especially not with the almighty King of France, who had an opulent embassy in Solothurn.

Obviously, if modern Europe is to adopt federalism, that would mean that the larger States, Germany and France, would have to accept sharing part of their influence and their advantages with the smaller States. This would only be temporary, for history

---

should pilot a sinking plane. Besides the fact that the premises of the problem are false (exercising democracy does not mean voting on operational or technical problems: one does not vote to designate the winner of a marathon, for instance), direct democracy always pays off in the long run. Despite some local regressions, the death penalty was democratically abolished in Switzerland a century before it was abolished in France. We do have to admit, however, that accepting women's suffrage was another, more tedious story.

The Scenario of Independence

has shown that if unity is strength, they would soon benefit from the new dynamic to maintain their relative prominence, as the case of Zurich illustrates so well. This is less true for Berne, for after having gotten its grasp on French-speaking Jura to compensate for having lost Vaud, it was compelled to give it back its independence in 1979 after 164 years of "occupation."

Between 1830 and 1848, Switzerland went through a period of continued democratic fermentation that prompted Tocqueville to remark, "The country has been in revolution for the past fifteen years!" This was true to the extent that tensions, as we have said, gave way to a brief civil war in 1847. The bubbling cauldron almost burst, but the heat quickly abated through the wise, revenge-free management of the crisis. The losers were forced to admit defeat, but no unbearable diktat was imposed on them: they continued to dispose of the same rights and duties as the victorious cantons within the new federation.

This was the crucible that over three generations gave birth to Switzerland, as we know it today. From this standpoint, federalism and semi-direct democracy are only 150 years old, or half a century younger than the American federal Constitution. But contrary to the US, its practice as a confederation has been much older. It started at the end of the 13th Century thanks to a tradition of popular and democratic assemblies. This form of state has been celebrated by numerous Enlightenment writers such as Jean-Jacques Rousseau, "citizen of Geneva Republic," and has also influenced the political thinkers and European and American democrats of that time.[18]

This represents a duration rarely equaled by another country and confirms the fact that its results are largely positive: the system survived all the social and political crises, two world wars and the wars between their neighbors (France-Prussia and Italy-Austria in the 1860s–1870s), and even came out stronger over time. This means that the Swiss system provides for the satisfactory

---

18 The story of William Tell, the swiss hero of independence and liberty, has been celebrated in the US at the end of the XVIIIth Century. Dramatic performances such as *Helvetic Liberty* and even a musical like *The Archers or Mountaineers of Switzerland* have been played in New York in 1796.

regulation of the relations between the citizens and the state on the one hand, and the federal and state/canton members on the other. We can point out that in France and Spain—to mention only these two countries—these matters were far from being solved in 2019. France still has great difficulty in handling its state-citizens relations as does Spain in managing its provinces, while the European Union has still not succeeded in determining its form of governance and the extent of its central authority.

A Brief Lesson in Federalism

Without writing a treatise on constitutional law, it is worth going through the basic principles of federalism and direct democracy for the readers who may not be particularly familiar with these terms.

According to Montesquieu, federalism completes the horizontal separation of powers by a vertical one. The object is to avoid concentrating all of the power into a single instance (presidency or parliament in a parliamentary regime). This moderates state power and lightens the tasks entrusted to the state. In Switzerland, federalism serves above all to guarantee the independence of the cantons vis-à-vis the Confederation. Like in the US, the Swiss states/cantons are very touchy about their rights and try to keep the balance with a federal state which tries to erode them.

The power of the Swiss federal state is limited by two major principles, known as subsidiarity (a principle anchored in Article 5a of the Federal Constitution) and proportionality.

The principle of subsidiarity requires entrusting the *lower* political levels with all the tasks that they can be able to perform. The higher authority should intervene only when the lower authorities are unable to tackle the issue in question. This means that in practice, the communal and cantonal levels (which would correspond to the nations in today's Europe) are endowed with much more power and competencies than those of a unitary, centralized state like France, for instance.

This principle is enhanced by the principle of proportionality that defines three conditions for the proper execution of state

The Scenario of Independence

measures: convenience (the means must be compatible with the nature of the goal); necessity (the means must be necessary, i.e., as lenient or as advantageous as possible); acceptability (to be legitimate, the intensity of the means must be adapted to the goal).

In virtue of these principles, only the problems that exceed the capacities of the smallest entities may be entrusted to a higher level. Thus we go from the individual to the family, to the commune, to the canton, and to the federal state, that can intervene only as a last resort.

The 26 cantons are sovereign in all the domains that are not limited by the Federal Constitution. As each has its own constitution, they are free to organize themselves as they see fit, on the legislative, judiciary and fiscal, and administrative levels. However, they cannot adopt a type of constitution that does not comply with the rules of democracy. In other words, the people must accept the constitution, and it must be amendable upon request by the canton's electoral body.

A given number of domains are thus managed only at the cantonal level, such as education (except the three federal universities), hospitals (except the communal and private hospitals), roadbuilding and maintenance of the major roads (except the highways and national roads), and the police (the army is federal). They also have control of direct taxation. Each canton has its own parliament (called *Great Council* in most of the French-speaking cantons) and government (called *State Council* in most of the French-speaking cantons) and their own courts.

The cantons themselves are subdivided into 2,551 communes that are more or less autonomous according to the different cantonal constitutions. They represent the smallest political entity in the country. Some cantons have an intermediary subdivision called district or borough that usually plays only an administrative role with no proper autonomy.

Direct democracy, as opposed to representative democracy, allows the people to exercise their political power directly. Swiss democracy combines both in what is called semi-direct democracy: the citizens elect their representatives to the various councils (communal, cantonal and Confederate) but also have their say in approving legislative or constitutional texts decided on by the councils (through referendum) or proposing constitutional or legal amendments through popular initiative. These popular consultations are generally organized four times a year at the federal level, always over the weekend. The Swiss population has always shown high satisfaction (around 80%) with this political system that allows the citizens to counterbalance and impact the executive and the political parties.

It does, however, somewhat slow down the process of political reforms, especially because any organization that disagrees with a bill can brandish the threat of referendum. In practice, the system therefore obliges the executives to widely consult the parties and the various intermediary bodies in order to reach a consensus before launching major legislative upheavals. Negotiations are ongoing. Direct democracy influences the Swiss political system as a whole, impelling the authorities to seek compromises early in the decision-making process to avoid a referendum that would attack the law. This style of national policy is known as "the concordance system." It is characterized by a proportional number of state organs, political forces integration, conflict rejection, and solutions that are negotiated rather than imposed by decree. Political scientists generally attribute it to the impact of referenda and popular initiative, integral bicameralism, federalism, and the electoral system that compels the political actors to minimize the risk of their projects failing before the people. Some also add the cultural differences that call for the widest possible minority representation.

Government homogeneity is guaranteed by the way the federal councilors are elected. They cannot lean exclusively on their party's votes and must therefore distance themselves from it in the hopes of bringing together majorities for their projects. No single party can impose its views or its candidates and therefore has to deal with the others in order to weigh in on the political game. Thus this is very far-removed from the American spoil system

The Scenario of Independence

whereby "the winner takes it all" and much closer to the European tradition of consultation.

Concordance and Coalitions at Every Level

In default of a true, common political program, the "guidelines" serve to replace it for the electoral period of a given legislature. This is one of the peculiarities of the Swiss system: the notion of majority and opposition or of power coalition after the elections does not exist. Majority and opposition take form topic-by-topic or even article-by-article at both the executive (Federal Council) and legislative levels. This point is essential for the proper functioning of the referendum system: the project contested is never that of a party or a governmental line, but of the parliament. In contrast with other countries, the referendum is therefore never an issue of staying in power or leaving it. An important point for the French, who are very mistrustful of this institution, is that a popular referendum as the Swiss practice it is never a plebiscite for or against the government.

Let us specify a few more points concerning direct democracy. If it is to function, the right to initiative and referenda must be effective and not simply declaratory like it is in France today, where it has existed since Nicolas Sarkozy was in office but is impracticable because of too many restrictions. In Switzerland, the number of signatures to be collected must not exceed a given percentage of the electorate (100,000 for initiatives and 50,000 for referenda for 5.3 million registered voters). The referendum's political commune is responsible for verifying the authenticity of each and every one of the signatories.

A popular initiative is a stronger political act (it implies modifying the cantonal or Confederate Constitution) and its scope is greater, especially if it is successful (which is rarely the case). But even when it fails and whatever its purpose, it has considerable symbolic scope either because it can be pointed to as having been rejected by the people or because there was a counterproposal to oppose it. We should point out for the record that since popular initiatives came into force in 1891, 215 have been put to the vote, of which only 22 have been successful. That comes to fewer than two votations (Swiss term for the voting process) per year for only one accepted every six years—which is far from an overdose! As for the federal referenda, there were 562 between 1848 and 2010, or an average of 3.4 votations per year. In all, the Swiss have been called upon to vote at the federal level 309 times in 162 years.

In their debates over the citizens' initiative referendum (CIR), the arrogant French intellectuals traditionally make fun of the Swiss system. According to them, it flatters the popular passions and can at times mobilize the citizens and the state around ridiculous issues.

In looking closely, however, we can see that this is absolutely untrue. What seem to be minor matters (like the 80km/hour speed limit on the national roads in France or the questions of cows' horns and the width of trucks in Switzerland) often hide major political issues. The votation on the protection of cows' horns, launched by a single, isolated peasant from the Bernese Jura (which goes to show what just one citizen can accomplish!) had everyone laughing for miles around. But it took a concern that was highly progressive and innovating, including for city dwellers, to the political level, foregrounding animal dignity and the treatment of domestic and wild animals in a world where they exist practically only in terms of meat for the industrial slaughterhouses.

As to the width of trucks, it revealed the people's apprehension of heavy truck invasion, highway concreting and the outrageous expense for that to be borne by the taxpayers, as well as the dismantling of the public rail service. This message was confirmed a few years later when surprisingly, another popular initiative that drastically limited the transport of private merchandise across the Alps was accepted.

The establishment of direct democracy presupposes that it be practiced on a regular basis: if referenda are only occasional, then indeed that mechanism runs the risk of shifting into a permanent political clash and not in actuality producing a system of direct democracy. In Switzerland, there are popular consultations three or four times a year on miscellaneous topics, such as professional taxes, prohibition of the burqa, age of retirement, electronic ID, free trade agreements and so on. Votes are linked with local consultations or elections in order to be more rationale and less costly.

In fact, the system is pretty simple, efficient and inexpensive. Voters need only say Yes or No. With votes machines controlled by due representation of the political parties' representatives in every county, the consolidated results of a national vote can be released within the five hours following the closing of the polls, whatever the number of voting people. This cost of the exercise of democratic choice is more than compensated by the absence of social and political unrest and a high degree of confidence in government and political leaders.

To be efficient, direct democracy must also be exercised at the double level, cantonal (national) and federal (European), and be backed by strong, dynamic political parties. The parties, unions, and civil society in general, relayed by the media, are both the political actors and the leaders of public debate through their opposition or support of the various topics submitted to popular vote. In contemporary France, whose traditional parties were pulverized by the *République en marche* and Emmanuel Macron's election, their reconstruction is critical. With no parties to embody the different popular opinions, democracy is but a fiction.

Innovative Taxation to Finance Federal Europe

One cannot discuss the federal construction of Europe without raising the question of how it is to be financed. Federalism should enable the creation of a viable, sustainable federal state endowed with its own resources. The unending debates on the European budget, national contributions and resource allocation, the financing of agricultural policy, and perhaps even soon a common defense, show that this is a fundamental issue.

The Swiss system is also quite simple and functional in this respect. It rests on the principle that the federal state is financed thanks to a quasi-monopoly of indirect taxation while the cantons and the lower echelons resort almost exclusively to direct taxation (income and wealth taxes levied on natural and legal persons) and hold the monopoly on tax collection (except for VAT, which is in federal hands). This principle does have its exceptions, but it serves as a general guideline.

The European federal state therefore has to find its own indirect revenue to finance its spending without subjecting the finances of the Member States to generalized attrition. There are solutions, as reported by *BFM Business* (bfmtv.com) in 2016 when they presented the proposal of Marc Chesney, finance professor at the University of Zurich, and his associate, financier Felix Bolliger.[19] To replace all the tax deductions in Switzerland, the partners recommend setting up a 0.2% general financial transaction tax that would cover all purchases from the French baguette to stocks, and are preparing an initiative in this respect.

To quote *BFM Business:*

> Concretely, Marc Chesney's idea is frightfully simple. Forget corporation tax, income tax and even VAT. There would be one, single 0.2% micro-tax on financial transactions. Mind you, it wouldn't be simply a matter of taxing capital movements in the markets, like in France today, but of taxing payments made by the economic actors (households, companies, etc.) as a whole.
>
> The current system is not well thought out. Instead of taxing labor, which is becoming scarce, financial transactions, which are more and more numerous, should be taxed. Imagine the time we would save with this, knowing that the US Tax Code comes to no fewer than 71,000 pages. The micro-tax would also be applicable to cash withdrawals. For a withdrawal of 100 Swiss francs, the bank would charge a tax of twenty centimes that would go to the state.
>
> With a rate of 0.2%, this micro-tax would garner 200 billion Swiss francs, which is more than the total amount

---

19 "An economist wants to replace all taxes by a single tax," (in French) https://bfmbusiness.bfmtv.com/monde/un-economiste-veut-remplacer-tous- les-impots-par-une-seule-taxe-1052525.html

The Scenario of Independence

of the annual Confederate fiscal income, about 170 billion. For France alone, the 0.2% rate would be enough to bring in 436 billion euros, which is much more than the sum of its fiscal revenue (292 billion euros according to the finance bill for 2017).

The tax is not progressive according to income, but it is nevertheless equal in that the very wealthy have securities portfolios, regularly buy and sell shares or obligations, and would therefore pay more. It's the same principle as for the highway tolls: the more you travel, the more you pay. And the rich travel around more, physically and financially and for larger amounts.

As for companies that make enormous transfers and buy and sell securities in the markets, whether it is the banks or the companies raising the funds, they would have no other tax to pay on financial transactions or capital gains. Only the large banks that use high frequency trading would lose, which wouldn't be so bad and would force the industry of finance to reconnect with the real economy and wealth-productive investments.

Finally, this system would also be egalitarian for the various Member States, as the small States would not be penalized in relation to the large ones because each would be taxed on the volume of transactions made on its territory.

All that would remain to be done would be setting the rate to finance a credible European budget, taking into account, for example, the fact that the Swiss federal budget corresponds to some 30% of public spending (73 billion francs in 2017), the cantonal budget to 40% (89 billion), and the communal budget to 21% (48 billion).[20] We should point out that this figure should reassure the national "sovereigntists" on the effectiveness of the principle of subsidiarity, for it shows clearly that the cumulated budget of the two lower levels, national and sub national, is twice as high as

---

20 The social insurance accounts (63 billion) are not included in these figures, for they are managed by other public entities.

the supranational budget. This formula of indirect taxation is not really complicated to implement because all of the financial transactions are already traceable and documented. It would allow not only the financing of ordinary spending, but also facilitate making transfers to disadvantaged regions according to a distribution key as yet to be defined. At the same time, there would be no restraint on the lower echelons to define their choices regarding their local education, safety, social, energy, health and even environmental policies; each would be free to do more than what is stipulated by the federal laws without putting the whole entity in danger.

The system would also have the advantage of not favoring one country at the expense of the others and of offering a sufficient critical mass to avoid a massive transfer of capital, for it covers all transactions, including those of Google, Amazon, Facebook, Apple and Microsoft and the future intelligent robots. Thus it is about setting up a new tax system, adapted to our contemporary economy and its developments, by tackling first consumption and expenditure rather than penalizing the labor force and the production tool.

European Sovereignty

In a Europe that is dependent on the United States, as Switzerland was formerly dependent on France or on Austria, this implies a keen awareness of the challenges at hand and of the best method to see them through. Like federalism, independence and sovereignty cannot be decreed; they must be conquered in progressive steps, and no state can be entirely free of the pressures that can be brought to bear by others.

Breaking off suddenly with the United States is out of the question due to its geopolitical and internal power relations with Europe and for Europe's own immediate security interests. A gradual emancipation over the medium term, however, is possible. There is a way, and it is efficient: non-alignment or the third way. Of course, even mentioning this perspective will touch off the fanatic Atlanticists and intellectuals who support Europe's purported humanitarian intervention and civilizing mission meant to bring the lights of democracy and human rights to the rest of the world plunged in the shadows of barbarity. To these avid crusader minds may we recall the fact that neutrality in no way prevents intervening on the international scene, and that even the best-intentioned intervention, if it was indeed such, has its limits and often leads to crime and misery (as witnessed in Libya and Syria).

As far as foreign policy goes, dynamic neutrality, diplomacy and win-win solutions will always be more effective and cost-efficient than bombing civilian populations and causing devastation, or unconditional alignment with a third power, or even total helplessness for want of internal consensus—perhaps particularly, going forward, in view of the global trend supported by China and Russia and much of the rest of the world favoring multilateralism, reflected in Germany's recent adherence to China's Regional Comprehensive Economic Partnership (RCEP), the world's largest free trade zone, along with 15 other Asia-Pacific countries.

Switzerland's perpetual neutrality is therefore an important part of its foreign policy and is supported, in good times and bad, by 80% to 90% of its inhabitants. If Swiss neutrality has acquired the status of a national myth, it is nevertheless not an absolute ethical principle. It is just a means, thought to be the best for the country, to reach its goals of independence and security. In practice, the Swiss policy of neutrality is not cast in bronze and has often evolved over time with the constraints of international policy.

Neutrality (or Non-alignment) as a Principle of Action

Neutrality is characterized by three major factors: it is perpetual inasmuch as it neither begins nor ends in wartime; it is freely chosen, for it is anchored in the Federal Constitution; it is armed, for Switzerland has a credible defense army. Switzerland was not born neutral. It became neutral because it wanted to. As we saw earlier, the territory that corresponds to central Switzerland belonged to the Habsburg family, and the original confederation had to fight hard for its independence, like at the Battle of Morgarten. Likewise, all through the Middle Ages and up until the end of the

16th century, Switzerland had to break free from the tutelage of the Holy Roman German Empire.

For all this time the different cantons were involved in many conflicts, such as the Burgundy War in which the victorious Swiss brought on the collapse of the Burgundian state, or the Italian Wars, where their defeat in Northern Italy in 1515 marked the end of the country's political expansion. Expansion evolved into neutrality in the 17th century, with the first official declaration of the Federal Diet in 1674. The Thirty Years' War that ravaged central Europe was sorely felt in Switzerland, divided between Catholics and Protestants. But while exporting arms and mercenaries to the belligerent nations, Switzerland managed to stay away from military operations until the Treaty of Vienna confirmed its neutrality in 1815.

Switzerland adopted neutrality for different reasons of internal or foreign policy. It was a small country surrounded by major powers, and remaining neutral prevented it from becoming Europe's permanent battlefield. And the neighboring powers could get the assurance that swiss territory will not be used as a possible road for a military invasion. At the same time, their ruling class and bourgeoisie could also enjoy a safe haven for their assets. It also ensured the cohesion between the various religious, linguistic and cultural currents within the country. With no armed commitment abroad, the cantons were able to reinforce their autonomy. And thanks to its neutrality, Switzerland also contributed to balancing Europe by keeping at an equal distance from the opposing forces instead of adding on to the tensions by siding with one or the other camp.[21]

With the ongoing rise in tensions, it is vital for peace that Europe remain neutral. If so, in a few decades or centuries, it would be in a position analogous to that of Switzerland between

---

21 Its geographic location, moreover, is another important factor in this regard. Situated on the Eurasian continent, the base of global demography and economy, it lies at the epicenter of tensions and cannot be ignored by any of the opposing camps, as we could see during the Cold War and the Euromissile crisis in the 1980s.

The Scenario of Independence

France, Germany and Austria during the past centuries—surely a development devoutly to be wished.

What might appear to be the sacrifice of international initiative and the dubious fruits of increasingly unsuccessful third-state aggression (witness France in Mali, the US across the Middle East, NATO in Afghanistan) is mitigated by the significant economic impacts entailed in maintaining high-level trade with the various potential belligerents. Non-alignment also enables a state to offer its good offices and play the role of mediator in settling international disputes or facilitating international agreements of general interest dealing with the climate, trade, health and human progress as a whole.

Switzerland was home to the headquarters of the Society of Nations and is home now to the world's major international organizations in Geneva. The country also hosted summits such as the "Big Four" in 1955 and Reagan-Gorbachev in 1985, and the signing of the Treaty of Lausanne that defined the borders of modern Turkey. Since 1953 it has participated in supervising the armistice between North and South Korea, representing American interests in Cuba and Iran, Russian interests in Georgia and Georgian interests in Russia, as well as peace negotiations between the Columbian government and the rebels.

Again, being neutral or non-aligned has nothing to do with being inactive or ineffective as insinuated by the masked partisans of an aggressive or warlike policy. The only real constraint boils down to having an exclusively defensive army (like Japan, for that matter) and refraining from any act of aggression towards third countries. From this standpoint, Donald Trump even opened a window of opportunity when he declared his distrust of NATO on the pretext that its European members did not pay their parts and threatened to pull out. Mind you, that was likely part of his campaign to increase European military expenditure for NATO—again, a doubtful positive from Europe's point of view.

But there is nothing to prevent Europe from catching the ball on the fly and direct its announced increase in spending toward a continental, strictly defensive military that would guarantee its independence and sovereignty, thus making Europe a significant factor in the pursuit of world peace and security. This defensive provision could be incorporated into the Constitution, similar to Article 9 of the Japanese Constitution.[22] However, a provision à la Swiss, with a true defense army, would be preferable.[23]

Europe: The Will Behind the Way

So, what if Europe chose a democratic reset inspired by 'the Swiss method? Reorienting European construction along the lines of a true federalism, far from being a regression, would be a prodigious step forward, a leap not into the unknown, but towards a horizon that we can already perceive. And it takes less daring than drive.

This book has outlined in detail what lies in store for Europe if it does not act now. It has also shown that the Europe's existential dilemma is as well a dilemma for the United States. The crucial questions are: do Europeans really want to end their story—indeed, their civilization—by helplessly giving in to a slow and irreparable dereliction, a gradual and programmed obliteration—until

---

22 This article stipulates that Japan renounces war forever: "Aspiring sincerely to an international peace based on justice and order, the Japanese people forever renounce war as a sovereign right of the nation and the threat or use of force as a means of settling international disputes. In order to accomplish the aim of the preceding paragraph, land, sea and air forces, as well as other war potential, will never be maintained. The right of belligerency of the state will not be recognized." The Japanese nationalists, beginning with Prime Minister Shinzo Abe, seek to repeal or amend this article so that Japan can build up a true offensive army.

23 Art. 57 and 58 of the Swiss Federal Constitution:
"The Confederation and the Cantons shall within the scope of their powers ensure the security of the country and the protection of the population. They shall coordinate their efforts in the area of internal security.
"Switzerland shall have armed forces. In principle, the armed forces shall be organized as a militia. The armed forces serve to prevent war and to maintain peace; they defend the country and its population. They shall support the civilian authorities in safeguarding the country against serious threats to internal security and in dealing with exceptional situations. Further duties may be provided for by law. The deployment of the armed forces is the responsibility of the Confederation."

they are ultimately downgraded into insignificance like the ancient Greeks?

Is Europe able to seize the opportunity offered by the new emerging world order to emancipate itself? Or does Europe prefer to continue letting an outside power, even if close ally, tell it what or what not to do? Will it remain embroiled in controversy over the wording of "Federation of Nation-States," the "Europe of Nations" or of sovereign Europe, without ever getting down to business?

This is the European existential dilemma, and it is primarily for Europeans to resolve.

EPILOGUE

Geneva, May 2021

Only one month has passed since the end of the last version of this book. The events and news follow and look the same, each more depressing for the future of a free, independent and sovereign Europe, making the scenario of the American tutelage ever closer to a self-fullfiling prophecy and the scenario of an independent Europe a wishful thinking.

Five weeks after the visit of Secretary of State Anthony Blinken to NATO summit in Brussels in March, the Norwegian NATO Secretary General Jens Stoltenberg and his Romanian deputy announced a rapprochement between NATO and the European Union, transforming de facto the EU into a junior military partner of NATO. In the meantime, the 27 European Union defense ministers approved for the first time the integration of non-members States (US, Canada and Norway) in the initiative on military mobility in Europe. This initiative aims to facilitate the movement of rapid interventions troops and equipment throughout Europe, across borders, in order to face the so-called "Russian threat."

"Non–EU Allies play an essential role in protecting and defending Europe," said Stoltenberg, while German Defense minister Annegret Kramp Karrenbauer endorsed this unprecedented decision: "Making sure that troops can be moved across borders is a very important issue not only for the European Union but also for NATO."

A few days later, the NATO website announced that four Swiss FA-18 Hornets would participate in the two-week military exercises Tiger Meet in Portugal, in order to increase the interoperability between NATO and its partners, which delighted the commander of the Swiss patrol, who could thus improve "his flight operational capabilities in all areas of air interventions, as well as electronic warfare, space and cyber scenarios." For a country which, as we have seen, has a constitution which obliges

Epilogue

it to maintain military neutrality, this doesn't lack spice... It is true that this cooperation is carried out in the name of the "Partnership for Peace" that NATO launched in 1996 towards non-members States. With such a magic name, who cares about neutrality ?[1]

And to end this little review, let us mention that, according to the last economic figures released after the 2020 pandemic crisis, the GNP of the 27 members of EU fell by 6.4% in 2020 while that of the US decreased only by 3.5%, that of Russia only by 3.1%, while that of China managed to rise by 2.3%.

We will have to be very, very patient to see a free and strong Europe...

---

1 Rick Rozoff, "NATO Consolidates European Union As Junior Military Partners," *news.antiwar.com*, May 7, 2021; and "Europe Without Neutrals: Switzerland Provides Combat Aircraft for NATO Exercise," *news.antiwar.com*, May 10, 2021.

INDEX

A
Afghanistan, 161, 162
anti-Russian propaganda, 145, 149–152, 195, 211
Aron, Raymond, 13, 174, 198
Assange, Julian, 214, 226
Austria, xi, 14, 35–37, 50–53

B
Balibar, Etienne, 119
Balkans, 9–12, 15, 154, 174
Barroso, Jose Manuel, xi, 13, 200
Belt & Road Initiative (New Silk Roads), xiii, 219, 235, 236
Biden, Joe, xi, xii, 211, 218, 219
Blinken, Anthony, 262
Bosnia, 8, 9
Brexit, xi, 16

C
Charlemagne, 21, 22, 26–29,
Chesney, Marc, 254
Chevènement, Jean-Pierre, 103, 104
China, xii, xiii, 100, 167, 196, 210, 219, 224, 225–227, 234–236, 257
Christianity, 24, 26–29, 218
Churchill, Winston, 21, 139, 146
Cold War, 4, 78, 101, 139–141
communism, 46–49, 72, 77
comitology, 115
confederation, 81–89, 248–254, 261
Corti, Eugenio, 6
Council of Europe, 188
Covid-19, coronavirus, xi, xii

D
De Gaulle, Charles, 21, 136, 142, 143
debt spiral, 132, 133
Delors, Jacques, 4, 100
democratic deficit, 116–120, 183–186
Diamond, Jared, 73
dictatorship, 99–135

direct democracy, 240–243, 246, 247, 251, 252
Dotézac, Arnaud, 104–135, 183–185

E
Eastern Europe, 126, 170, 175
EEA, EFTA, 6, 7, 187
Enzensberger, H.-M., 120, 121, 165
European Commission, Community, Union, xi, 25, 90, 99–135, 177–183
European Court of Justice, 110, 177
European Defence Community, 122, 140–142
European Federal State, 223, 238–261
European sovereignty, 256, 257
European Ttreaties, 177–182

F
federalism, *See* confederation
France, xi, 4, 166–170, 259
Fukuyama, Francis, 17, 212

G
GAFAM (Google, Amazon, Facebook, Apple and Microsoft), 135, 193, 220, 256
GATT, 102, 103, 187
Germany, xi, 3, 14, 75, 92, 102, 147, 148, 163–173, 257
Gorbachev, Mikhail, 146–148
Greece, xii, 3, 91
Greece, Ancient, 54–89, 90
Grossman, Vladimir, 6

H
Habermas, Jürgen, 112
Habsburgs, 35, 36
Hallstein, Walter, 100
Hegel G.H.F., 37
Hitler, Adolf, xii, 38–42, 47, 49, 73, 93, 94, 107

Index

Holy Roman Empire, xii, 29–36, 46, 50–53, 90, 173, 258
Hungary, xi, 4

I
illiberalism, 130
imperialism, 67–68, 105
inequalities, 125, 130–132
India, 193
Industrial Revolution 1, 2.0, 3.0, 4.0; 22, 133, 135
innovative taxation, *See* microtax
Iran, 162
Iraq, 9, 161, 162
Italy, xi, 3

J
Japan, 65, 94, 260
Juncker, Jean-Claude, xi, 99, 113,

K
Khaldun, Ibn, 215
Kennan, George, 139, 141
Kennedy, Paul, 225, 226
Keynes, John Maynard, 101,
Kissinger, Henry, 136
Kosovo, 11, 155–159

L
Laïdi, Zaki, 118, 119, 121
Lasch, Christopher, 214
Latin America, 213
Levi, Primo, 6, 76
Lincoln, Abraham, 99

M
Macedonia, 69–70, 93, 173
Macron, Emanuel, 114, 172, 253
Marshall Plan, 101
Mélenchon, Jean-Luc, 128, 165, 166
Mendès-France, Pierre, 99
Merkel, Angela, 171, 172, 212, 223, 226
micro-tax, 253–256
migrations, 120, 127
Mitterrand, François, 103, 125, 147

Monnet, Jean, 100, 105, 107–109, 111, 122, 141, 185
Monti, Mario, 112
Morin, Edgar, 205

N
Napoleon, xii, 37–38, 45
NATO, 7, 10, 78, 140, 142, 144–149, 151, 152, 155–160, 186, 187, 188, 262, 263
Nazis, Nazism, *See* Hitler
Netherlands, xi
neutrality, 257–260
Nietzsche, Friedrich, 21

O
OECD, 187–189
Otto of Saxony, 29

P
Peloponnesian War, 62–67
Pericles, 62
Piketty, Thomas, 129, 130
Poland, xi, 4, 175
populism, populists, xi, 6, 126, 190–193
Putin, Vladimir, xii, 195, 218, 219

R
Roman Republic, Empire, xii, 55, 85–89, 207, 208, 216, 217
Romania, 8
Rougemont, Denis de, 24, 138
Royal, Ségolène, 114
Russia, xii, 149–152, 161, 194–196

S
Salais, Robert, 101
Schuman, Robert, 102
Serbia, 8, 10, 153, 155–159, 228
Sloterdijck, Peter, 14, 17
Snowden, Edward, 214, 226
sovereignty, 256, 257, 261
Soviet Union, 6, 8, 48, 76, 127, 138
Spengler, Oswald, 73
Stalin, Josef, xii, 21, 38–45, 49, 137
Starwars, 206, 207

265

Stoltenberg, Jens, 262
Syria, 11, 162
Sweden, xi
Switzerland, xiv, 4, 238–261, 262

T
Theorem of Cylon, 95
Thibaudet, Albert, 54, 55, 62
Thucydides, 54, 55, 64
TINA, 118
Tocqueville, Alexis, 143
Treaty of Rome, 102, 175, 177
Trump, Donald, xi, xii, 16, 95, 214, 219, 226, 259
Turkey, 182, 189, 193

U
Ukraine, 11, 159, 160, 163
United Kingdom, xi, 77, 134, 145
United States, xiii, 16, 74, 75, 92, 93, 94, 137, 142, 143, 193, 197–200, 225–234
US Constitution, 198, 226
US empire, 199, 206–222

V
vassalization, 144–146
Védrine, Hubert, 176
Von der Leyen, Ursula, xi

W
World Economic Forum, 221
World War I, II; 55, 63–65, 94, 209

Y
Yellow Jackets, xi, 134, 192, 227
Yugoslavia, 4, 8, 153–160